THE HARDEST PATH IS THE EASIEST

EXPLORING THE WISDOM LITERATURE WITH
PASCAL,
BURKE,
KIERKEGAARD
AND CHESTERTON

Gary Furnell

Connor Court Publishing

Published in 2021 by Connor Court Publishing Pty Ltd
Revised Second Edition in 2023 by Connor Court Publishing Pty Ltd

Copyright © Gary Furnell

All rights reserved. No part of this book may be reproduced or transmitted in any form or by any means, electronic or mechanical, including photocopying, recording or by any information storage and retrieval system, without prior permission in writing from the publisher.

Connor Court Publishing Pty Ltd
PO Box 7257
Redland Bay QLD 4165
sales@connorcourt.com
www.connorcourtpublishing.com.au
Phone 0497-900-685

Printed in Australia

ISBN: 9781922449757

Front Cover Design by Tash

Printed in Australia
Excerpts from *A Kierkegaard Anthology*, edited by Robert Bretall. 1959; republished with permission of Princeton University Press, permission conveyed through Copyright Clearance Centre, Inc.

Excerpts from *Purity of Heart* by Soren Kierkegaard, Douglas Steere. English translation copyright 1938 by Harper & Brothers, renewed (c)1966 by Douglas V. Steere. Used by permission of HarperCollins Publishers.

Excerpts from *Works of Love* by Soren Kierkegaard. English language translation copyright (c) 1962 by Howard Hong. Used by permission of HarperCollins Publishers.

Dedicated to the seekers after Spirit and wisdom

Joseph Pieper considered them "Untimely Inopportunes"

Jacques Maritain called them a "Prophetic Shock Minority"

Soren Kierkegaard honoured them as "Knights of Faith"

Certain authors, speaking of their works, say, "My book," My commentary," "My history", etc. They resemble middle-class people who have a house of their own, and always have "My house" on their tongue. They do better to say: 'Our book," "Our commentary," "Our history," etc., because there is in them usually more of other people's than their own. Pascal, *Pensees,* 43.

CONTENTS

1. A Difficult Beginning — 7
2. The Search for Wisdom — 39
3. Four Follies to Avoid — 59
   - i. The Folly of Adultery — 59
   - ii. The Folly of Insurrection — 81
   - iii. The Folly of Lazyness — 104
   - iv. The Folly of Pride — 110
4. Wisdom and Wealth — 123
5. Wisdom and Asset Management — 131
6. Wisdom and Government — 145
7. Wisdom and Relationships — 169
8. Wisdom and Reverence — 199
   - i. Reverence and the puzzle of man. — 201
   - ii. Reverence and the puzzle of God. — 217
   - iii. Reverence and double-mindedness. — 236

Bibliography — 249

1

A DIFFICULT BEGINNING

"What times and what customs!" exclaimed Cicero after observing grotesque behaviour in Imperial Rome. In every age, the shrewd observer of human habits will find much that is astonishing and ridiculous. One of the absurdities of contemporary Western culture is the odd belief that greater freedom, functionality and justice can be achieved by repudiating custom and tradition. This idea has itself become a tradition that developed from one of the central tenets of the Enlightenment which proposed that clever individuals, guided by autonomous reason rather than by their forebears or religion, could solve the problems of life and determine an appropriate reconfiguration of society and values.

This reconfiguration, especially in Europe, led to the disparagement of the beliefs and customs of ordinary people and the imposition of the visionary ideals of intellectual and cultural elites. It was truly a revolution in human affairs. For most of history, in most cultures, precedent guided the present, but – according to the Enlightenment's principles – precedent was the problem, tradition was the stumbling-block, and a rational vision of the future was expected to provide guidance for the present. Too often, these visionary ideas were regarded as more important than the people who were merely alive and bound to tradition. Their hopes and priorities were disregarded where they obstructed the rush to a happier, idealised future. The result is well-known (even some artists and a few intellectuals eventually acknowledged it) – the common people paid the price for the implementation of the intellectuals' vision. At worst, the commoners paid with their lives; at best, they paid with their freedoms and suffered a desperately diminished quality of life all the while being harangued by propaganda telling them how much better off they were under the new regime.

This change in societal expectations has been profound; we are living with the consequences. For example, medieval people expected, based on the traditional teaching of the Church, that the returning Christ would institute a fair, peaceful and just society. In contrast, French and German Enlightenment thinkers taught that man, unaided by the divine, was capable of inaugurating a fair, peaceful and just society. After twenty centuries of Christianity and three centuries of the Enlightenment project, this happy society hasn't arrived; and disillusionment with these promises of a perfected world is one of the reasons for post-modernism's bitter attitude.

In the early decades of the twentieth century – a time of tumult with communists, socialists and fascists agitating to enact their visions – G.K. Chesterton reminded people that there is a direct link between democracy and tradition; tradition is democracy extended through time. Tradition is the continued enfranchisement of the dead; tradition honours their values and choices. Through tradition, previous generations of people are allowed to speak and their opinions and customs are respected.

> Tradition may be defined as an extension of the franchise. Tradition means giving votes to the most obscure of all classes, our ancestors. It is the democracy of the dead. Tradition refuses to submit to that arrogant oligarchy who merely happen to be walking about. All

> democrats object to men being disqualified by the accident of birth; tradition objects to their being disqualified by the accident of death.
> From *Orthodoxy*.

In addition, tradition helps protect ordinary people from the ill-judged agendas of philosophers, economists, academics and politicians. These people frequently want society to embrace the latest ideas, as if what they thought this Friday is necessarily better than what the rest of humanity had thought – and found workable – for the previous twenty centuries. In other words, tradition protects people from the slavery of intellectual fashion. Fashion is wonderful in less important things like hairstyles, clothes, décor, cars, television shows, sport and pop music. In these things, fashion provides us with invigorating variety and opens avenues for creativity, but fashion is dangerous in consequential affairs like politics, philosophy, ethics, and the direction of society. In these things, fashion leads to instability; to individual, familial and societal dysfunction, and to wasted resources as the efforts of people and vast amounts of money are directed and re-directed to constantly changing programs. And the speed with which these programs are changed is itself a problem: thought is lacking, truth is neglected, evidence is overlooked, direction is obscured, people are frightened. The constant change is an expression of rigidity, like a train hurtling along its anchored tracks. Chesterton made the analogy.

> Now, in spite of the wildest claims to independence, the intellectual life of today still strikes me as being mainly symbolised by the train or the track or the groove. There is any amount of fuss and vivacity about certain fixed fashions or directions of thought; just as there is any amount of rapidity along the fixed rails of the railway-track. But if we begin to think about really getting off the track, we shall find what is true of the train is equally true of the truth. We shall find it is actually harder to get out of the groove, when the train is going fast, than when the train is going slowly. We shall find that rapidity is rigidity; that the very fact of some social or political or artistic

movement going quicker and quicker means that fewer people have the courage to move against it. And at last perhaps nobody will make a leap for real intellectual liberty, just as nobody will jump out of a railway-train going eighty miles an hour. This seems to me the primary mark of what we call progressive thought in the modern world. It is in the most exact sense of the term limited. It is all in one direction. It is limited by its progress. It is limited by its speed.
From *The Common Man*.

Of course, not all tradition is worthy of respect. The traditional belief in some African cultures that disabled children are cursed, or the quaint but persistent belief in Western cultures that plutocrats embody success are examples of traditional beliefs that need to be reformed. But reform of unworthy traditional beliefs should not be undertaken according to whatever is currently fashionable; the result would be one unworthy belief being replaced by another unworthy belief. The wisdom literature, and this book focuses on *Proverbs* and *Ecclesiastes*, provides the best basis for beneficial change: in any reform the key values are prudence, experience, concern for one's neighbour and justice.

Allied to this respect for tradition is respect for parents and elders who are the custodians of tradition. This respect is everywhere promoted in wisdom literature; it's closely linked to promises of long life, well-being, honour and knowledge. Alternatively, disrespect for parents and elders is linked to early death, shame, self-destructiveness and impoverishment. Honouring parents and elders is in sharp contrast to the cult of youth prevalent in our society. Today, parents are routinely portrayed by the popular media as uncool, incompetent, and crass; often they are perceived as bigger and older but less savvy adolescents; frequently they're examples of arrested development. Elders and grandparents are portrayed by the popular media in a denigrating manner: they are regarded as irrelevant, sentimental and burdensome.

It's an appalling reflection on our society that the elderly are so undervalued. All their experience, expertise, and skill, together with their sense of perspective and balance on many different aspects of life, developed over many decades, are foolishly considered less than precious. Too often the elderly are considered an hindrance and a cost to society rather than an immensely sensible and stabilising gift to the rest of society.

Proverbs is more balanced. It recognises that both the young and the old have much to contribute to their families and to society.

> The glory of young men is their strength, but the beauty of old men is their gray head. 20:29

The young possess abundant strength, energy and passion but lack experience; their decisions may be impulsive and naive, with destructive results. Older, mature people tend to make more prudent decisions with constructive results, but lack strength and energy. Thus, each generation has their respective attributes and contribution to make to society: young people bring strength and vitality while older people bring experience and expertise to guide the energy of the young.

It's immediately obvious that *Proverbs*, in particular, is a type of moral philosophy. Immanuel Kant defined the goal of philosophy; it must consider three primary questions: What do I know? What may I hope? What should I do? While *Proverbs* and *Ecclesiastes* do not neglect to direct our hopes, and they do consider what we can know (and cannot know), they're mainly concerned with the latter question: What should I do? Good self-management should be everybody's first concern.

Chesterton understood that in a pluralist culture the individual had to work hard to sift opinions, distinguish between reality and faddish fantasies, and identify what was worthwhile and what was worthless.

> The true task of culture today is not a task of expansion, but very

decidedly of selection – and rejection. From *What's Wrong with the World*.

A society largely composed of individuals who are skilled at self-management, including the task of selecting worthy activities and rejecting unrealistic options and ideas, has a stable basis. Where there are significant numbers of people who are careless and unskilled at self-management, then society suffers in proportion to their numbers and their degree of carelessness. *Proverbs* and *Ecclesiastes* provide essential wisdom so anybody attendant to it can build a fruitful, loving life.

The moral philosophy of the wisdom literature is based on a particular theological understanding which is assumed or presupposed rather than demonstrated or proved. It's always best to uncover the presuppositions of a particular person or philosophy (including our own presuppositions) so they can be considered and defended, abandoned or amended. When *Proverbs* and *Ecclesiastes* are explored we discover that, consistent with their Hebraic origins, they presuppose that the cosmos is created (it is a result of divine intention); that essence precedes existence; it is personal rather than impersonal; it is moral because it is based on the moral character of the creator; it is reasonable rather than irrational or absurd (that the universe is absurd is a fashionable contemporary belief); it is complicated in the particular sense that life is an admixture of good and evil with man free to choose between them, and complex too in the sense that man is not a monist materialistic entity (another fashionable contemporary belief) but a composite being of body, soul and spirit. That man may, and often does, choose to ignore his sacred stamp is the main cause of his discord; this is another of the presuppositions of the Hebrew wisdom literature. Mankind's complexity, and mystery, is compounded by the presupposition that man is free to choose his own course, yet the sovereignty of the creator is maintained – a paradox that does not sit well with modern man, who is, however, able to speak about choice and freedom with one breath and then proclaim that man is a bio-chemical machine with the next breath. The wisdom literature further proposes that when a person acts selfishly, violently, unjustly or irreverently they diminish their own self. Likewise, when a person chooses to act justly, truthfully, equitably and reverently they fulfil their self. Consequently, within the parameters set by the creator we can choose our own level of ontological fulfilment.

This is a uniquely human quality; it's one of the qualities that differentiates humanity from animals. An elephant, for example, will always behave in a consistently elephantine manner; nothing it does will be inconsistent with its nature; its ontology is set. But man can act in a way that dehumanises himself or in a way that fulfils his humanity. Man is unique because, to a significant extent, he can progressively create or destroy himself. And we do this every day by the decisions we make. *Proverbs* makes this plain.

> A man who is kind benefits himself, but a cruel man hurts himself. 11:17.
>
> He who is steadfast in righteousness will live, but he who pursues evil will die. 11:19.
>
> He who gets wisdom loves himself; he who keeps understanding will prosper. 19:8.
>
> He who keeps the commandment keeps his life; he who despises the word will die. 19:16.
>
> An evil man is ensnared in his transgression, but a righteous man sings and rejoices. 29:6.

Chesterton saw that the unique ability of man to choose his own level of fulfilment differentiated him from all other creatures.

> If you leave off looking at books about beasts and men, if you begin to look at beasts and men then (if you have any humour or imagination, any sense of the frantic or the farcical) you will observe the startling thing is not how like man is to the brutes, but how unlike he is. It is the monstrous scale of his divergence that requires an explanation. That man and brute are like is, in a sense, a truism; but

that being so like they should then be so insanely unlike, that is the shock and the enigma. That an ape has hands is far less interesting to the philosopher than the fact that having hands he does next to nothing with them; does not play knuckle-bones or the violin; does not carve marble or carve mutton. People talk of barbaric architecture and debased art. But elephants do not build colossal temples of ivory even in rococo style; camels do not paint even bad pictures, though equipped with the material of many camel's-hair brushes. Certain modern dreamers say that ants and bees have a society superior to ours. They have, indeed, a civilization; but that very truth only reminds us that it is an inferior civilization. Who ever found an ant-hill decorated with the statues of celebrated ants? Who has seen a bee-hive carved with the images of gorgeous queens of old? No; the chasm between man and other creatures may have a natural explanation, but it is a chasm. We talk of wild animals; but man is the only wild animal. It is man that has broken out. All other animals are tame animals; following the rugged respectability of the tribe or type. All other animals are domestic animals; man alone is ever undomestic, either as a profligate or a monk ... From *Orthodoxy*.

Our decisions make us responsible, and this responsibility is one of the defining characteristics of humanity. Responsibility makes our own history significant. Swiss theologian Emil Brunner, deeply influenced by Kierkegaard, explained that if man is not responsible, then our own history – our life – is insignificant: the deeds and misdeeds of yesterday, of decades ago, of half a century ago have little or no weight or consequence. If this is the case, our being really is unbearably light. But if we are responsible for each and every one of our deeds and misdeeds then our own life and its history is loaded with significance. This is consistent with the wisdom literature.

To properly honour our life and to appreciate the gravity of our power of choice we may need to consider our lives again and see our acts not as buried by changes and the passing years but forever standing prominently to demean or dignify us. Man exists in time and beyond time.

> I have seen the business that God has given to the sons of men to be busy with. He has made everything beautiful in its time; also he has put eternity into man's mind, yet so that he cannot find out what God has done from the beginning to the end. *Ecclesiastes* 3:10,11.

Kierkegaard commented on this verse.

> It is eternally false, that guilt is changed by the passage of a century. To assert anything of this sort is to confuse the Eternal with what the Eternal is least like – with human forgetfulness. From *Purity of Heart is to Will One Thing*.

He further expounded on the eternity-seeking aspect of man that King Solomon had highlighted.

> If there is, then, something eternal in a man, it must be able to exist and to be grasped within every change. Nor can it be wisdom to say, indiscriminately, that this something eternal has its time like the perishable, that it makes its circle like the wind that never gets further; that it has its course like the river that never fills up the sea. Nor can it be wisdom to talk of this eternal element in the same vein as if one were talking about the past, as if it is past and past in the sense that it can never, not even in repentance, relate itself to a present person but only to an absent one. For repentance is precisely the relation between something past and someone that has his life in the present time ... But for the eternal, the time never comes when a man has grown away from it, or has become older – than the Eternal. From *Purity of Heart is to Will One Thing*.

Kierkegaard thought seeking forgiveness was one way to honour the eternal quality of man's being because our responsibility is not changed by time, or senility. He called remorse, repentance and confession *eternity's emissaries* to man.

Because we live in time and beyond time, it's wise to acknowledge our moral faults rather than to deny their existence. Mercy and forgiveness upon repentance are as real as our responsibility and guilt. This is good news for humanity. We possess possibility; we are not locked into fate, transgression, guilt, addiction, compulsion or despair. Our moral nature is renewable. *Proverbs* urges honesty.

> He who conceals his transgressions will not prosper, but he who confesses and forsakes them will obtain mercy. 28:13.

A flippant disregard of our own past is a flippant disregard of our own life and significance. Of course, we're ready to consider our past as void because to carry around the garlands of our goodness would be burden enough but to carry around, in addition, the guilt of our misdemeanors and cruelties would be crushing. We are therefore selectively forgetful: we remember our good deeds, yet discount our folly and selfishness. *Proverbs* is not blind to our selective memories.

> All the ways of a man are pure in his own eyes, but the LORD weighs the spirit. 16:2.

We tend to exonerate ourselves; to forget what injures our sense of our goodness – to the detriment of our own life's meaning and weight. *Proverbs* is alert to this tendency too; it observes the discrepancy between what most people proclaim and the less glorious reality.

> Many a man proclaims his own loyalty, but a faithful man who can find? 20:6.

This distance between our sense of ourselves as good, just and loving people and the reality in which elements of selfishness and injustice are ever-present in our lives is addressed.

> Who can say, "I have made my heart clean; I am pure from my sin"? 20:9.

> Surely there is not a righteous man on earth who does good and never sins. *Ecclesiastes* 7:20.

Of course, if one admits that our life has significance and that we are responsible for our past decisions, then no one can say they are free from sin. Hence, the wisdom literature insists on humility and right moral action, with reverence for the creator of all to whom we are responsible.

To some extent, this offends our sensibilities. It seems too much: is every person responsible for all their moral decisions? Can our lives really be that significant? It seems to load us down with too much meaning and a disturbingly profound gravity. We could perhaps concede, even joyfully concede, that our lives have meaning and significance, but to load them with this level of personal, historical, detailed significance seems unreasonable and unlikely. It takes a good idea much too far, and so many people reject this idea; it causes offense. But other people, choosing not to be offended, find it liberates them from futility and insignificance.

A consequence of our responsibility and immense significance is the need to actively seek wisdom. Here custom and tradition can be at fault. We see so few other people consciously and consistently seeking wisdom that we become complacent and seek it half-heartedly or not at all. We're content to follow the norms and attitudes of our culture.

From our earliest years we're given much to learn and do, and we labour – often very honourably – at the roles given to us. We also willingly embrace the diversions offered to us and we constantly desire new diversions all the while paying scant attention to what is immediately important to us: how to live a good life. We live without considering how to live. The result is that along with enacting much good, we also harm ourselves and others. We underestimate the meaning of our lives and slide towards death oblivious of our real significance.

We might also be ignoring the richness and responsibility of our individuality. *Proverbs* affirms that the benefits of wisdom, and the consequences of foolishness, are borne first of all by the individual who acts wisely or foolishly.

> If you are wise, you are wise for yourself; if you scoff, you alone will bear it. 9:12.

Pascal made a similar point, but went further and reflected on the conflict of loyalties that faces us. He asked: do we love ourselves enough to seek wisdom or do we seek only the love of our companions and, being content with that, abandon the difficult search for wisdom? Our mortality and fragility add urgency to this question.

> We are fools to depend upon the society of our fellow-men. Wretched as we are, powerless as we are, they will not aid us; we shall die alone. We should therefore act as if we were alone, and in that case should we build fine houses, etc.? We should seek the truth without hesitation; and, if we refuse it, we show that we value the esteem of men more than the search for truth. 211

Kierkegaard was a champion of the individual. He wanted each person to embrace their unique identity and path in life. He had an acute sense of each person's need to search for wisdom and truth in quietness and humble patience, even if it meant the distress of social isolation. He thought that submitting to the crowd, trying to submerge ourselves in the mass of mankind was an futile attempt to abdicate personal responsibility. The consequence was a forfeited existence, and all of these choices had a sacred context.

> Above all, the one, who in truth wills the Good must not be "busy." In quiet patience he must leave it to the Good itself, what reward he shall have, and what he shall accomplish. He dare not allow himself a single word of compromise, not a glance. He dare not ask the slightest relief from the world. He has only to give himself up to the Good and to that thing and to that person that might possibly be helped by him. He is no judge. On the contrary, he is just the opposite, he is the one who is judged. He effects a judgment only in

the sense that the surrounding world becomes manifest by how it judges him. From *Purity of Heart is to Will One Thing*.

Proverbs contains many warnings about leaving the way of wisdom to embrace a destructive companionship; of not being prepared to draw aside from the crowd. But there's also the promise of reward for those who do draw aside to seek wisdom.

> For the LORD gives wisdom; from his mouth come knowledge and understanding; he stores up sound wisdom for the upright; he is a shield to those who walk in integrity, guarding the paths of justice and preserving the way of his saints. Then you will understand righteousness and justice and equity, every good path; for wisdom will come into your heart, and knowledge will be pleasant to your soul; discretion will watch over you; understanding will guard you; delivering you from the way of evil, from men of perverted speech, who forsake the paths of uprightness to walk in the ways of darkness, who rejoice in doing evil and delight in the perverseness of evil; men whose paths are crooked, and who are devious in their ways. 2:6-15.

The significance and responsibility of the individual, together with the fact of mortality, seems strangely a matter of little concern to most of us. Pascal lamented the apathy of so many people to these profound matters.

> But as for those who pass their life without thinking of this ultimate end of life, and who, for this sole reason that they do not find within themselves the lights which convince them of it, neglect to seek them elsewhere, and to examine thoroughly whether this opinion is one of those which people receive with credulous simplicity, or one of those which, although obscure in themselves, have nevertheless a solid and immovable foundation, I look upon them in a manner quite different.
>
> This carelessness in a matter which concerns themselves, their eternity, their all, moves me more to anger than pity; it astonishes

and shocks me; it is to me monstrous. I do not say this out of the pious zeal of a spiritual devotion. I expect, on the contrary, that we ought to have this feeling from principles of human interest and self-love; for this we need only see what the least enlightened persons see. 194.

We search with assiduousness for a parking spot in the morning, we hope fervently that our favourite football team will win the game this weekend or that a person we find attractive will notice us, but do we search for wisdom, do we wish fervently for prudence and for knowledge about ourselves and our world? Too often the answer is no: oddly, smaller things consume us but larger issues are neglected, as Pascal saw.

The sensibility of man to trifles, and his insensibility to great things, indicates a strange inversion. 198.

Apart from the fact that we see so few other people searching diligently for wisdom, there are two other problems that commonly discourage the search: the fact that wisdom is disputed, and the intoxicating pleasures of diversion. A dispute about the wisdom in *Proverbs* and *Ecclesiastes* could begin with disagreement about presuppositions. For example, if one believes, as many people do, that the universe is uncreated and unintentional, a product of chance, then much so-called wisdom is irrelevant. Some Proverbial wisdom may be helpful, such as the admonitions to avoid being surety for another person's debt, but the sacred context could be considered nonsense if the cosmos is ultimately impersonal. Again, if one is committed to one of the world's religions that presuppose the dissolution of individual personal consciousness, such as Hinduism or Buddhism, then much of the wisdom in *Proverbs* and *Ecclesiastes* could likewise be disputed. Of course, the opposite also applies – if one presupposes the sacred, moral, and personal context of these two books, then certain aspects of the wisdom of Hinduism or Buddhism or secularism could be questioned.

Given the complexity of reality and the crucial role of our presuppositions in shaping our understanding of it, it's no wonder that contentions arise about the nature of wisdom. The main reason for contention is that not one of us has a consistently sure and certain means of determining justice, right action, or exact truth. Pascal made this precise point in a sardonic manner.

> Justice and truth are two such subtle points, that our tools are too blunt to touch them accurately. If they reach the point, they either crush it, or lean all around it, more on the false than the true. Man, then, is so happily constituted that he has no exact principle of truth, and several excellent ones of falsehood. Let us see now how many. 82

Pascal identified our imagination as the chief determinant of what we value. But imagination has no immediate or necessary link to truth.

> *Imagination.* – It is that deceitful part in man, that mistress of error and falsity, the more deceptive that she is not always so; for she would be an infallible rule of truth, if she were an infallible rule of falsehood. But being most generally false, she gives no sign of her nature, impressing the same character on the true and the false.
>
> I do not speak of fools, I speak of the wisest men; and it is among them that the imagination has the great gift of persuasion. Reason protests in vain; it cannot set a true value on things.
>
> This arrogant power, the enemy of reason, who likes to rule and dominate it, has established in man a second nature to show how all-powerful she is. She makes men happy and sad, healthy and sick, rich and poor; she compels reason to believe, doubt, and deny; she blunts the senses, or quickens them; she has her fools and sages; and nothing vexes us more than to see that she fills her devotees with a satisfaction far more full and entire than does reason. Those who have a lively imagination are a great deal more pleased with themselves than the wise can reasonably be. They look down upon

> men with haughtiness; they argue with boldness and confidence, others with fear and diffidence; and this gaiety of countenance often gives them the advantage in the opinion of the hearers, such favour have the imaginary wise in the eyes of judges of like nature. Imagination cannot make fools wise; but she can make them happy, to the envy of reason which can only make its friends miserable; the one covers them with glory, the other with shame.
>
> What but this faculty of imagination dispenses reputation, awards respect and veneration to persons, works, laws, and the great? How insufficient are all the riches of the earth without her consent! 82.

It's easy to avoid the search for wisdom by claiming that man is inevitably confused, truth is disputed, presuppositions are subjective, and the social and religious or irreligious circumstances in which one was born routinely determine what one believes. This is a common protestation. It's also a common excuse for intellectual and spiritual lazyness. Medieval people had a word for this type of torpor: *acedia*. It's a neglected, nearly forgotten word today, which is particularly ironic – but not surprising – because spiritual lassitude is one of the chief vices of contemporary Western culture. Pascal observed this stubborn complacency in his age.

> Those who do not love the truth take as a pretext that it is disputed, and that a multitude deny it. And so their error arises only from this, that they do not love either truth or charity. Thus they are without excuse. 261.

There are two related failures here: an imprudent trust in the opinions of others, and a refusal to take responsibility for one's own opinions. It's also a commitment, not to a neutral position about truth or wisdom – such neutrality doesn't exist – but to scepticism. Put another way, one can't avoid adopting a particular philosophy or idiosyncratic way of looking at the world. Pascal noted this predicament.

> So there is open war among men, in which each must take a part,

and side either with dogmatism or scepticism. For he who thinks to remain neutral is above all a sceptic. This neutrality is the essence of the sect; he who is not against them is essentially for them. [In this appears their advantage.] They are not for themselves; they are neutral, indifferent, in suspense as to all things, even themselves being no exception. 434.

We must choose; not choosing is a choice: it's a commitment to scepticism. But scepticism is itself is open to dispute; no one is ever a consistent sceptic. Belief in many things underpins scepticism; for example, a sceptic could never be a determinist, nor a monist. A sceptic must affirm some measure of free-will and some form of differentation – a sceptic must be free to choose, and possess an individual consciousness that is confronted by something else we call the cosmos. But these beliefs are themselves contentious: so even to choose not to choose means affirming something of doubtful credibility. This is a distressing predicament. Most people avoid thinking about it.

Not thinking about ourselves, our lives, and what it means to live a good, worthwhile life has developed into an art form. Distracting ourselves from difficult existential questions is one of the things humanity spends much time and effort to achieve. We are excellent at avoiding profound, necessary but disconcerting and puzzling questions. And that is another factor that harms the search for wisdom: our love of diversion.

Pascal's *Pensees* contain many reflections on our desire for diversion. Pascal observed that we would not hunger for diversion if we were satisfied, fulfilled beings. We'd rest at home, doing nothing but reflecting on our happiness if we were truly happy. But we aren't consistently, deeply happy, not enough to enjoy long and unalloyed rest. Our barely articulated and achingly unfulfilled longings drive us to activity for two reasons: we know intuitively that it is outside of ourselves that satisfaction and meaning are found, and because we want to distract ourselves from a vague sense of emptiness, confusion and anxiety. A sample of these *Pensees* helps us follow Pascal's thoughts on the role of diversion.

> *Diversion.* – If man were happy, he would be the more so, the less he was diverted, like the Saints and God. – Yes; but is it not to be happy to have a faculty of being amused by diversion? – No; for that comes from elsewhere and from without, and thus is dependent, and therefore subject to be disturbed by a thousand accidents, which bring inevitable griefs. 170
>
> *Misery.* – The only thing which consoles us for our miseries is diversion, and yet this it the greatest of our miseries. For it is this which principally hinders us from reflecting upon ourselves, and which makes us insensibly ruin ourselves. Without this we should be in a state of weariness, and this weariness would spur us to seek a more solid means of escaping from it. But diversion amuses us, and leads us unconsciously to death. 171.
>
> *Thoughts.* – *In omnibus requiem quæsivi.* [I have sought tranquility everywhere]. If our condition were truly happy, we would not need diversion from thinking of it in order to make ourselves happy. 165.
>
> *Diversion.* – As men are not able to fight against death, misery, ignorance, they have taken it into their heads, in order to be happy, not to think of them at all. 168.
>
> *Weariness.* – Nothing is so insufferable to man as to be completely at rest, without passions, without business, without diversion, without study. He then feels his nothingness, his forlornness, his insufficiency, his dependence, his weakness, his emptiness. There will immediately arise from the depth of his heart weariness, gloom, sadness, fretfulness, vexation, despair. 131.
>
> *Diversion.* – Men are entrusted from infancy with the care of their honour, their property, their friends, – and even with the property and the honour of their friends. They are overwhelmed with business, with the study of languages, and with physical exercise; and they are made to understand that they cannot be happy unless

their health, their honour, their fortune and that of their friends be in good condition, and that a single thing wanting will make them unhappy. Thus they are given cares and business which make them bustle about from break of day. – It is, you will exclaim, a strange way to make them happy! What more could be done to make them miserable? – Indeed! what could be done? We should only have to relieve them from all these cares; for then they would see themselves: they would reflect on what they are, whence they came, whither they go, and thus we cannot employ and divert them too much. And this is why, after having given them so much business, we advise them, if they have some time for relaxation, to employ it in amusement, in play, and to be always fully occupied.

How hollow and full of ribaldry is the heart of man! 143.

Like Pascal, Kierkegaard drew a connection between busyness and inward confusion. Kierkegaard wasn't a solitary homebody; he liked country carriage rides, daily walks through Copenhagen, and frequent restaurant dinners. But he knew that anybody always rushing around lost clarity about vital things.

> That the one who wills the Good only to a certain degree, that he is double-minded, that he has a distracted mind, a divided heart, scarcely needs to be pointed out. But the reason may need to be explained and set forth, why in the press of busyness there is neither time nor quiet to win the transparency that is required to understand oneself in willing one thing, or even for a preliminary understanding of oneself in one's confusion. Nay, the press of busyness into which one enters further and further, and the noise in which the truths continually slips more and more into oblivion, and the mass of connections, stimuli, and hindrances, these make it ever more impossible for one to win any deeper knowledge of himself. It is true that a mirror has the quality of enabling a man to see his reflection in it, but for this he must stand still. If he rushes hastily by, he sees nothing. Suppose a man should go about with a mirror in his possession which he does not take out, how should such a

man get to see himself? In this fashion a busy man hurries on, with the possibility of understanding himself in his possession. But the busy man keeps on running and it never dawns upon him that this possibility which he has in his possession is rapidly fading from his memory. And yet one hardly dares say this to one of the busy ones, for however rushed he otherwise may be, yet upon occasion he has plenty of time for a multitude of excuses by the use of which he becomes worse than he was before: excuses whose wisdom is about the same as when a sailor believes it is the sea, not the ship, that is moving. From *Purity of Heart is to Will One Thing*.

Diversion in the right measure is an adjunct to life, allowing us to refresh our minds and bodies, explore new things, to develop new skills. But unrestrained diversion is an enemy of humanity, leading us to death, keeping us sufficiently involved with lesser things while neglecting the most important aspects of our lives: the discovery of ourselves and our place in the cosmos. Chesterton defined religion as that which puts first things first. Endless diversion puts frivolity first and leaves no time or energy for the search for wisdom. This is self-defeating behaviour which *Proverbs* recognised.

> He who tills his land will have plenty of bread, but he who follows worthless pursuits has no sense. 12:11

Chesterton was a man who worked incredibly hard when he had to work; but he knew there was a time for doing nothing and he cherished this time. This wasn't diversion; it was a meditative engagement with himself and the wondrous world. It was the sort of fruitful doing nothing that was practiced by the desert monks in their hermitages. Chesterton thought it was the best kind of leisure, better than the two alternatives of active leisure: doing nothing was better than doing something, and better than doing anything. Avoiding busy diversions allowed the sub-conscious freedom to operate fruitfully.

> And as for the third form of leisure, the most precious, the most consoling, and holy, the noble habit of doing nothing at all – that is being neglected in a degree that seems to me to threaten the degeneration of the whole race. It is because artists do not practice, patrons do not patronize, crowds do not assemble to reverently worship the great work of Doing Nothing, that the world has lost its philosophy and even failed to invent a new religion. From *On Leisure*.

Kierkegaard wanted to give one gift to the world: silence, so that men and women could encounter themselves, feel their dependence and lack of fulfillment, and then seek lasting satisfaction. But news, noise and activity are what men and women desire to avoid encountering themselves, feeling their sense of dependence and becoming conscious of their lack of fulfillment. Despite our complaints about our harried and busy lives, the possibility is that we don't want too much free time and peace in our lives: we would become distressed about ourselves. It's better therefore to skim along the surface of life. Reflective solitude is among our deepest needs, but we treat solitude like it's a punishment instead of a means of encountering ourselves and the reality we inhabit. Kierkegaard wrote about this odd perspective.

> Generally the need for solitude is a sign that there is spirit in a man after all, and it is a measure for what spirit there is. The pure twaddling inhuman and too-human men are to such a degree without feeling for the need of solitude that, like a certain species of social birds (the so-called love birds), they promptly die if for an instant they have to be alone. As this little child must be put to sleep with a lullaby, so these men need the tranquilizing hum of society before they are able to eat, drink, sleep, pray, fall in love, etc. But in ancient times as well as in the Middle Ages people were aware of this need for solitude and had respect for what it signifies. In the constant sociability of our age people shudder at solitude to such a degree that they know no other use to put it to but (oh, admirable

> epigram!) as a punishment for criminals. But after all it is a fact that in our age it is a crime to have spirit, so it is natural that such people, the lovers of solitude, are included in the same class with criminals. From *The Sickness unto Death*.

It takes a remarkable level of courage, honesty, determination and vulnerability to put first things first, to be an individual linked to eternity, to take responsibility for one's values and decisions, to see beyond the ostensible offensiveness of paradoxical ideas, to keep diversion from dominating one's life in order to seek the rich humanity, the vibrant life and the joy that wisdom will give those who persist in the search for it.

> Happy is the man who finds wisdom, and the man who gets understanding, for the gain from it is better than gain from silver and its profit better than gold. She is more precious than jewels, and nothing you desire can compare with her. Long life is in her right hand; in her left hand are riches and honor. Her ways are ways of pleasantness, and all her paths are peace. She is a tree of life to those who lay hold of her; those who hold her fast are called happy. 3:13-18

In this exploration of wisdom four sometimes neglected, somewhat misunderstood thinkers will be consulted: Blaise Pascal, Edmund Burke, Soren Kierkegaard and Gilbert Keith Chesterton. All were outsiders, to a lesser or greater extent, because each proclaimed to their culture that the fashionable philosophies were faulty and dangerous. This is a heroic role but not one that will garner much favour with the arrogant cliques who promote the inadequate, baleful philosophies. Further estranging these four men, not one of them was a professional philosopher or even an academic. Pascal was an amateur mathematician, a scientist and a man of letters. Burke was a parliamentarian. Kierkegaard was a writer and lay churchman. Chesterton was a journalist. This unprofessional dabbling in philosophy is another mark against them. To make matters worse, all four were pious. Their lives and their thinking were formed by Christian orthodoxy.

Blaise Pascal (1623-1662), a Frenchman, was a child prodigy. He published significant treatises on mathematics while still a teenager. In his twenties, he undertook experiments that established the basic principles of hydraulics, and he designed and built a machine that could add, subtract, multiply and divide – one of the forerunners of the computer. His friends were gamblers and they sparked his interest in games of chance. The result was Pascal's pioneering work on the mathematics of probability and statistical analysis. In addition, he promoted the idea of public transport, with many of his suggestions included in every public transport system now in existence: a set route, stops at set times, and prices set according to distance travelled.

However, Pascal lived in a tumultuous time. France was beset with religious troubles as the Crown and the Catholic majority sought to minimise the impact of various protestant movements, including reforming movements within the Catholic Church. Jansenism was one of these, and it was a Jansenist abbey, *Port Royal des Champs*, that Pascal went for religious retreats and instruction. Pascal's father and sisters first came into intimate contact with Jansenism when his father broke his arm and came under the ministrations of two bone-setters who were Jansenists. The Pascal family were impressed by the skill and tenderness of these men and the family moved from nominal Catholicism to ardent Christianity. Blaise had an intense Pentecost-like spiritual experience that he called his "night of fire." Like Simone Weil three centuries later, Pascal didn't find God – God found him in an unmistakable, life-changing manner. Pascal's devout commitment to Christianity was cemented by the experience – he kept a written record of it in a specially-made pocket of his jacket. But Jansenists, a tiny minority within French Catholicism, were viewed with grave suspicion. As momentum against those at Port Royal gathered weight under the auspices of the French sovereign and Church hierarchy, Pascal wrote in defense of the movement and his Jansenist friends. *The*

Provincial Letters was his first work of literature; in it he posed as a Parisian explaining the religious controversy to a fascinated provincial man. *The Provincial Letters* was a polemic sensation and demonstrated that Pascal was not only a scientist, mathematician, and inventor of the first rank, but a prose writer of the highest quality. Despite the wit, reason and intelligence of the work, it was not successful in forestalling official condemnation. The abbey at Port Royal was destroyed and its adherents forced to scatter. Blaise and his sisters, Josephine and Gilbertine, were distraught at the destruction of their spiritual home. Josephine died soon after, and Blaise, already a sick man, went to live with Gilbertine and her family.

Pascal had long considered writing a defense of Christianity for the benefit of its sophisticated detractors, many of whom were his friends, and he began to make notes for the work. But he became increasingly ill and died before he could complete his book. We're left with the notes, some gathered according to theme, others unclassified. They were published as *Pensees*; one of the most distinctive spiritual books written by a European. It influenced thinkers, writers and artists as diverse as Albert Camus, Simone Weil, Hannah Arendt, Takashi Nagai, Ignace Lepp, Georges Rouault, Graham Greene, and T.S. Eliot.

Edmund Burke (1729-1797), born a century after Pascal, was an Irishman who lived most of his life in England. He became involved in politics as secretary to a Whig statesman. In 1774, Burke entered Parliament as member for Bristol. He was a practical politician, suspicious of abstractions, of social and political theories, and wary of the danger of revolutionary thought. Burke wrote a treatise urging a conciliatory attitude toward the American colonies. He called for an acknowledgment of their legitimate grievances and an enlarged role for them in government. His advice was ignored. The War of Independence broke out, and England lost a rich, vibrant colony.

In 1784, England was seeking to lower its prison population by establishing penal colonies in Gambia. Burke spoke against that particular plan, accurately describing tropical Africa as a deathtrap for Europeans. He won the point. Within a few years convicts were sent, instead, to build their own prison camp at a far more salubrious place: Botany Bay. The penal colony seeded a nation, Australia.

Burke was a reformer, but he believed that reform required great patience – and was best undertaken by those who loved rather than despised the complexities that time and custom had built in society. He travelled to France numerous times, growing to love the country and its people. He knew the administration of France needed to rectify obvious injustices and inefficiencies, but he looked on with alarm as the French Revolution resulted in the overthrow of a government willing to change. Appalled, he saw the French nation impoverished, valuable traditions deliberately destroyed, and the population subjugated by pretentious intellectuals who were incompetent, divisive, excessively violent and in all ways unfit for rule. He wrote his masterpiece of political thought *Reflections on the Revolution in France* in 1790. One year into the revolution, he foresaw that the sure repercussions of a hasty taste for wholesale revolt would be the bankruptcy of the nation's treasuries, the rise of a dictatorship, the slaughter of people and the betrayal of their hopes as the state assumed greater control over their lives. Further, he saw that the champions of rationality and equality would meet their opponents, not with reasoned discourse and compromise, but with musket-balls and cannon fire. He was correct in his analysis. His mature understanding of society and his political acumen are of immense value.

Soren Kierkegaard (1813-1855) was a Danish writer of theological, psychological and philosophical works. He wrote in the context of two powerful and influential movements: Hegel's system of thought which posited that everything in existence was moving in a dialectical pattern towards comprehensive Spirit and Reason; and a state-sanctioned Lutheran Christianity that provided a comfortable, but largely inauthentic religious setting for Danes. Kierkegaard argued against Hegel's philosophical system because it robbed the individual of freedom, responsibility and significance. He argued with the Danish Lutheran Church because it had, in his words, "exchanged the strong whiskey of the gospel for lemonade". Kierkegaard thought Christendom – he differentiated Christianity from Christendom – invited complacency, conformity and faithlessness.

Kierkegaard is regarded as the father of existentialism, and this may be the case but it nonetheless reflects a distortion. Those who claim Kierkegaard as the forerunner of existentialism often ignore the clear and abundant evidence in Kierkegaard's own works that he was, consistent with his Christianity, an essentialist to the core. Certainly, he examined the existential life of the individual, but the governing essential truth was that every individual existed in a relationship with God (with the relationship either embraced or ignored) in a world created, not by chance or necessity or by the individual, but by God. It is because of these different presuppositions – Kierkegaard believed essence preceded existence, whereas the atheist existentialists such as Martin Heidegger and Jean-Paul Sartre believed that existence preceded essence – that Christian philosopher Gabriel Marcel, who revered Kierkegaard, described himself as a "philosopher of existence" or as a neo-Socratic rather than call himself an existentialist.

Kierkegaard focused on the individual rather than on society, the class, the tribe, nation or species because he knew we're unique individuals possessing rich self-consciousness and a sacred centre. This puts Kierkegaard in a class by himself in the middle of the nineteenth century compared to Hegel, Marx and Engels, John Stuart Mill, Auguste Comte or Charles Darwin. The fact that he was anomalous to the strains of thought that brought so much grief, directly or indirectly, to so many in the twentieth century establishes that he is worthy of deep respect. Kierkegaard said that what differentiated him and other theologically-centred thinkers from the mass of philosophers was that he and his devout antecedents began with paradox and mystery. Other thinkers refused this beginning and it was no surprise that inconsistencies and fragmentation in their philosophical projects soon revealed themselves. The philosophers have worked long and hard – they've worked for centuries, in fact – but they have achieved less than they imagine that is credible, helpful or lasting because they refuse to admit paradoxes. They will not knot the thread so their work can profitably begin. As a consequence, speculative thought has become a procession of theories which have their short time of prominence before unravelling, replaced by the next theory that also soon unravels. Kierkegaard exclaimed:

> The secret of speculative thought is exactly that it sews without fastening the end, without knotting the thread, and that is why it can keep on sewing and sewing: by pulling the thread through. Christianity, in contrast, has knotted the thread with the help of the paradox. From *The Sickness unto Death*.

Speculative philosophy refuses to admit paradoxes because paradoxes make assertions that seem contradictory; they confound human understanding and defy convention. Paradoxes are an offense to human understanding which insists on its own limited understanding as the ultimate standard of validity. Christianity, as Kierkegaard repeatedly emphasised, is based on paradoxes: it is thick with ideas that confound human comprehension. Christianity is therefore offensive in some way to every person who makes their own understanding the measure of validity rather than acknowledging that they are a creature "before God", a favourite phrase of Kierkegaard's because it describes man's essential characteristic and privileged position. Ludwig Wittgenstein was provoked and challenged as he read Kierkegaard. Wittgenstein said Kierkegaard was "by far the most interesting philosopher of the nineteenth century".

Gilbert Keith Chesterton (1874-1936) battled in the early twentieth century like a jouster in a public tournament, and his opponents were the systems of thought formulated in the late nineteenth century: determinism, the growing power of the state over the individual, nihilism, eugenics, Darwinism, Marxism, imperialism, materialism, and those who disliked babies, families, festivities, homes and beer. He fought against life-denying things because he believed in positive things: reason, play, religion, good traditions, the dignity of everybody, joy, friendship, feasting, home life, creativity and responsibility.

Chesterton was not a distinguished student; one of his teachers considered him a dull boy with few prospects: a stunning misjudgment. He studied art at the Slade School, but soon veered towards journalism, the trade in which he happily worked for the rest of his life. Journalism trained him, and gave him the opportunity, to write about a bewildering range of subjects. Eyebrows, Robert Louis Stevenson, war memorials, Communism, bad poetry, Jonathon Swift, industrialism, Darwinism, suicide, monsters, love, and pagan religion are just some of the subjects from one of his many books of essays (*All I Survey*). Chesterton enjoyed the rush and currency of writing newspaper articles, but somehow between the demands of journalism, lecture tours, the love of rowdy discussions in pubs and devotion to his wife, Frances, he also found time to write poems, many novels and short stories and hundreds of essays. He also wrote a neglected play, *Magic*, that was not neglected by at least one person: Ingmar Bergman cited it as a key influence. Chesterton was beloved by figures as varied as Ernest Hemingway, Franz Kafka, Jorge Luis Borges, Flannery O'Connor, Jacques Maritain, E.F. Schumacher, Dorothy Sayers, Clive James, Josef Pieper and Martin Amis. He was a loyal but combative friend of some of the giants of English modernism, most famously with H.G. Wells and George Bernard Shaw.

Chesterton was received into the Catholic Church in 1922, but was committed to Christianity long before that point. He described himself as a pagan as a child and an agnostic as a young man. *Orthodoxy* outlines the story of, and the reasons for, his conversion and is the most popular of his many non-fiction works. When Chesterton died, Pope Pius XI described him as "a gifted defender of the faith". C.S. Lewis said that Chesterton was the wisest man in England. The fact that he is so largely forgotten today is testament to the lack of wisdom of our times. But we have the freedom to refuse being entirely defined by our times.

Proverbs and *Ecclesiastes* are products of ancient Jewish culture. There are other Jewish wisdom books of very great value and interest, especially *The Book of Wisdom* and *Wisdom of Sirach*, but these are not included in the Hebrew scriptural canon. The Jews, because of the *diaspora* and the careful garnering of their traditions, shared the wisdom books with many other cultures, enriching those cultures that were receptive to them and their literature.

Pascal considered the Jews a unique people with an incredible history. He was intrigued by their story, their religious customs and laws, their prophets, their fantastic longevity. He thought part of the clue to the puzzle of life was contained in Jewish culture. Certainly he thought the complexities and contradictions they embodied merited special attention. Pascal's observations form one more reason to focus on the wisdom literature of this extraordinary people.

> Advantages of the Jewish people. – In this search the Jewish people at once attracts my attention by the number of wonderful and singular facts which appear about them.
>
> I first see that they are a people wholly composed of brethren, and whereas all others are formed by the assemblage of an infinity of families, this, though so wonderfully fruitful, has all sprung from one man alone, and, being thus all one flesh, and members one

of another, they constitute a powerful state of one family. This is unique.

This family, or people, is the most ancient within human knowledge, a fact which seems to me to inspire a peculiar veneration for it, especially in view of our present inquiry; since if God had from all time revealed Himself to men, it is to these we must turn for knowledge of the tradition.

This people is not eminent solely by their antiquity, but is also singular by their duration, which has always continued from their origin till now. For whereas the nations of Greece and of Italy, of Lacedæmon, of Athens and of Rome, and others who came long after, have long since perished, these ever remain, and in spite of the endeavours of many powerful kings who have a hundred times tried to destroy them, as their historians testify, and as it is easy to conjecture from the natural order of things during so long a space of years, they have nevertheless been preserved (and this preservation has been foretold); and extending from the earliest times to the latest, their history comprehends in its duration all our histories [which it preceded by a long time].

The law by which this people is governed is at once the most ancient law in the world, the most perfect, and the only one which has been always observed without a break in a state. This is what Josephus admirably proves, against Apion, and also Philo the Jew, in different places, where they point out that it is so ancient that the very name of law was only known by the oldest nation more than a thousand years afterwards; so that Homer, who has written the history of so many states, has never used the term. And it is easy to judge of its perfection by simply reading it; for we see that it has provided for all things with so great wisdom, equity, and judgment, that the most ancient legislators, Greek and Roman, having had some knowledge of it, have borrowed from it their principal laws; this is evident from what are called the Twelve Tables, and from the other proofs which Josephus gives.

But this law is at the same time the severest and strictest of all in respect to their religious worship, imposing on this people, in order to keep them to their duty, a thousand peculiar and painful observances, on pain of death. Whence it is very astonishing that it has been constantly preserved during many centuries by a people, rebellious and impatient as this one was; while all other states have changed their laws from time to time, although these were far more lenient.

The book which contains this law, the first of all, is itself the most ancient book in the world, those of Homer, Hesiod, and others, being six or seven hundred years later. 619.

Proverbs and *Ecclesiastes*, although very ancient, were compiled several centuries after the Pentateuch. Debate around the exact author(s) and dating of these books is not relevant to the personal embrace of the wisdom they contain and encourage. We must keep first things first.

2

THE SEARCH FOR WISDOM

The search for wisdom is prolonged and arduous, requiring complete and persistent dedication. This is because the wisdom outlined in *Proverbs* and *Ecclesiastes* is counter-cultural in many ways, with noisy opponents. To be more accurate, the wisdom contradicts many of the values of modernity and post-modernity. The easily-remembered sayings of *Proverbs* and *Ecclesiastes* were for many centuries among the guiding tenets of all levels of European, Levantine and Byzantine culture. But the tenets are routinely disputed today, and the disputers often own or operate the film and music studios, the newspapers and magazines, digital media, the television and radio stations, the intellectual journals and the publishing houses. The people disputing the value of the wisdom literature often have the ear of government when they don't actually sit in government. They determine the curricula of public schools and state universities, and control much of the wealth of the nation.

The voices disparaging this wisdom are powerful, not with truth and insight, but with the confidence and arrogance that are the trappings of wealth and status. Many people, easily taken in by a brash and convincing display, will mistake this confidence and assurance with strength of argument. In debate, the powerful will often seem to outwit and defeat the wise because the wise will be slow to answer, silent in reflection, humble in spirit and gentle in tone which hasty people, unimpressed by such a poor display, will mistake for stupidity and inadequacy. The powerful usually speak without concern for the dignity of those with no power. The wise speak hesitantly and courteously because they want to honour the dignity of everybody, especially those who oppose them and who, by doing so, degrade their own dignity.

The wise further fail to impress the popular imagination because they speak in stories, in paradoxes, in prayers and in actions without seeking to draw attention to themselves. They're likely to remain unacknowledged; they're not interested in self-promotion and self-publicity. Many people, especially if they want power, influence or celebrity are interested in little else.

In addition, the search for wisdom, if undertaken seriously, may be lonely because there are few cenobitic settings to support the search. Unfortunately, monasteries, convents, and abbeys do not dot the landscape as they once did in Europe, for example. They are, however, slowly being re-established: a very welcome development. One may perhaps find a book club or church that provides some encouragement in the search for wisdom, but even there it will probably proceed indirectly rather than intentionally. Ultimately, it's a neglected search and an individual search. In Pascal's assessment it's a search that requires the total commitment of real love.

> Truth is so obscure in these times, and falsehoods so established, that unless we love the truth we cannot find it. 863.

The wisdom literature itself says wisdom is the best possible investment; nothing is more valuable. Acquiring it is imperative.

> To get wisdom is better than gold; to get understanding is to be chosen rather than silver. 16:16.

> Buy truth, and do not sell it; buy wisdom, instruction, and understanding. 23:23.

It's an individual, passionate, and probably an anonymous search. Wisdom is unlikely to be rewarded with popularity, nor is a wise person often remembered; a reality the wise themselves acknowledge.

> I have also seen this example of wisdom under the sun, and it seemed great to me. There was a little city with few men in it; and a great king came against it and besieged it, building great siegeworks against it. But there was found in it a poor wise man, and he by his wisdom delivered the city. Yet no one remembered that poor man. But I say that wisdom is better than might, though the poor man's wisdom is despised, and his words are not heeded. The words of the wise heard in quiet are better than the shouting of a ruler among fools. *Ecclesiastes* 9:14-17.

In part, any wisdom attained will go unrecognised because its validity is disputed, and also because people are generally too busy (or diverted) to notice wisdom even when it saves their lives. An encounter with wisdom may change history, but not often to the extent that its remarkable achievements are celebrated. To give one example: every single person in the Western world, at some level, owes the gentleness, the stimulating lessons and the effectiveness of their schooling to a nearly forgotten man, John Amos Comenius. His is hardly a household name anywhere except in his native Czech Republic. In the seventeenth century, Comenius changed children's formal education from a harsh system that used frequent beatings and repetition without explanation as the basic teaching tools into a system that acknowledged the natural curiosity of the child. Comenius understood that gentleness achieved more than harshness and that due recognition inspired effort. Nearly every European nation that embraced the Reformation also embraced at least part of his system. Through the legacy of his influence and the good sense of his pedagogical approach, Comenius permanently changed the school experience of hundreds of millions of people. Yet today, even teachers and educational theorists would struggle to recognise his name and identify his achievements.

Besides the disputed nature of wisdom and common distractions, there's another reason why people don't seek wisdom: they dislike reproof and correction. The pain felt when one's failings are identified, even when the failings are minor, are highlighted privately and only so improvement can be made, is too great for some people and they refuse to listen. They stop where they are in terms of skills, experience and expertise and will not develop much further. They're apprentices who scorn their instructors, athletes who sack their candid coaches. They conflate humility with humiliation and want encouragement but not correction. They fear the pain of honest self-perception more than they fear the pain of stubborn self-deception. It's a serious fault. Pascal wrote of the blinding nature of self-love in regard to reproof.

> *Self-love.* – The nature of self-love and of this human Ego is to love self only and consider self only. But what will man do? He cannot prevent this object that he loves from being full of faults and wants. He wants to be great, and he sees himself small. He wants to be happy, and he sees himself miserable. He wants to be perfect, and he sees himself full of imperfections. He wants to be the object of love and esteem among men, and he sees that his faults merit only their hatred and contempt. This embarrassment in which he finds himself produces in him the most unrighteous and criminal passion that can be imagined; for he conceives a mortal enmity against that truth which reproves him, and which convinces him of his faults. He would annihilate it, but, unable to destroy it in its essence, he destroys it as far as possible in his own knowledge and in that of others; that is to say, he devotes all his attention to hiding his faults both from others and from himself, and he cannot endure either that others should point them out to him, or that they should see them.
>
> Truly it is an evil to be full of faults; but it is a still greater evil to be full of them, and to be unwilling to recognise them, since that is to add the further fault of a voluntary illusion. We do not like others to

deceive us; we do not think it fair that they should be held in higher esteem by us than they deserve; it is not then fair that we should deceive them, and should wish them to esteem us more highly than we deserve.

Thus, when they discover only the imperfections and vices which we really have, it is plain they do us no wrong, since it is not they who cause them; they rather do us good, since they help us to free ourselves from an evil, namely, the ignorance of these imperfections. We ought not to be angry at their knowing our faults and despising us; it is but right that they should know us for what we are, and should despise us, if we are contemptible.

Such are the feelings that would arise in a heart full of equity and justice. What must we say then of our own heart, when we see in it a wholly different disposition? For is it not true that we hate truth and those who tell it us, and that we like them to be deceived in our favour, and prefer to be esteemed by them as being other than what we are in fact? One proof of this makes me shudder. The Catholic religion does not bind us to confess our sins indiscriminately to everybody; it allows them to remain hidden from all other men save one, to whom she bids us reveal the innermost recesses of our heart, and show ourselves as we are. There is only this one man in the world whom she orders us to undeceive, and she binds him to an inviolable secrecy, which makes this knowledge to him as if it were not. Can we imagine anything more charitable and pleasant? And yet the corruption of man is such that he finds even this law harsh; and it is one of the main reasons which has caused a great part of Europe to rebel against the Church.

How unjust and unreasonable is the heart of man, which feels it disagreeable to be obliged to do in regard to one man what in some measure it were right to do to all men! For is it right that we should deceive men?

There are different degrees in this aversion to truth; but all may perhaps be said to have it in some degree, because it is inseparable from self-love. It is this false delicacy which makes those who are under the necessity of reproving others choose so many windings and middle courses to avoid offence. They must lessen our faults, appear to excuse them, intersperse praises and evidence of love and esteem. Despite all this, the medicine does not cease to be bitter to self-love. It takes as little as it can, always with disgust, and often with a secret spite against those who administer it.

Hence it happens that if any have some interest in being loved by us, they are averse to render us a service which they know to be disagreeable. They treat us as we wish to be treated. We hate the truth, and they hide it from us. We desire flattery, and they flatter us. We like to be deceived, and they deceive us.

So each degree of good fortune which raises us in the world removes us farther from truth, because we are most afraid of wounding those whose affection is most useful and whose dislike is most dangerous. A prince may be the byword of all Europe, and he alone will know nothing of it. I am not astonished. To tell the truth is useful to those to whom it is spoken, but disadvantageous to those who tell it, because it makes them disliked. Now those who live with princes love their own interests more than that of the prince whom they serve; and so they take care not to confer on him a benefit so as to injure themselves.

This evil is no doubt greater and more common among the higher classes; but the lower are not exempt from it, since there is always some advantage in making men love us. Human life is thus only a perpetual illusion; men deceive and flatter each other. No one speaks of us in our presence as he does of us in our absence. Human society is founded on mutual deceit; few friendships would endure if each knew what his friend said of him in his absence, although he then spoke in sincerity and without passion.

Man is then only disguise, falsehood, and hypocrisy, both in himself and in regard to others. He does not wish any one to tell him the truth; he avoids telling it to others, and all these dispositions, so removed from justice and reason, have a natural root in his heart. 100.

Accepting reproof and correction is a key prerequisite in the search for wisdom; but for proud people instruction in the form of reproof is unacceptable. Proud people prefer to do things badly or unjustly rather than suffer the blow to the vision of themselves that comes by accepting the truth of their limitations, inexperience or selfishness. In contrast, people who are realistic about their need for knowledge and instruction usually possess the humility to accept correction. And this humility is needed because *Proverbs* insists reproof and correction are integral to wisdom.

> Give heed to my reproof; behold, I will pour out my thoughts to you; I will make my words known to you. 1:23.
>
> He who heeds instruction is on the path to life, but he who rejects reproof goes astray. 10:17.
>
> Whoever loves discipline loves knowledge, but he who hates reproof is stupid. 12:1.
>
> Poverty and disgrace come to him who ignores instruction, but he who heeds reproof is honored. 13:18.

Reproof and correction are best delivered with sensitivity, but given the reality of human egotism and the pressure of priorities, it's probable that correction and reproof will on occasion be somewhat severe and therefore offensive. Even Jesus, who deeply loved his disciples, sometimes offended them with his reproofs; many ceased following him for this reason. Sometimes the risk of danger calls for a degree of severity. Sometimes great folly invites firm rebuke. But a gentle rebuke is best with care taken to minimise the possibility of offense.

> Do not reprove a scoffer, or he will hate you; reprove a wise man, and he will love you. 9:8.

> Whoever loves discipline loves knowledge, but he who hates reproof is stupid. 12:1.
>
> A rebuke goes deeper into a man of understanding than a hundred blows into a fool. 17:10.

We learn by accumulating skills, knowledge and experience; it's a slow process where practice, mistakes, correction and learning go hand-in-hand. A prudent man sees his need to increase knowledge; he knows he is not, never will be, wholly capable and comprehensively informed. Constant learning, constant reflection and constant refinement of understanding and perspective are required.

> Do not reprove a scoffer, or he will hate you; reprove a wise man, and he will love you. Give instruction to a wise man, and he will be still wiser; teach a righteous man and he will increase in learning. 9:8,9.

There is no such thing as Instant Wisdom in therapeutic, mystical, pharmaceutical or philosophical form. Learning from experience, good teaching, humility, and persistently seeking sagacity over decades are required. This doesn't suit our culture which doubts the expediency of life-defining commitments, long perseverance or plodding effort for a disputed knowledge. The writer of *Ecclesiastes* – a man divinely gifted with wisdom – perceived the realities of life "little by little". Our experience will surely be the same, discovering truths gradually over long periods of time; not weeks and months but years and decades.

Facing and overcoming these difficulties, especially the difficulty of attending to reproof, will be rewarded. It's the right path, light slowly and gradually dawning on it.

> But the path of the righteous is like the light of dawn, which shines brighter and brighter until full day. The way of the wicked is like deep darkness; they do not know over what they stumble. 4:18, 19.
>
> He whose ear heeds wholesome admonition will abide among the

wise. He who ignores instruction despises himself, but he who heeds admonition gains understanding. 15:31, 32.

The hardest thing to see is our own weaknesses; we are weakened by our inability or unwillingness to see our frailties. Simply because we have succeeded in school and university, in a trade or a career, or because we have passed through childhood to adolescence and adulthood, we tend to assume that we're able independently to determine the best way to live. Our achievements and successes encourage us to believe that we are not ignorant, but they don't give us enough knowledge to recognise our real level of ignorance. Pascal categorised this position as a ruinous half-way house of the mind. It's the condition of many people; it is especially the condition of most young university graduates and earnest activists.

> The sciences have two extremes which meet. The first is the pure natural ignorance in which all men find themselves at birth. The other extreme is that reached by great intellects, who, having run through all that men can know, find they know nothing, and come back again to that same ignorance from which they set out; but this is a learned ignorance which is conscious of itself. Those between the two, who have departed from natural ignorance and not been able to reach the other, have some smattering of this vain knowledge, and pretend to be wise. These trouble the world, and are bad judges of everything. 327.

Proverbs identifies this inclination to proud self-sufficiency as common but calamitous. It's repeatedly addressed in negative terms.

> There is a way which seems right to a man, but its end is the way to death. 14:12.

> Do you see a man who is wise in his own eyes? There is more hope for a fool than for him. 26:12.

> He who trusts in his own mind is a fool; but he who walks in wisdom will be delivered. 28:26.

Imagining we are self-sufficient is the delusion of bunglers. They assume there's no need for advice from people with more experience and skills; they think what they already know will suffice for the challenges ahead. They believe, incorrectly, that the superior individual will triumph.

Their self-confidence is abetted by the Enlightenment's philosophy which still frames much of the culture of the West. It extols the ratiocination of the individual, disparaging tradition and religion as vital sources of knowledge. Not surprisingly, self-centredness as a basis for one's epistemology leads naturally to self-centredness in action, with deleterious results for oneself, one's family and community. Complete self-confidence is a trap; it's better to be guided by a healthy level of self-diffidence.

Humility is not only a moral or spiritual ideal but a vital epistemological ideal because it's open to new perspectives and fresh possibilities. Humility is an aid to pragmatism; it encourages submitting to experience without insisting on comprehensive understanding before adopting an effective strategy. This is important and honours the fact that our practical knowledge may well run ahead of our theoretical understanding. For example, in the seventeenth and eighteenth centuries, thousands of new mothers died unnecessarily from puerperal fever as doctors moved straight from autopsies to attending women in childbirth; unwittingly, the doctors carried deadly bacteria from the cadavers to the healthy women and infected them. In 1847, Ignaz Semmelweiss, an Hungarian doctor, made the connection between the autopsies and the infections. He found that hand-washing in a chlorinated-lime solution greatly lessened the mortality rate of birthing women attended by doctors. However, he couldn't offer an acceptable scientific explanation for his observations. The medical fraternity was loath to adopt laborious hand-washing habits because they didn't seem logical. The necessary rational link – Pasteur's discovery of the existence and effects of bacteria – hadn't yet been formulated. The doctors, proud and busy professionals, continued to scorn hand-washing.

And they infected thousands more new mothers creating thousands more needless tragedies.

Proverbs and *Ecclesiastes* are based on a simple yet direct form of empiricism: one looks at the world, reflects on experience and draws conclusions about life. This process is possible because man and the world complement each other; they have the same creator. It's a form of rationalism but it's far removed from the idealistic Rationalism lauded by speculative thinkers.

The wisdom literature is much more inclined towards empiricism rather than idealism. It's a practical understanding that engages with everyday life. It doesn't seek to build an abstract map of reality based on causal laws, a project beloved by many philosophers of previous centuries, although now it's fashionable to discount such grandiose visions.

Proverbs and *Ecclesiastes* present an existential understanding of life, but one that is based firmly on essences: an individual explores and develops their given essence throughout their existence. Our essence is sacred personhood; our existential task is to express this essence in our unique individuality. We advance or retard this task through the big and small decisions we make every moment of every day. We gradually unfold or distort our essence in our existence.

This unfolding process takes time; all our life, in fact. Accordingly *Proverbs* demands respect for devout, functional, balanced elders. Of course, many older people have not bothered much to develop these qualities – *acedia* has defined their lives – but even these torpid elders may have at least some valuable lessons that are worth hearing.

Chesterton defended the reasonableness of appealing to humanity's senses – our engagement with the concretion of things – and contrasted this with the abstractions of idealism. The invitation in *Proverbs* to come to Wisdom's feast rather than Wisdom's lecture typifies its seemingly prosaic approach. For Chesterton, this is a sign of authenticity.

> If any one wandering about wants to have a good trick or test for separating the wrong idealism from the right, I will give him one on the spot. It is a mark of false religion that it is always trying to express concrete facts as abstract: it calls sex affinity; it calls wine alcohol; it calls brute starvation the economic problem. The test of true religion is that its energy drives exactly the other way; it is always trying to make men feel truths as facts; always trying to make abstract things as plain and solid as concrete things; always trying to make men, not merely admit the truth, but see, smell, handle, hear, and devour the truth. All great spiritual scriptures are full of the invitation not to test, but to taste; not to examine but to eat.
>
> From *The Appetite of Earth*.

Comprehensive knowledge of the world is simply beyond us; we are limited, mortal, and dependent creatures prone to self-deception, to confusion, to temptation. We don't fully understand ourselves, and we cannot even predict what will happen tomorrow. Pascal honoured man's faculties of thought and observation but, like *Proverbs* and *Ecclesiastes*, he scoffed at the over-reaching, pretentious thinking of proud men. He knew we are limited, mysteries to ourselves living amid immense mysteries.

> We know ourselves so little, that many think they are about to die when they are well, and many think they are well when they are near death, unconscious of approaching fever, or of the abscess ready to form itself. 175.

> The last proceeding of reason is to recognise that there is an infinity of things which are beyond it. It is but feeble if it does not see so far as to know this. But if natural things are beyond it, what will be said of supernatural? 267.

Pascal wrote that one purpose of *Ecclesiastes* is to demonstrate that man's faculties, although magnificent, are incapable of delivering wisdom or happiness. The endless enigmas of creation and the contradictions of man's nature are against him.

> *Ecclesiastes* shows that man without God is in total ignorance and inevitable misery. For it is wretched to have the wish, but not the power. Now he would be happy and assured of some truth, and yet he can neither know, nor desire not to know. He cannot even doubt. 389.

In *Proverbs*, naivety is synonymous with immaturity. Sentimentality sees naivety as a sweet form of innocence, but it isn't in any way commendable or excusable. The naive person overlooks the prevalence of unforeseen factors and events; he discounts the impact of the unknown, assuring himself that it won't affect his plans. But there is so much we can't control, don't imagine will happen and don't understand. Naivety is a dangerous lack of knowledge *about our lack of knowledge;* it leaves the simple person vulnerable to adverse circumstances and exploitation by self-centred people. The wisdom literature is distinctly unsentimental.

> How long, O simple ones, will you love being simple? How long will scoffers delight in their scoffing and fools hate knowledge? 1:22.

> The simple believes everything, but the prudent looks where he is going. 14:15.

> The simple acquire folly, but the prudent are crowned with knowledge. 14:18.

A judicious person will consider his limits, knowing he cannot foresee and control everything. Mystery surrounds us because we are dependent creatures in a universe not of our making. Part of the mystery is that we are responsible for our acts, but the partly-hidden creator is sovereign, his intents and actions inscrutable. Our plans will not likely proceed as we expect. Constantly in human affairs the importance of time, chance and change is underestimated. Often, however, they are decisive.

> A man's mind plans his way, but the LORD directs his steps. 16:9.

The lot is cast into the lap, but the decision is wholly from the LORD. 16:33.

Many are the plans in the mind of a man, but it is the purpose of the LORD that will be established. 19:21.

A man's steps are ordered by the LORD; how then can man understand his way? 20:24.

The horse is made ready for the day of battle, but the victory belongs to the LORD. 21:31.

Whatever your hand finds to do, do it with your might; for there is no work or thought or knowledge or wisdom in Sheol, to which you are going. Again I saw that under the sun the race is not to the swift, nor the battle to the strong, nor bread to the wise, nor riches to the intelligent, nor favor to the men of skill; but time and chance happen to them all. For man does not know his time. Like fish which are taken in an evil net, and like birds which are caught in a snare, so the sons of men are snared at an evil time, when it suddenly falls upon them. *Ecclesiastes* 9:10-12.

As you do not know how the spirit comes to the bones in the womb of a woman with child, so you do not know the work of God who makes everything. In the morning sow your seed, and at evening withhold not your hand; for you do not know which will prosper, this or that, or whether both alike will be good. *Ecclesiastes* 11:5, 6.

The wisdom literature advises careful thought before starting any venture or project. Expending labour, capital and assets without adequate forethought and on-going management is careless and usually profitless. Experience and knowledge provide the best basis for evaluating the utility of any undertaking, and then for the appropriate allocation of time, capital, assets and effort. Because we are not fully in control of our own circumstances, flexibility and patience are required. Prudence – reason in action – is advocated, while impetuosity and complacency are condemned.

> In everything a prudent man acts with knowledge, but a fool flaunts his folly. 13:16.
>
> An intelligent mind acquires knowledge, and the ear of the wise seeks knowledge. 18:15.

Asking advice from worthy people is one of the best ways to gain knowledge and insight. But we need to get advice from mature people, because dysfunctional people are often eager to instruct. This is common. The loudest people, the most opinionated people, and those prone to self-promotion are quick to speak, but there's a catch: they're unlikely to say much that survives scrutiny. In contrast, the truly shrewd are quiet and easily overlooked; in their humility they may not step forward to speak. But their lives commend them: if they are married, their marriages last; they work to maintain themselves and their family rather than depend on welfare and handouts; their children grow into productive adults; the sacred is central to their lives; they are hospitable and good neighbours; they appreciate beauty but are not enthralled by material goods; they are honest; they are not gulled by fashionable opinion; they speak quietly and listen attentively. These, rather than people who shout their views and praise themselves, are the people to ask for advice.

> He who walks with wise men becomes wise, but the companion of fools will suffer harm. 13:20.
>
> The lips of the wise spread knowledge; not so the minds of fools. 15:7.
>
> A fool takes no pleasure in understanding, but only in expressing his opinion. 18:2.

Good decisions require advice from more than one person. A multiplicity of perspectives and experiences is best. And the greater the gravity, the more important this principle becomes. For example, in tense foreign relations when the nation's independence is threatened and war is possible, it's imperative to gain the guidance of many perceptive people. *Proverbs* advocates a multiplicity of counselors.

> Where there is no guidance, a people falls; but in an abundance of counselors there is safety. 11:14.
>
> Without counsel plans go wrong, but with many advisers they succeed. 15:22.
>
> Plans are established by counsel; by wise guidance wage war. 20:18.
>
> A wise man is mightier than a strong man, and a man of knowledge than he who has strength; for by wise guidance you can wage your war, and in abundance of counselors there is victory. 24:5,6.

The principle remains valid in the individual's life; none of us alone has sufficient wisdom, knowledge and experience to make consistently excellent decisions. Parents, grand-parents and good-living teachers are a ready source of counsel. The onus is on the learner to receive instruction, which may be contrary to his preferences. Several proverbs address this theme.

> A wise son hears his father's instruction, but a scoffer does not listen to rebuke. 13:1.
>
> Give instruction to a wise man, and he will be still wiser; teach a righteous man and he will increase in learning. 9:9.
>
> The wise of heart will heed commandments, but a prating fool will come to ruin. 10:8.

A person seeking wisdom will not be naive, nor will they be an incorrigible sceptic. True wisdom is a third position that avoids the extremes of simplicity and cynicism, of believing anything or believing nothing. These extreme positions are invitations to incapacity.

> A scoffer seeks wisdom in vain, but knowledge is easy for a man of understanding. 14:6.

> The mind of him who has understanding seeks knowledge, but the mouths of fools feed on folly. 15:14.

Wisdom doesn't come naturally with the passage of years; sapience isn't forced to keep company with greying hair and yellowing teeth. Wisdom is a spiritual quality and like all spiritual qualities it requires constant, diligent cultivation. Kierkegaard knew the difference between growing old and growing mature; he didn't conflate the categories.

> In the main it is a great folly, and precisely a lack of sense as to what spirit is, and moreover a failure to appreciate that man is spirit, not merely an animal, when one supposes that it might be such an easy matter to acquire faith and wisdom, which come with the years as a matter of course, like teeth and a beard and such like. No, whatever it may be that a man as a matter of course comes to, and whatever it may be that comes to a man as a matter of course – one thing it is not, namely, faith and wisdom. From *The Sickness unto Death*.

Continuing the life-long search for wisdom is an on-going choice. Old age is included.

> A hoary head is a crown of glory; if it is gained in a righteous life. 16:31.

> Listen to advice and accept instruction, that you may gain wisdom for the future. 19:20.

> My son, eat honey, for it is good, and the drippings of the honeycomb are sweet to your taste. Know that wisdom is such to your soul; if you find it, there will be a future, and your hope will not be cut off. 24:13, 14.

Searching for wisdom can also be abandoned. This isn't a neutral position; it's stumbling backwards into obtuseness.

> Why should a fool have a price in his hand to buy wisdom, when he has no mind? 17:16.

> Cease, my son, to hear instruction only to stray from the words of knowledge. 19:27

Just as there is always a pathway, a series of choices, that lead away from reverence and wisdom, so there is always a pathway that leads back. In this sense, an individual's path to wholeness is always provisional, paved with choice. Human free-will and dignity are founded on the grace and severity of God who allows each of us to choose and then re-choose the direction of our lives again and again and who always honours our choices. In Psalm 107, an account is given of delinquencies leading to disorder and then of the restored life that is possible: we choose. As long as we live, there is way back to goodness. The psalm concludes: "He who is wise will observe these things and they will understand the loving-kindness of the Lord".

We possess great skills and gifts, and the immense dignity of choosing our own level of fulfillment, but we need guidance, first from our creator and then from the accumulated wisdom of our community. The search for wisdom is individual but not individualistic. I alone must seek wisdom but I don't seek it in isolation; other people are my teachers, examples, helpers. In *Proverbs* and *Ecclesiastes* wisdom is expressed largely through life in community – financial relationships, sacred relationships, familial and work relationships, friendship and neighbourly relationships, political, managerial and administrative relationships. It's primarily in these settings that maturity is measured. A sapient person is ensconced in his community, consciously contributing to its vibrancy and goodness. A trouble-maker is abrasive and self-centred; they frustrate their community and are unworthy of serious responsibilities in it.

The first and most important of our relationships is with our family. In the modern West we tend to define the family (when we don't dismantle it) as the nuclear family, but it's the whole family – aunts, uncles and especially grand-parents – that *Proverbs* assumes to have a central role in our life.

It locates the family home as the primary place for instruction. Parents are the first and should be the finest teachers of their children, and they have the responsibility to guide, instruct, reprove, and warn. Parents who neglect these responsibilities do not love their children as they ought.

> He who spares the rod hates his son, but he who loves him is diligent to discipline him. 13:24.
>
> Discipline your son while there is hope; do not set your heart on his destruction. 19:18.
>
> Train up a child in the way he should go, and when he is old he will not depart from it. 22:6.
>
> Discipline your son, and he will give you rest; he will give delight to your heart. 29:17.

Actions which damage the integrity and functionality of the family are serious faults, with adultery being obviously destructive. However, adultery is only one of several very serious follies that harm our lives, families and communities.

3

FOUR FOLLIES TO AVOID

Proverbs and *Ecclesiastes* provide both admonitions to follow and warnings about villainies to avoid. Repeated warnings are given to avoid ruinous practices such as drunkenness, bribery, and slander. But there are four particularly insensate yet common follies addressed in a varied and dramatic manner: adultery, insurrection, lazyness and pride. Warnings are pointed because they're humanity's common vices. We are all in danger of failing to relate creditably to our family, our society, to our tasks and ourselves.

i. THE FOLLY OF ADULTERY

Life is both short and long. Essentially, life is short. Even if we live to ripe old age, our years are few against the whole of human history and as nothing compared to eternity. Existentially, life is long, or it seems long because of the unending tension between the polarities – freedom and necessity, the physical and the spiritual, the temporal and the eternal – that constitute our nature. Further, passing time brings manifold opportunities and challenges to us, adding the pressure of making countless decisions that form or deform our life.

The principal author of *Proverbs*, King Solomon, reflects on the confusion and brevity of life and the inevitability of death in *Ecclesiastes*. (The extent of his authorship of *Proverbs* and *Ecclesiastes* varies according to different traditions).

> For every matter has its time and way, although man's trouble lies heavy upon him. For he does not know what is to be, for who can tell him how it will be? No man has power to retain the spirit, or authority over the day of death; there is no discharge from war, nor will wickedness deliver those who are given to it. *Ecclesiastes* 8:6-8.

Pascal uses more direct, unpleasant images to convey our mortal state.

> Let us imagine a number of men in chains, and all condemned to death, where some are killed each day in the sight of the others, and those who remain see their own fate in that of their fellows, and wait their turn, looking at each other sorrowfully and without hope. It is an image of the condition of men. 199.

> The last act is tragic, however happy all the rest of the play is; at the last a little earth is thrown upon our head, and that is the end for ever. 210.

> We run carelessly to the precipice, after we have put something before us to prevent us seeing it. 183.

> When I consider the short duration of my life, swallowed up in the eternity before and after, the little space which I fill, and even can see, engulfed in the infinite immensity of spaces of which I am ignorant, and which know me not, I am frightened, and am astonished at being here rather than there; for there is no reason why here rather than there, why now rather than then. Who has put me here? By whose order and direction have this place and time been allotted to me? *Memoria hospitis unius diei prætereuntis.* [Remembrance of a guest who tarried but a day.] 205.

> The power of flies; they win battles, hinder our soul from acting, eat our body. 367.

We all know this is true although we prefer not to think about it. It's disturbing to realise that life is short, our death certain and our being mysterious. Pascal focused on this reality, too often neglected, in order to move us to search for wisdom. Pascal's strategy was similar to the strategy of the wisdom literature: the ambiguities and difficulties of life, including the unpleasant fact of our mortality, encourage us to search for wisdom; our search for wisdom leads us to God and God in turn provides wisdom.

> My son, if you receive my words and treasure up my commandments with you, making your ear attentive to wisdom and inclining your heart to understanding; yes, if you cry out for insight and raise your voice for understanding, if you seek it like silver and search for it as for hidden treasures; then you will understand the fear of the LORD and find the knowledge of God. For the LORD gives wisdom; from his mouth come knowledge and understanding; he stores up sound wisdom for the upright; he is a shield to those who walk in integrity, guarding the paths of justice and preserving the way of his saints. 2:1-8.

Time is an environment in which we live, and the gift of time is that every instant brings something new, never before seen in history. There are constant blessings and challenges. Our sexuality is a blessing that brings many pressing challenges.

We are sexual beings all our lives; every cell of our body expresses our sexuality, our maleness or femaleness. Our sexual drive is powerful and difficult to control; it is mysterious; it soaks both our conscious and unconscious being. It brings intense, unique pleasures; and our sexuality is intimately connected to our sense of self and self-value. Our sexuality gives us the privilege of expressing ourselves, and of demonstrating our power to bring forth or destroy new life.

Human sexuality is a wonder. Contemporary secular society portrays sex as natural, which is correct, and as ordinary, which is incorrect. Sex is extraordinary; it's something necessary and common yet enigmatic and profound. And when sex is uncoupled from ethics, artificially separated from a firm moral framework and especially from marriage and the family, then it threatens to become a tyrant, ruling our minds, our bodies, our money and our time. It invades and dominates areas of life where it has always properly existed but in a controlled and measured way; for example, in dance, music, art, theatre, literature, fashion, advertising. Unchecked, sexuality quickly assumes – because it has primal, attractive power – a disproportionate significance in these areas of life. Certainly, it should provide energy to all these creative enterprises but when uncontrolled by ethics and taboos, sex tends to fill the frame at the expense of the prior, primary intent.

Chesterton, writing in the early decades of the twentieth century, saw where sexuality divorced from traditional values would lead and he would not be surprised, although likely dismayed, to see porn stars becoming celebrities, sex used to sell everything from chocolate milk to motor scooters, simulated intercourse a staple scene in many movies, and attention-hungry celebrities exposing their breasts at the slightest promise of publicity or notoriety. Chesterton knew that one reason sex quickly usurped good sense was because paganism had an insufficient depth of mystic possibilities beyond the mysteries of nature: sex, death, growth. But natural mysteries are not sufficient by themselves to satisfy humanity; we need a richer and deeper supernatural mysticism to stay balanced and sane. Chesterton reviewed the mystical limitations of ancient Greek and Roman civilizations, and the principle he highlighted also applies to our increasingly shallow, narrow culture.

> What was the matter with the whole heathen civilization was that there was nothing for the mass of men in the way of mysticism, except that concerned with the nameless forces of nature, such as sex and growth and death. In the Roman Empire also, long before

the end, we find nature-worship inevitably producing things that are against nature. Cases like that of Nero have passed into proverb when Sadism sat on a throne brazen in the broad daylight. But the truth I mean here is something much more subtle and universal than a conventional catalogue of atrocities. What happened to the human imagination, as a whole, was that the whole world was coloured by dangerous and rapidly deteriorating passions; by natural passions becoming unnatural passions. Thus the effect of treating sex as only one innocent natural thing was that every other innocent natural thing became soaked and sodden with sex. For sex cannot be admitted to a mere equality among elementary emotions or experiences like eating and sleeping. The moment sex ceases to be a servant it becomes a tyrant. There is something dangerous and disproportionate in its place in human nature, for whatever reason; and it really does need a special purification and dedication. The modern talk about sex being free like any other sense, about the body being beautiful like any tree or flower, is either a description of the Garden of Eden or a piece of thoroughly bad psychology, of which the world grew weary two thousand years ago. From *St. Francis of Assisi*.

Mankind wants some form of mysticism, whether he knows it or not. When the defined and consciously-held mysticism of religion is embraced – through prayer, sacraments, fasting, saying grace before meals, and acts of contrition or worship, for example – then this appetite for mysticism is satisfied in good ways. When an undefined and largely unconscious mysticism prevails then it is potentially harmful; nature is deified, death glorified and sex multiplied. In the absence of spiritual mysticism, the natural mysteries surrounding growth, death and sex become dominant. In part, through the natural appetite of sex we hope to connect with mystery.

However, treating sex as an innocent appetite like any other soon leads to a jaded appetite. The sense of wonder associated with sexuality is lost. Fidelity and self-control become more difficult as the idea of sex with only one person – the marriage spouse – loses its appeal. Jaded taste desires new, more exotic and strange pleasures to remain stimulated. Chesterton saw this, too, and observed that an obsession with sex leads to a strange sort of thoughtlessness about sex. In this passage, Chesterton addressed polygamy, but the same lack of wonder applies to recreational sex, infidelity and sex addiction.

> Estates are sometimes held by foolish forms, the breaking of a stick or the payment of a peppercorn. I was willing to hold the whole huge estate of earth and heaven by any such feudal fantasy. It could not well be wilder than the fact that I was allowed to hold it at all. At this stage I give only one ethical instance to show my meaning. I could never mix in the common murmur of the rising generation against monogamy, because no restriction on sex seemed so odd and unexpected as sex itself. To be allowed, like Endymion, to make love to the moon and then to complain that Jupiter kept his own moons in a harem seemed to me (bred on fairy tales like Endymion's) a vulgar anticlimax. Keeping to one woman is a small price for so much as seeing one woman. To complain that I could only be married once was like complaining that I could only be born once. It was incommensurate with the terrible excitement of which one was talking. It showed, not an exaggerated sensibility to sex, but a curious insensibility to it. A man is a fool who complains that he cannot enter Eden by five gates at once. Polygamy is a lack of the realization of sex; it is like a man plucking five pears in mere absence of mind. From *Orthodoxy*.

This sense of wonder and gratitude for sexual expression is echoed in *Proverbs* which extols satisfaction with the charm, beauty and sexuality of our spouse.

> Drink water from your own cistern, flowing water from your own

well. Should your springs be scattered abroad, streams of water in the streets? Let them be for yourself alone, and not for strangers with you. Let your fountain be blessed, and rejoice in the wife of your youth, a lovely hind, a graceful doe. Let her affection fill you at all times with delight, be infatuated always with her love. 5:15-19.

Adultery is one of the greatest enemies of marriage. Marriages can survive many troubling things, but few can survive repeated adultery. Sexual and romantic expression is explored through the love of our husband or wife, not another person's spouse, a prostitute or a seductive single man or woman. In the wisdom literature, infidelity and irresponsible sex are portrayed as profligate scorn for that which is near to us, the scattering of that which is precious. This is particularly the case when careless single men and women beget children who grow up estranged from one of their parents and very likely estranged from their grand-parents as well: a double loss. These children are often robbed of the love and instruction of a parent, and the absent parent is robbed of their responsibility, or carelessly neglects, to cherish and instruct the very person – their child – who should be a treasure to them. The absent parent's role may be undertaken, often without the required love by someone else: a step-parent, a short-term lover, or the school counselor. In many cases (certainly not all), these will be wholly inadequate substitutes. Sometimes they will prove dangerous and sordid substitutes for the natural father or mother.

Proverbs insists that parents teach their children right from wrong, including extensive teaching about marriage, with warnings about infidelity and promiscuous sexuality. This shouldn't be shirked: specific instruction is required. Leaving our maturing young people unprepared to face the temptations of smooth seducers, prostitutes, or adulterers is irresponsible. This instruction is provided in multiple passages, emphasising that repeated warnings are required. The matter is serious, the consequences grave.

My son, be attentive to my wisdom, incline your ear to my

> understanding; that you may keep discretion, and your lips may guard knowledge. For the lips of a loose woman drip honey, and her speech is smoother than oil; but in the end she is bitter as wormwood, sharp as a two-edged sword. Her feet go down to death; her steps follow the path to Sheol; she does not take heed to the path of life; her ways wander, and she does not know it. 5:1-6.
>
> My son, give me your heart, and let your eyes observe my ways. For a harlot is a deep pit; an adventuress is a narrow well. She lies in wait like a robber and increases the faithless among men. 23:26-28.

The parents' teaching must include the beauty of wise sexual expression and its contrary, the ugliness of selfish sexual expression. This isn't the government or the school's responsibility, although it has been increasingly arrogated by educationalists or lazily surrendered by parents to an aggressively secular state who will teach their own faddish, imbalanced values to children.

Here, advocating the traditional seven virtues and an awareness of the seven vices is a great benefit. Many people run to ruin simply because they don't have clarity about what values to pursue and what vices to avoid. Those who embrace greed and adultery will find harm and some level of personal disintegration. Those who embrace faith and temperance will find security and maintain their credibility.

> My son, keep your father's commandment, and forsake not your mother's teaching. Bind them upon your heart always; tie them about your neck. When you walk, they will lead you; when you lie down, they will watch over you; and when you awake, they will talk with you. For the commandment is a lamp and the teaching a light, and the reproofs of discipline are the way of life, to preserve you from the evil woman, from the smooth tongue of the adventuress. Do not desire her beauty in your heart, and do not let her capture you with her eyelashes; for a harlot may be hired for a loaf of bread, but an adulteress stalks a man's very life. 6:20-26.

> A foolish woman is noisy; she is wanton and knows no shame. She sits at the door of her house, she takes a seat on the high places of the town, calling to those who pass by, who are going straight on their way, "Whoever is simple, let him turn in here!" And to him who is without sense she says, "Stolen water is sweet, and bread eaten in secret is pleasant." But he does not know that the dead are there, that her guests are in the depths of Sheol. 9:13-18.

The proper place for rich, varied and life-long sexuality – including the begetting and instruction of children – is affectionate marriage because sex isn't its only concern. Marriage places sex in its proper relation to all life's other varied, important aspects. Chesterton saw sex as the gate to a great house and it's the house, not the gate, which has primacy. However, this is no reason to disregard the excitement and romance of the gate.

> Sex is an instinct that produces an institution; and it is positive and not negative, noble and not base, creative and not destructive, because it produces this institution. That institution is the family; a small state or commonwealth which has hundreds of aspects, when it is once started, that are not sexual at all. It includes worship, justice, festivity, decoration, instruction, comradeship, repose. Sex is the gate of that house; and romantic and imaginative people naturally like looking through a gateway. But the house is very much larger than the gate. There are indeed a certain number of people who like to hang about the gate and never get any further. From *G.K.'s Weekly*.

Chesterton understood the wonder of sexuality; he also understood the wonder of children, formed by sexuality. He described the fundamental trio of man, woman and child as a necessary triangle – the most basic and persistent part of any human society, and any state that harmed this trio harmed itself. Their home, however humble, is critical for humanity's essential freedoms and the vast richness of domestic creativity.

> Now a child is the very sign and sacrament of personal freedom. He is a fresh free will added to the wills of the world; he is something

that his parents have freely chosen to produce and which they freely agree to protect. They can feel that any amusement he gives (which is often considerable) really comes from him and from them, and from nobody else. He has been born without the intervention of any master or lord. He is a creation and a contribution; he is their own creative contribution to creation. He is also a much more beautiful, wonderful, amusing and astonishing thing than any of the stale stories or jingling jazz tunes turned out by the machines. When men no longer feel that he is so, they have lost the appreciation of primary things, and therefore all sense of proportion about the world. People who prefer the mechanical pleasures, to such a miracle, are jaded and enslaved. They are preferring the very dregs of life to the first fountains of life. From *The Well and the Shadows*.

Maintaining our sexual integrity throughout life is an immense challenge. Marriage is a peculiar challenge and not everyone is suited, by personality or maturity, to marriage. Many marriages end in divorce because marriage was not a wise choice in the first place for one or both people. An individual may be gifted for marriage or gifted for single-hood, as Jesus made plain. Discerning our gifts in this area is one of the most important responsibilities we face. And the discerning process may be undertaken more than once in life. After divorce or bereavement, for example, we may need to re-evaluate our inclinations and capabilities and decide anew if remarriage or singleness is best for us.

Unfortunately, in much of the Western world a commitment to a sacred singleness, or to sacred marriage for that matter, is not encouraged. In wiser centuries than ours, communities of single men or single women existed to encourage one another, support one another and provide security for one another in monasteries and priories. And they in turn provided a model of contented and fruitful singleness to others who, although not suited to monastic life, still refrained from marriage. This example hardly exists anymore. A person living in a pleasure-seeking society who wants to maintain their sexual integrity but discerns their gifts and inclinations don't lead them to marriage must be a determined and resilient soul.

A person choosing marriage also must be a determined and resilient soul. Trying day in and day out to maintain caring fidelity to a spouse who will at times be irritating, distant, distracted, battling with their own emotions, temptations, desires, questions, goals or relationships, and who certainly will be aging and therefore continuously changing is not simple or easy. Nevertheless, *Proverbs* has a positive view of marriage, if entered with prudence and discernment.

> He who finds a wife finds a good thing, and obtains favor from the LORD. 18:22.

Choices about marriage and singleness need to be made in consultation with people who love us and with the invitation of sacred guidance, as in other areas of life. This is a principle routinely neglected by contemporary popular culture. No matter; a wise person does not follow the speculative ideas of superficial commentators.

> House and wealth are inherited from fathers, but a prudent wife is from the LORD. 19:14.

It takes abundant determination, a commitment to love, and constant grace to honour one's spouse every day in all circumstances over decades. *Proverbs* praises the married people who achieve this, and warns against behaviours and attitudes that undermine one's spouse. Both husband and wife need to treat each other with tenderness, avoiding actions and attitudes that belittle, humiliate or embarrass. This requires thoughtfulness and self-restraint.

> A good wife is the crown of her husband, but she who brings shame is like rottenness in his bones. 12:4.

> Wisdom builds her house, but folly with her own hands tears it

down. 14:1.

A single person faces the challenge of isolation. A married person faces the challenge of constant loyalty amid endless personal change. Pascal made these observations about our mutability and the difficulties attendant to it.

> The weariness which is felt by us in leaving pursuits to which we are attached. A man dwells at home with pleasure; but if he sees a woman who charms him, or if he enjoys himself in play for five or six days, he is miserable if he returns to his former way of living. Nothing is more common than that. 128.
>
> Time heals griefs and quarrels, for we change and are no longer the same persons. Neither the offender nor the offended are any more themselves. It is like a nation which we have provoked, but meet again after two generations. They are still Frenchmen, but not the same. 122.
>
> He no longer loves the person whom he loved ten years ago. I quite believe it. She is no longer the same, nor is he. He was young, and she also; she is quite different. He would perhaps love her yet, if she were what she was then. 123.
>
> *Inconstancy.* – We think we are playing on ordinary organs when playing upon man. Men are organs, it is true, but, odd, changeable, variable with pipes not arranged in proper order. Those who only know how to play on ordinary organs will not produce harmonies on these. We must know where [the keys] are. 111.

The many changes that occur in every marriage make marriage a constantly exciting adventure. Sometimes we may wish for a little less adventure, but the changes underline the need for an unchanging sacred framework. We will change, but there is constancy in the wisdom that comes from the unvarying nature and purposes of our creator. We seek God's wisdom and it provides a solid basis for our lives; if both partners in a marriage have this same commitment, then the possibilities are heightened for a fruitful, enjoyable marriage that accepts and manages the changes and chances of life.

Many problems in relationships have an epistemological cause: in the absence of any uniting ethos, an agreed set of constant values, how may disagreements be resolved? How can we know the person behind the continuously changing screen of words and gestures? Assured knowledge of another person is facilitated by a firm commitment to a shared ethical framework; each may then have confidence in the other's motives and trust the transparency of their words and actions. *Proverbs* and *Ecclesiastes*, largely written by a Jewish king for his Jewish nation, assumed a common commitment to the books of the Pentateuch, and especially to the Decalogue; these universal commands form the basis for trusting communities. The Decalogue also establishes that marriage is not a contract or a mood, but a sacred covenant underpinned by vows of commitment.

Vows are important to marriage because the heart is mutable. Maintaining fidelity and loving-kindness within marriage requires the encouragement, the support and at times the sharp prod of the vows made at the wedding. Exchanging vows before witnesses is an unequivocal benefit; it publishes commitment and invites accountability. A set of public promises is evaded in *de facto* relationships: one more reason for their frequent failure.

We don't always feel like treating our spouse with love and respect; vows push us towards our duty when our inconstant heart would lead us to behave with petulant selfishness. Moreover, most people want to make promises to their beloved and want their beloved to make promises to them. Chesterton wrote about lovers' vows and their role in marriage.

> The revolt against vows has been carried in our day even to the extent of a revolt against the typical vow of marriage. It is most amusing to listen to the opponents of marriage on this subject. They appear to

> imagine that the ideal of constancy was a yoke mysteriously imposed on mankind by the devil, instead of being, as it is, a yoke consistently imposed by all lovers on themselves. They have invented a phrase, a phrase that is a black and white contradiction in two words—'free-love'—as if a lover ever had been, or ever could be, free. It is the nature of love to bind itself, and the institution of marriage merely paid the average man the compliment of taking him at his word. Modern sages offer to the lover, with an ill-favoured grin, the largest liberties and the fullest irresponsibility; but they do not respect him as the old Church respected him; they do not write his oath upon the heavens, as the record of his highest moment. They give him every liberty except the liberty to sell his liberty, which is the only one that he wants. From *The Defendant*.

Modern movies and television comedies often portray marriage as a war, and truly many battles must be fought and won. In marriage there must be battles with our own selfishness; battles with the isolating differences between a man and a woman; battles with our lazyness; battles with a loss of wonder; battles with jaded appetite, with routine, with temptation from within the heart of husband or wife and temptations from would-be seductresses and playboys. Not everyone is a warrior, so not everyone should be married, especially if they don't have the heart, the head or the gifts to fight these battles. Chesterton was cheerful but unsentimental about these sorts of conflicts.

> The fairy tales said that the prince and the princess lived happily ever afterwards: and so they did. They lived happily, although it is very likely that from time to time they threw the furniture at each other. Most marriages, I think, are happy marriages; but there is no such thing as a contented marriage. The whole pleasure of marriage is that it is a perpetual crisis. From *Appreciations*.

> The principle is this: that in everything worth having, even in every pleasure, there is a point of pain or tedium that must be survived, so that the pleasure may revive and endure. The joy of battle comes

after the first fear of death; the joy of reading Virgil comes after the bore of learning him; the glow of the sea-bather comes after the icy shock of the sea bath; and the success of the marriage comes after the failure of the honeymoon. All human vows, laws, and contracts are so many ways of surviving with success this breaking point, this instant of potential surrender.

In everything on this earth that is worth doing, there is a stage when no one would do it, except for necessity or honor. It is then that the Institution upholds a man and helps him on to the firmer ground ahead. Whether this solid fact of human nature is sufficient to justify the sublime dedication of Christian marriage is quite another matter, it is amply sufficient to justify the general human feeling of marriage as a fixed thing, dissolution of which is a fault or, at least, an ignominy. The essential element is not so much duration as security. Two people must be tied together in order to do themselves justice; for twenty minutes at a dance, or for twenty years in a marriage. In both cases the point is, that if a man is bored in the first five minutes he must go on and force himself to be happy. Coercion is a kind of encouragement; and anarchy (or what some call liberty) is essentially oppressive, because it is essentially discouraging. If we all floated in the air like bubbles, free to drift anywhere at any instant, the practical result would be that no one would have the courage to begin a conversation. It would be so embarrassing to start a sentence in a friendly whisper, and then have to shout the last half of it because the other party was floating away into the free and formless ether. The two must hold each other to do justice to each other. If Americans can be divorced for "incompatibility of temper" I cannot conceive why they are not all divorced. I have known many happy marriages, but never a compatible one. The whole aim of marriage is to fight through and survive the instant when incompatibility becomes unquestionable. For a man and a woman, as such, are incompatible. From *What's Wrong with the World.*

Married people must fight, not so much with each other, although this is inevitable if people are honest with one another. Arguments are necessary to clarify issues and arrive at an understanding, but the main battle is the fight *for* one's marriage with husband and wife as intimate allies.

Adultery is a sneaky enemy; it is entrancing yet destructive, and its dangers are compounded because we don't have to seek an adulterous partner – they will come looking for us, their hook baited with sensuality, beauty, secrecy and suggestion.

> For at the window of my house I have looked out through my lattice, and I have seen among the simple, I have perceived among the youths, a young man without sense, passing along the street near her corner, taking the road to her house in the twilight, in the evening, at the time of night and darkness. And lo, a woman meets him, dressed as a harlot, wily of heart. She is loud and wayward, her feet do not stay at home; now in the street, now in the market, and at every corner she lies in wait. She seizes him and kisses him, and with impudent face she says to him, "I had to offer sacrifices, and today I have paid my vows; so now I have come out to meet you eagerly, and I have found you. I have decked my couch with coverings, spreads of Egyptian linen; I have perfumed my bed with myrrh, aloes, and cinnamon. Come, let us take our fill of love till morning; let us delight ourselves with love. For my husband is not at home; he has gone on a long journey; he took a bag of money with him; at full moon he will come home." With much seductive speech she persuades him, with her smooth talk she compels him. All at once he follows her; as an ox goes to the slaughter, or as a stag is caught fast till an arrows pierces its entrails; as a bird rushes into a snare, he does not know it will cost him his life. 7:6-23.

Adultery is a temptation likely to visit every one of us at some point in our lives. But its prevalence doesn't mitigate its violence or lessen the scale of consequences. Adultery destroys integrity, corrupts the conscience, and undermines health and prosperity. It sometimes takes the life of people who pursue it.

Proverbs identifies four consequences of marital infidelity: a loss of wealth to people outside our family; the loss of health through disease and stress; the loss of happiness as remorse and self-loathing grow; and the loss of respect from people around us. In the following passage we again hear a parent warning young people about infidelity, providing good reasons to heed the lesson, including lost family wealth, diminished freedom and lacerating regret.

> And now, O sons, listen to me, and do not depart from the words of my mouth. Keep your way far from her, and do not go near the door of her house; lest you give your honor to others and your years to the merciless; lest strangers take their fill of your strength, and your labors go to the house of an alien; and at the end of your life you groan, when your flesh and body are consumed, and you say, "How I hated discipline, and my heart despised reproof! I did not listen to the voice of my teachers or incline my ear to my instructors. I was at the point of utter ruin in the assembled congregation." 5:7-14.
>
> Like a bird that strays from its nest, is a man who strays from his home. 27:8.

It's a measure of sexual temptation's power that there is no sure defence against it. Intelligence, power, security, prestige, wealth, health, confidence, loving relationships, family, friends, a fulfilling vocation and creative gifts – all the strengths and resources that humanity possesses – are no sure protection against the flash of legs, the shape of breasts, the smell of perfume or aftershave, the whispered suggestion, the lustre of eyes. It isn't just weak, insecure and irresolute people who commit adultery; individuals at the peak of their strength and abilities, at the top of their profession, people who have solid personal, spiritual, and moral credentials are also vulnerable. *Proverbs* is realistic.

> Now therefore listen to me my children; pay attention to the words of my mouth: do not let your heart turn aside to her [the seducer's] paths, do not stray into her paths; for she has cast down many

wounded, and all who were slain by her were strong men. Her house is the way to hell, descending to the chambers of death. 7:24-27.

Chesterton linked the prevalence of divorce – of which adultery is a prime cause – with three freedom-destroying tendencies: the loss of independence through decreased private wealth, the impoverishment of our children, and the growth of the intrusive state. He observed that most sociologists and social workers are not interested in the idea of marriage as much as the peculiar circumstances of individual divorces. He suggested this is because they believe, not necessarily in marriage, but certainly in bureaucratic meddling.

> The truth is that these sociologists are not at all interested in promoting the sort of social life that marriage does promote. The sort of society which marriage has always been the strongest pillar is what is sometimes called the distributive society; the society in which most of the citizens have a tolerable share of property, especially property in land. Everywhere, all over the world, the farm goes with the family and the family with the farm. Unless the whole domestic group hold together with a sort of loyalty or local patriotism, unless the inheritance of property is logical and legitimate, unless the family quarrels are kept out of the courts of officialism, the tradition of family ownership cannot he handed on unimpaired. On the other hand, the Servile State, which has always been the opposite of the distributive state, has always been rather embarrassed by the institution of marriage. From *The Sentimentalism of Divorce.*

The primary loyalty of marriage is to the new family unit that two people have freely formed. Stubborn family loyalty is generally an inconvenience to the state which doesn't want any other loyalty compromising people's subservience to its own agenda. Strong marriages and firm families are among society's best defences against extension of government power. It's one reason the state is usually loosening the bonds of marriage with the goal, it trumpets, of extending sexual liberties. Freedom of speech, of congregation, of the press; freedom of belief and conscience; freedom from arbitrary arrest and the right to own firearms all threaten state power, but not sexual freedoms. They are among the few liberties the state promotes because they pose no direct threat to its power. Indeed, sexual liberties create more dependents on state welfare. Chesterton preferred independent households to interfering houses of parliament.

> Marriage makes a small state within the state, which resists all such regimentation. That bond breaks all other bonds; that law is found stronger than all later and lesser laws. They desire the democracy to be sexually fluid, because the making of small nuclei is like the making of small nations. Like small nations, they are a nuisance to the mind of imperial scope. In short, what they fear, in the most literal sense, is home rule. From *The Superstition of Divorce*.

Home rule is the best rule. One reason people are eager to finish work for the day and get home, or anticipate the weekend or their holidays or retiring from work altogether is because they sense, correctly, that their greatest freedom and most enjoyable creativity are found at home not at work, not under the watch of a supervisor, not in the rush-hour commute. Men and women, and children too are freest at home where the rules are informal, framed with love and often enforced with humour. Peaceful home life is to be treasured, not least for the relief it brings from deadlines, inflexible routines, quotas, bosses, performance indicators, regulations, policies, assessment processes and timetables. Chesterton favoured the wider freedoms of a privately-owned home. These liberties shouldn't be harmed either by governments or by the inhabitants of the home.

> Public life must be rather more regulated than private life; just as a man cannot wander about in the traffic of Piccadilly exactly as he wander about in his own garden. Where there is traffic there will be regulation of traffic; and this is quite true, or even more true, where it is what we should call an illicit traffic; where the most modern governments organise sterilization today and may organise

> infanticide tomorrow. Those who hold the modern superstition that the State can do no wrong will be bound to accept such a thing as right. If individuals have any hope of protecting their freedom, they must protect their family life. At the worst there will be rather more personal adaptation in an household than in a concentration camp; at the best there will be rather less routine in a family than in a factory. In any tolerably healthy home the rules are at least partly affected by things that cannot possibly affect fixed laws; for instance, the thing we call a sense of humour. From *The Well and the Shadows*.

Chesterton understood, too, that relaxing divorce laws would encourage imprudent marriages because people knew they could easily divorce when marriage became difficult. Prudence, the evaluation of character and habits, and judicious caution would be increasingly abandoned in the choice of husband or wife.

> The obvious effect of frivolous divorces will be frivolous marriages. If people can be separated for no reason they will feel it all the easier to be united for no reason. From *The Superstition of Divorce*.

Legislation intended to make divorce less traumatic results in divorces becoming more common as marriage is less hedged about by any expectation of endurance or high levels of commitment. In the modern West, most employers are more tightly bound by law to their employees than anybody is bound to their husband or wife. There are adjudication boards and courts to deal with unfair dismissal of employees; there's nowhere wronged husbands or wives who find themselves facing divorce can seek justice. Divorce is thus a tragedy of injustice in many cases, but because of the nobility of the idea of marriage it is, at least, a noble tragedy and not a ridiculous tragedy. The aim was high and good even if the achievement was not. Chesterton acknowledged this and wrote about the fundamental injustice inherent in many divorces.

> The doctors of divorce, with an air of the frank and friendly realism of men of the world, are always recommending and rejoicing in a sensible separation by mutual consent. But if we are really to dismiss our dreams of dignity and honour, if we are really to fall back on the frank realism of our experience as men of the world, then the very first thing that our experience will tell us is that it very seldom is a separation by mutual consent; that is, that the consent very seldom is sincerely and spontaneously mutual. By far the commonest problem in such cases is that in which one party wishes to end the partnership and the other does not. And of that emotional situation you can make nothing but a tragedy, whichever way you turn it. With or without marriage, with or without divorce, with or without any arrangements that anybody can suggest or imagine, it remains a tragedy. The only difference is that by the doctrine of marriage it remains both a noble and a fruitful tragedy; like that of a man who falls fighting for his country, or dies testifying to the truth. From *The Superstition of Divorce*.

Adultery is no longer addressed in our legal system; a reckless lapse. Someone through their own uncontrolled lust can massively harm an entire family yet he or she faces no examination, is not held accountable and is not required to make any restitution. This judicial indifference is contrary to the wisdom of *Proverbs*, which requires restitution at least be paid, and the stripping of some privileges and responsibilities. If our society required an adulterer to pay a huge fine for each marriage they harmed – with the money transferred to the innocent party of the marriage – and if the guilty person suffered weekend detention, together with their citizenship or passport being temporarily suspended and any welfare payments rescinded, for example, then many more irresponsible men and women would think twice before removing their underpants.

Images of acute pain, remorse and loss describe the repercussions of adultery.

> Can a man carry fire in his bosom and his clothes not be burned? Or can one walk upon hot coals and his feet not be scorched? So is he who goes in to his neighbor's wife; none who touches her will go unpunished. Do not men despise a thief if he steals to satisfy his appetite when he is hungry? And if he is caught, he will pay sevenfold; he will give all the goods of his house. He who commits adultery has no sense; he who does it destroys himself. Wounds and dishonor will he get, and his disgrace will not be wiped away. For jealousy makes a man furious, and he will not spare when he takes revenge. He will accept no compensation, nor be appeased though you multiply gifts. 6:27-35.

Adultery is a betrayal not only of one's spouse but also of God. The sacred relationship in which each of us lives (whether we like it or not and whether we recognise it or not) is seriously affected by our behavior. Adultery invites a disciplining judgment from God, not least being allowing the consequences of our sin to hurt us. We injure and punish ourselves. It's a mercy if nothing worse befalls us. The commandment, *Thou shalt not commit adultery* forbids the act not to restrict our freedom and pleasures, but to guarantee them and protect us from many painful consequences. Always, wisdom is for us not against us.

> Why should you be infatuated, my son, with a loose woman and embrace the bosom of an adventuress? For a man's ways are before the eyes of the LORD, and he watches all his paths. The iniquities of the wicked ensnare him, and he is caught in the toils of his sin. He dies for lack of discipline, and because of his great folly he is lost. 5:20-23.

> A man who wanders from the way of understanding will rest in the assembly of the dead. 21:16.

A wise person knows the attractions and pleasures of sexual waywardness don't last, quickly giving way to grief and suffering. Medications (the recourse of many a guilt-ridden person) may mask, or at least moderate grief and guilt's effects on the psyche, but they don't remove it; only divine grace and human forgiveness can permanently heal the distressed person. Better by far to maintain integrity, develop self-control and enjoy untroubled sleep.

> My son, keep sound wisdom and discretion; let them not escape from your sight, and they will be life for your soul and adornment for your neck. Then you will walk on your way securely and your foot will not stumble. If you sit down, you will not be afraid; when you lie down, your sleep will be sweet. 3:18–23.

ii. THE FOLLY OF INSURRECTION

Like adultery and pride, insurrection is today seen less as a folly and more an action possessing a certain cachet. Rebellion is considered a noble act reflecting a vigourous autonomy and a commendable defiance: the revolutionary is a hero. Nothing in *Proverbs* or *Ecclesiastes* ratifies this celebration of the rebel. Rather, the insurrectionist and the rebel are portrayed as dangerous to themselves and to others; their plots and subversive acts are regarded on the whole as instruments, not of justice, but of injustice.

The sense of pride, of deserving merit, among those who aspire to rule in place of another is a sure cause of instability. A nation led by kings or queens who gain their power through hereditary succession is relatively stable precisely because it ignores pretenders to the throne who proclaim their right to rule because they're sure of their merit – merit which will always be disputed by others proclaiming their superior merit. Pascal commented on the benefits of regal rule, and the relative instability of merit-based rule.

> Civil wars are the greatest of evils. They are inevitable, if we wish to reward desert; for all will say they are deserving. The evil we have to

fear from a fool who succeeds by right of birth, is neither so great nor so sure. 313.

The wisdom literature dates from a time when monarchs ruled tribes and nations. The monarch had power of life and death, and while a suite of advisors joined the royal court, the monarch's authority was behind the laws; the ruler defended the kingdom, and fostered arts and religion. In return, fealty was demanded. This form of social organisation is not questioned; instead the wisdom literature affirms the dignity and power of the monarch.

> Three things are stately in their tread; four are stately in their stride: the lion, which is mightiest among beasts and does not turn back before any; the strutting cock, the he-goat, and a king striding before his people. 30:29-31.

As we will see, the ruler is expected to ensure justice and security, acting with prudence, sobriety and compassion to build peace and stability in the realm. Yet even under the best governments, there will be aggrieved people and their grievances, real or imagined, will provoke enmity against the established hierarchy. Antagonism towards leaders is as ancient as humanity.

Edmund Burke, in his magisterial 1790 work, *Reflections on the Revolution in France*, wrote this about resistance to government.

> The speculative line of demarcation, where obedience ought to end and resistance must begin, is faint, obscure and not easily definable. It is not a single act, or a single event, which determines it. Governments must be abused and deranged indeed, before it can be thought of; and the prospect of the future must be as bad as the experience of the past. When things are in that lamentable condition, the nature of the disease is to indicate the remedy to those whom nature has qualified to administer in extremities this critical, ambiguous, bitter potion to a distempered state. Times,

and occasions, and provocations will teach their own lessons. The wise will determine from the gravity of the case; the irritable, from sensibility to oppression, the high-minded, from disdain and indignation at abusive power in unworthy hands; the brave and bold, from the love of honourable danger in a generous cause: but, with or without right, a revolution will be the very last resource of the thinking and the good.

Proverbs warns against joining any rebellion because the prevailing powers are likely to exact a deadly revenge and because there are better ways to address grievances.

> An evil man seeks only rebellion, and a cruel messenger will be sent against him. 17:11.
>
> A king's wrath is like the growling of a lion, but his favor is like dew upon the grass. 19:12.
>
> The dread wrath of a king is like the growling of a lion; he who provokes him to anger forfeits his life. 20:2.

Rebels provoke rulers to violence, and then the rebels highlight the violence as another reason to despise the rulers; rebels help to create what they say they lament. Edmund Burke observed that, "Kings will be tyrants from policy, when subjects are rebels from principle."

A government confronted by violent dissent will become oppressive to quell the dissent, with harmful results felt through society: death, confiscation of rights and property, curfews, intimidation and incarceration. A government enjoying the fundamental loyalty and confidence of its people has no reason to be oppressive. Rulers may oppress without provocation, but rulers must oppress if there are rebellious people fomenting subversion; the government has no choice but harsh action. The action may be fatal for the insurrectionists and their associates.

Burke understood that a great deal of a society's stability and clemency

– that which made its hard edges softer and fairer – came from the kind manners and chivalry of its people. Rulers were honoured, but the rulers themselves displayed common kindness; obedience to them was thereby dignified because they were courteous, to sufficient extent. Likewise, through good manners, parents, the elderly, women, teachers and employers received respect, and they treated others with respect in return.

Good manners and common courtesies are hugely important to the smooth operation of any society and should not be under-estimated, nor ever undermined. It's the responsibility of everyone to maintain the traditions of courtesy and chivalry; it's one of the most important things children must be taught in the home and school.

The courtesies and chivalry that permeated European society – dating back to the Middle Ages – were suddenly subverted in France by the 1789 revolution, with disastrous results. Burke wrote about this tradition and its demolishing.

> This mixed system of opinion and sentiment had its origin in the ancient chivalry; and the principle, though varied in its appearance by the varying state of human affairs, subsisted and influenced through a long succession of generations, even to the time we live in. If it should ever be extinguished, the loss I fear will be great. It is this which has given its character to modern Europe. It is this which has distinguished it under all its forms of government, and distinguished it to its advantage, from the states of Asia, and possibly from those states which flourished in the most brilliant periods of the antique world. It was this, which, without confounding ranks, had produced a noble equality, and handed it down through all the gradations of social life. It was this opinion which mitigated kings into companions, and raised private men to be fellows of the king. Without force, or opposition, it subdued the fierceness of pride and power; it obliged sovereigns to submit to the soft collar of social esteem, compelled stern authority to submit to elegance, and gave a

domination vanquisher of laws, to be subdued by manners.

But now all this is to be changed. All the pleasing illusions, which made power gentle, and obedience liberal, which harmonized the different shades of life, and which, by a bland assimilation, incorporated into politics the sentiments which beautify and soften private society, are to be dissolved by this new conquering empire of light and reason. All the decent drapery of life is to be rudely torn off. All the super-added ideas, furnished from the wardrobe of a moral imagination, which the heart owns, and the understanding ratifies, as necessary to cover the defects of our naked shivering nature, and to raise it to dignity in our own estimation, are to be exploded as a ridiculous, absurd, and antiquated fashion.

On this scheme of things, a king is but a man; a queen is but a woman; a woman is but an animal; and an animal not of the highest order. All homage paid to the sex in general as such, and without distinct views, is to be regarded as romance and folly. Regicide, and parricide, and sacrilege, are but fictions of superstition, corrupting jurisprudence by destroying its simplicity. The murder of a king, or a queen, or a bishop, or a father, are only common homicide; and if the people are by any chance, or in any way gainers of it, a sort of homicide much the most pardonable, and into which we ought not to make too severe a scrutiny.

The violence and recklessness of insurrectionists, and the calamities they unleash on themselves are presented in these two passages.

> Be not envious of evil men, nor desire to be with them; for their minds devise violence, and their lips talk of mischief. 24:1, 2.

> My son, fear the LORD and the king, and do not disobey either of them; for disaster from them will rise suddenly, and who knows the ruin that will come from them both? 24:21, 22.

Here, *Proverbs* is concerned with the life of the individual. Edmund Burke was more concerned with the life of the culture.

> By this unprincipled facility of changing the state as often, and as much, and in as many ways as there are floating fancies or passions, the whole chain and continuity of the commonwealth would be broken. No one generation could link with the other. Man would become little better than flies of the summer.

Moreover, Burke saw that appealing to the passing fancies of cultured cliques and the crudest desires of the population – that is, turning politics into a popularity contest – was not conducive to good policies. In fact, it almost ensured poor policies and the extension of frustrating bureaucracies.

> But when the leaders choose to make themselves bidders at an auction of popularity, their talents, in the construction of the state, will be of no service. They will become flatterers instead of legislators; the instruments, not the guides of the people. If any of them should happen to propose a scheme of liberty, soberly limited, and defined with proper qualifications, he will be immediately outbid by his competitors, who will produce something more splendidly popular. Suspicions will be raised of his fidelity to his cause. Moderation will be stigmatized as the virtue of cowards; and compromise as the prudence of traitors; until, in hopes of preserving the credit which may enable him to temper and moderate on some occasions, the popular leader is obliged to become active in propagating doctrines, and establishing powers, that will afterwards defeat any sober purpose at which he ultimately might have aimed.

Rapid and dramatic changes in a culture are deeply unsettling, and those at the lowest levels of society suffer most. Therefore, wisdom advises a deep respect for those good things that previous generations have achieved; scorning the edicts, customs and institutions built by the many sacrifices of parents, grandparents and great-grandparents is not supported. Rather, each generation is given the task of protecting and renovating the achievements of their parents and grandparents, and their more ancient ancestors.

The priority is social, cultural and political preservation, rather than innovation in any important matter. This doesn't mean resistance to all change; but it does mean a sober hesitation and consideration before change, especially in profound matters of society, polity and communal values. Conserving the best customs and facilities of the past is the goal, respecting the hard work previous generations undertook to build a stable, workable society. This legacy would be squandered without qualm by impatient and idealistic – but not realistic – people.

Renovation of existing good is necessary in any society. Indeed, the need to renovate is the best argument to be progressive, and an argument against conservatism, which might leave good things to degenerate. Chesterton outlined the principle.

> We have remarked that one reason offerred for being a progressive is that things naturally tend to grow better. But the only real reason for being a progressive is that things naturally tend to grow worse. The corruption in things is not only the best argument for being progressive; it is also the only argument against being conservative. The conservative theory would really be quite sweeping and unanswerable if it were not for this one fact. But all conservatism is based upon the idea that if you leave things alone you leave them as they are. But you do not. If you leave a thing alone you leave it to a torrent of change. If you leave a white post alone it will soon be a black post. If you particularly want it to be a white post you must be always painting it again; that is, you must always be having a revolution. Briefly, if you want the old white post you must have a new white post. But this which is true even of inanimate things is in a quite special and terrible sense true of all human things. An almost unnatural vigilance is really required of the citizen because of the horrible rapidity with which human institutions grow old. From *Orthodoxy*.

Even traditional customs and prejudices need to be renovated because they often have a latent, reasonable basis. Burke portrayed England as a place where customs were maintained and even common prejudices were recognised as valuable. They were not scorned, but reaffirmed, especially when criticised by rebels: people who don't want to repaint the dirty white post, but dig it up and burn it without asking why it was placed there.

> We are afraid to put men to live and trade each on his own private stock of reason; because we suspect that this stock in each man is small, and that the individual would do better to avail themselves of the general bank and capital of nations, and of ages. Many of our men of speculation, instead of exploding general prejudices, employ their sagacity to discover the latent wisdom that prevails in them. If they find what they seek, and they seldom fail, they think it more wise to continue the prejudice, with the reason involved, than to cast away the coat of prejudice, and to leave nothing but the naked reason; because prejudice, with its reason, has a motive to give action to that reason, and an affection which will give it permanence. Prejudice is of ready application in an emergency; it previously engages the mind in a steady course of wisdom and virtue, and does not leave a man hesitating in a moment of decision, skeptical, puzzled, and unresolved. Prejudice renders a man's virtue his habit; and not series of unconnected acts. Through just prejudice, his duty becomes a part of his nature.

Burke contrasted this good sense with the arrogance and haste he saw among the revolutionary leaders in France and some of the so-called enlightened people of England.

> Your literary men, and your politicians, and so do the whole clan of the enlightened among us, essentially differ in these points. They have no respect for the wisdom of others; but they pay it off by a very full measure of confidence in their own. With them it is a sufficient motive to destroy and old scheme of things because it is an old one. As to the new, they are in no sort of fear with regard to

the duration of a building run up in haste; because duration is of no object to those who think little or nothing has been done before their time, and who place all their hopes in discovery.

Preserving existing good is a priority; stability is thereby maintained, and the level of justice that already pertains is secured.

> Remove not the ancient landmark which your fathers have set. 22:28.

> Do not remove an ancient landmark or enter the fields of the fatherless; for their Redeemer is strong; he will plead their cause against you. 23:10.

Chesterton realised that education in literature and history aided a deeper and broader understanding of one's time and culture, and an appreciation of what is good and bad about it. This knowledge guides what might be amended and what should be renovated.

> I mean that to train a citizen is to train a critic. The whole point of education is that it should give a man abstract and eternal standards, by which he can judge material and fugitive conditions. If the citizen is to be a reformer, he must start with some ideal which he does not obtain merely by gazing reverently at the unreformed institutions. And if any one asks, as so many are asking: "What is the use of my son learning all about Ancient Athens and remote China and mediaeval guilds and monasteries, and all sorts of dead and distant things, when he is going to be a superior scientific plumber in Pimlico?" the answer is obvious enough. "The use of it is that he may have some power of comparison, which will not only prevent him from supposing that Pimlico covers the whole planet, but also to enable him, while doing full credit to the beauties and virtues of Pimlico, to point out that, here and there, as revealed by alternative experiments, even Pimlico may conceal somewhere a defect." From *On Business Education*.

Parents and teachers should help children appreciate the virtues and beauties of their culture, without ignoring its defects. Children, in turn, should love and respect their parents, teachers, grandparents, aunts and uncles rather than scorning and interrogating them. This mutual responsibility forms the basis for a reasonable and just society – as much as any society can be reasonable and just. The imperfections of society do not justify its destruction, wasting all that forebears have contributed.

Always, managing one's own life well is the best way to change society for the better, and this requires instruction and example from those who have lived and learned. Those unfortunate individuals who haven't had careful parents loving, instructing, helping and guiding them – because their parents were lazy, absent or stoned – must make even greater efforts to learn from their parents' mistakes, seek skilled role models and do better themselves. Still, they must honour their parents for whatever good they did however haphazard the manner.

> Grandchildren are the crown of the aged, and the glory of sons is their fathers. 17:6.
>
> A stupid son is a grief to a father; and the father of a fool has no joy. 17:21.
>
> A foolish son is a grief to his father and bitterness to her who bore him 17:25.
>
> He who does violence to his father and chases away his mother is a son who causes shame and brings reproach. 19:26.
>
> A righteous man who walks in his integrity – blessed are his sons after him! 20:7.
>
> If one curses his father or his mother, his lamp will be put out in utter darkness. 20:20.
>
> Hearken to your father who begot you, and do not despise your mother when she is old. 23:22.
>
> The father of the righteous will greatly rejoice; he who begets a wise son will be glad in him. Let your father and mother be glad, let her

who bore you rejoice. 23:24, 25.

He who robs his father or his mother and says, "That is no transgression," is the companion of a man who destroys. 28:24.

Chesterton thought celebrating, and then augmenting good things was the best and most natural disposition of humanity. Helpful changes come from love, not from embittered antagonism. He observed that a mother doesn't wash her son's face and put ribbons in her daughter's hair hoping she might find her appalling children more tolerable; rather, mothers deeply love their children and delight to enhance their young beauty. The noblest instincts of change are like this: people love a place, a house, a village, a region, a nation and this love delights in making it beautiful. Good is preserved and celebrated. Affection advances the existing qualities in ways that are consistent with them.

Those who hate existing conventions and the *status quo* want them overthrown, but they struggle to build anything good in their place. Revolt soon falls into confusion and exhausted lassitude. Chesterton explained the entropy.

> At first sight it would seem that the pessimist encourages improvement. But in reality it is a singular truth that the era in which pessimism has been cried from the house-tops is also that in which almost all reform has stagnated and fallen into decay. The reason of this is not difficult to discover. No man ever did, and no man ever can, create or desire to make a bad thing good or an ugly thing beautiful. There must be some germ of good to be loved, some fragment of beauty to be admired. The mother washes and decks out the dirty and careless child, but no one can ask her to wash and deck out a goblin with a heart like hell. No one can kill the fatted calf for Mephistopheles. The cause which is blocking all progress today is the subtle skepticism which whispers in a million ears that things are not good enough to be worth improving … things must be loved first and improved afterwards. Preface from *The Defendant*.

In our day, in the West at least, violent revolution is for the moment out of favour, and revolution by social engineering – with young people being particular targets – is the popinjays' preferred means of imposing their vision on society and culture. Chesterton thought the priority for educating of children, and the proper preparation of them for life, should the enduring truths of humanity and not passing intellectual fashions. The best things to teach to children are the things they can teach their children and grand-children – and which will still be true.

> The general truth remains that we should teach, to the young, men's enduring truths, and let the learned amuse themselves with their passing errors. From *The Duty of the Historian*.

Chesterton knew that teaching children enduring truths was difficult when the curricula is controlled by an unaccountable oligarchy.

> The trouble with too many of our modern schools is that the State, being controlled so specially by the few, allows cranks and experiments to go straight to the schoolroom when they have never passed through the Parliament, the public house, the private house, the church, or the marketplace. Obviously, it ought to be the oldest things that are taught to the baby. But in a school today the baby has to submit to a system that is younger than himself. The flopping infant of four actually has more experience, and has weathered the world longer, than dogma to which he is forced to submit. Many a school boasts of having the last ideas in education, when it has not even the first idea; for the first idea is that even innocence, divine as it is, may learn something from experience. But this, as I say, is all due to the mere fact that we are managed by a little oligarchy; my system presupposes that men who govern themselves will govern their children. Today we all use Popular Education as meaning education of the people. I wish I could use it to mean education by the people. From *What's Wrong with the World*.

When education is controlled by a fad-driven coterie the ideas of a few powerful people are taught, while the requirements and values of the parents are shirked or scorned. This isn't good for society. Ordinary, decent people don't like to be told, through their children, that their values are bone-headed and their understanding of life all wrong, and in bad taste to boot. Chesterton supported the embattled parents, not the education department bureaucrats.

> In the lower classes the school-master does not work for the parent, but against the parent. Modern education means handing down the customs of the minority, and rooting out the customs of the majority. Instead of their Christlike charity, their Shakespearean laughter and their high Homeric reverence for the dead, the poor have imposed on them the mere pedantic copies of the prejudices of the remote rich. From *What's Wrong with the World*.

Proverbs favours the maintenance of the current system of government, with gradual improvements to the administration undertaken only by those loyal to the incumbent government. Burke recognised this precept. He knew recklessly experimenting with society was always destructive.

> ... But in this, as in most questions of state, there is a middle. There is something else than the mere alternative of absolute destruction or unreformed existence. *Spartam nactum es, hanc exorna*. [You have obtained Sparta, adorn it]. This is, in my opinion, a rule of profound sense, and ought never to depart the mind of an honest reformer. I cannot conceive how any man can have brought himself to that pitch of presumption, to consider his country nothing but *carte blanche*, upon which he may scribble whatever he pleases. A man full of warm speculative benevolence may wish his society otherwise constituted than he finds it; but a good patriot, and a true politician, always considers how he shall make the most of the existing materials of his country. A disposition to preserve, and an ability to improve, taken together, would be my standard of a statesman. Every thing else is vulgar in the conception, perilous in the execution.

Burke said, further echoing *Proverbs*, that it's stupid allowing people hostile to an organisation to effect its amendment.

> We shall never be such fools as to call in an enemy to the substance of any system to remove its corruption, to supply its defects, or to perfect its construction. If our religious tenets should ever want a further elucidation, we shall not call in atheism to explain them.

Insurrection is an shambolic way to correct defects of government. The best way to influence rulers is through diligent ministration. An administrator, public servant or advisor who works with consistent excellence is in a unique position, born of demonstrated ability and fidelity, to gain the ear of their superior. Conversely, a person whose service is sloppy is likely to engender, not the ruler's respect, but his frustration and anger. An opportunity for advocacy is lost because of the servant's obvious incompetence. Diligence brings opportunities to influence rulers.

> A servant who deals wisely has the king's favor, but his wrath falls on one who acts shamefully. 14:35.

> Do you see a man skillful in his work? He will stand before kings; he will not stand before obscure men. 22:29.

The skillful man will not flatter the ruler. He will carefully, gently present a case. The wisdom literature condemns flattery; it affirms respectful, measured truth-telling by tactful, competent people.

> He who loves purity of heart, and whose speech is gracious, will have the king as his friend. 22:11.

> With patience a ruler may be persuaded, and a soft tongue will break a bone. 25:15.

The emphasis is on subtle persuasion, patient delivery of one's thoughts, and a desire to change only a specific policy not the government's status or the ruler's authority. This isn't a project for anybody who is greedy, impulsive, deceitful, inept or inexperienced. Government is no place at all for such people: too much is at stake.

Edmund Burke made this exact point in the next two passages. He observed the bungling of inexperienced (but proud) men in revolutionary France's National Assembly. He knew their first priority would be to operate to their own advantage. He then discussed the proper qualifications for exercising power and influence.

> Who could flatter himself that these men, suddenly, and, as it were, by enchantment, snatched from the humblest rank of subordination, would not be intoxicated with their unprepared greatness? Who could conceive, that men who are habitually meddling, daring, subtle, active, of litigious dispositions and unquiet minds, could easily fall back into their old condition of obscure contention, and laborious, low, unproductive chicane? Who could doubt that, at any expense of the state, of which they understood nothing, they must pursue their private interests, which they understood but too well? It was not an event depending on chance or contingency. It was inevitable; it was necessary; it was planted in the nature of things. They must *join* (if their capacity did not permit them to *lead*) in any project which could procure for them a litigious constitution; which could lay open to them those innumerable lucrative jobs which follow in the train of all great convulsions and revolutions in the state, and particularly all great and violent permutations of property, whose existence had always depended upon whatever render property questionable, ambiguous and insecure? Their objects would be enlarged with their elevation, but their disposition and habits, and mode of accomplishing their designs, must remain the same.
>
> There is no qualification for government, but virtue and wisdom, actual or presumptive. Wherever they are actually found, they have, in whatever state, condition, profession or trade, the passport of Heaven to human place and honour. Woe to the country which would madly and impiously reject the service of the talents and virtues, civil, military, or religious, that are given to grace and to serve it; and would condemn to obscurity every thing formed to diffuse lustre and glory around a state. Woe to that country too, that

> passing into the opposite extreme, considers a low education, a mean contracted view of things, a sordid occupation, as a preferable title to command. Every thing ought to be open; but not indifferently to every man. No rotation; no appointment by title; no mode of election operating in a spirit of sortition or rotation, can be generally good in a government conversant with extensive objects. Because they have no tendancy, direct or indirect, to select the man with a view to duty, or to accommodate the one to the other, I do not hesitate to say, that the road to eminence and power, ought not to be made too easy, nor a thing too much of course. If rare merit be the rarest of all are things, it ought to pass through some sort of probation. The temple of honour ought to be seated on an eminence. If it be open through virtue, let it be remembered too, that virtue is never tried but by some difficulty, and some struggle.

A wise ruler and a wise nation will ensure that individuals who are clueless, dishonest and cocky never get anywhere near the levers of power. If they're already present and have influence, their prompt removal is recommended.

> Take away the dross from the silver, and the smith has material for a vessel; take away the wicked from the presence of the king, and his throne will be established in righteousness. 25:5.

Gradual amendment is much better than sudden rearrangement because society is intricate. Modest change allows modifications to be evaluated so they don't damage existing good. The unforeseen consequences – positive or negative – can then be managed. Time is allowed to do its work of revealing shortcomings, unintended results and unanticipated reactions. Burke knew patience was important.

> But you might object—'A process of this kind is slow. It is not fit for an assembly, which glories in performing in a few months the work of ages. Such a mode of reforming, possibly might take up many years.' Without question it might; and it ought. It is one of the excellencies of a method in which time is amongst the assistants, that its operation is slow, and in some cases almost imperceptible.

If circumspection and caution are a part of wisdom, when we work only upon inanimate matter, surely they become part of duty too, when the subject of our demolition and construction is not brick and timber, but sentient beings, by the sudden alteration of whose state, condition, and habits, multitudes might be rendered miserable ... The true lawgiver ought to have a heart full of sensibility. He ought to love and respect his kind, and to fear himself. It may be allowed to his temperament to catch his ultimate object with an intuitive glance; but his movements towards it ought to be deliberate. Political arrangement, as it is a work for social ends, is to be only wrought by social means. There, mind must conspire with mind. Time is required to produce that union of minds which time alone can produce all the good that we aim at. Our patience will achieve more than our force ... I have never yet seen any plan which has not yet been mended by the observations of those who were much inferior in understanding to the person who took the lead in the business. By a slow but well-sustained progress, the effect of each step is watched; the good or ill success of the first gives light to us in the second; and so, from light to light, we are conducted with safety through the whole series. We see the parts or the system through the whole series. We see that the parts or the system do not clash. The evils latent in the most promising contrivances are provided for as they arise. One advantage is as little as possible sacrificed for another. We compensate, we reconcile, we balance. We are enabled to unite into a consistent whole the various anomalies and contending principles that are found in the minds and affairs of men. From hence arises, not an excellence in simplicity, but one far superior, an excellence in composition.

This excellence in composition is counted as nothing compared to the 'rights agenda' of presumptuous people. They promote the rights of their preferred suffering minority, whom, of course, they don't really care for; the suffering is useful because it helps them maneuver opponents into a defensive position. It doesn't matter that a country is reasonably well governed and allows a wide prosperity; usurpers want power and will highlight faults, manipulate language and allege abuses to gain power for themselves, even if they impair many other people. Burke was alert to this duplicitous strategy.

> They despise experience as the wisdom of unlettered men; and as for the rest, they have wrought under-ground a mine that will blow up at one grand explosion all examples of antiquity, all precedents, charges and acts of parliament. They have 'the rights of man'. Against these there can be no prescription; against these no agreement is binding: these admit no temperament, and no compromise; any thing withheld from their full demand is so much fraud and injustice. Against these their rights of men let no government look for security in the length of its continuance, or in justice and lenity of its administration. The objections of these speculatists, if its forms do not quadrate with their theories, are as valid against such an old and beneficent government as against the most violent tyranny, or the greenest usurpation. They are always at issue with government, not on a question of abuse, but a question of competency, and a question of title.

Burke didn't dispute that people had rights only that total rights, expressed in the abstract by contentious and conceited women and men, would erode the limited but workable rights, preserved by custom and tradition that the great majority already enjoyed.

> In denying their false claim of rights, I do not mean to injure those which are real, and are such as their pretended rights would totally destroy. If civil society be made for the advantage of men, all the advantages for which it is made become his right. It is an institution of beneficence; and law itself is only beneficence acting by a rule. Men have a right to live by that rule; they have a right to justice; as between their fellows, whether their fellows are in politic function or in ordinary occupation. They have a right to the fruits of their industry; and to the means of making that industry fruitful. They

have a right to the acquisitions of their parents; to the nourishment and improvement of their offspring; to instruction in life, and to consolation in death. Whatever each man can separately do, without trespassing upon others, he has a right to do for himself; and he has a right to a fair portion of all which society, with all its combinations of skill and force, can do in his favour. In this partnership all men have equal rights; but not to equal things. He that has but five shillings in the partnership has as good right to it, as he that has five hundred pounds has to his larger proportion. But he has not a right to an equal dividend in the product of the joint stock; and as to the share of power, and authority, and direction which each individual ought to have in the management of the state, that I must deny to be amongst the direct original rights of man in civil society; for I have in my contemplation the civil social man, and no other. It is a thing to be settled by convention.

Far from the totalisation of abstract rights which encourage a man to determine his own entitlements and then fight to gain them, Burke emphasised the many and necessary compromises in supposed rights that everyone must make to exist peacefully together. This included an external restriction on each person's selfish passions, especially their grasping acts born of envy. Burke noted that "Men cannot enjoy the rights of a civil and uncivil state together." He went on to say:

> Government is not made in virtue of natural rights, which may and do exist in total independence of it; and exist in much greater clearness, and in much greater degree of abstract perfection: but their abstract perfection is their practical defect. By having a right to everything they want everything. Government is a contrivance of human wisdom to provide for human wants. Men have a right that these wants should be provided for by this wisdom. Among these wants, is to be reckoned the want, out of civil society, of a sufficient restraint upon their passions. Society requires not only that the passions of individuals should be subjected, but that even in the mass and body as well as in the individuals, the inclinations of

men should frequently be thwarted, their will controlled, and their passions brought into subjection. This can only be done by a power outside of themselves; and not, in the exercise of its function, subject to that will and to those passions which is its office to bridle and subdue. In this sense the restraints on men, as well as their liberties, are to be reckoned among their rights. But as the liberties and the restrictions vary with times and circumstances, and admit of infinite modifications, they cannot be settled upon any abstract rule; and nothing is so foolish as to discuss them upon that principle.

Envy is an impulse which disrupts social order. Discontented people want the power and privilege of other people, imagining that they themselves deserve the positions and benefits. Simple envy is behind many social ills, including insurrections and rebellions. And envy is easily aroused by commercial and political propaganda. Of course, envy isn't regarded as much of a vice anymore. In fact, the whole apparatus of advertising, which one hundred years ago largely conveyed the merits of a product or service, now escalates envy so we're propelled by this base motive to want, to change, to buy.

Kierkegaard regarded envy as an insidious temptation that could rob a person of their individuality. And they may not know they've lost their individuality, nor may anyone else notice the profound loss.

> The biggest danger, that of losing oneself, can pass off in the world as if it were nothing; every other loss, an arm, a leg, five dollars, a wife, etc. is bound to be noticed. From *The Sickness unto Death*.

One way we lose our self is by measuring our self, not in the light of God, but in the light of society. And here envy agitates. Dissatisfied with ourselves because we're not as talented as we wish, or as intelligent or rich or esteemed or loved as we wish, we seek to escape our inadequate self by imitating the choices, values and vocation of someone else: someone more successful, someone luckier, someone richer or more respected.

And we may want to take by law, force or revolution what other people have gained. We justify our selfish desires by talking about our rights, and we highlight the injustices, real or invented, perpetrated by those whose position or goods we want. Envy, inflamed by agitprop, is usually skulking around discontent and riot.

Envious people are not generous people; they covet what other people have, but they will not share what they have with the genuinely needy. Covetousness is a powerfully destructive vice. It's self-destroying, like bone cancer.

> A worthless person, a wicked man, goes about with crooked speech, winks with his eyes, scrapes with his feet, points with his finger, with perverted heart devises evil, continually sowing discord; therefore calamity will come upon him suddenly; in a moment he will be broken beyond healing. 6:12-15.
>
> A tranquil mind gives life to the flesh, but passion makes the bones rot. 14:30.
>
> All day long the wicked covets, but the righteous gives and does not hold back. 21:26.

To protect ourselves from losing ourselves through envy, we're commanded, "Thou shalt not covet your neighbour's house; you shall not covet your neighbour's wife, or his manservant, or his maidservant, or his ox, or his ass, or anything that is your neighbour's." This injunction protects our neighbour from our greed. Equally important, it preserves our inner freedom to be a unique individual. It also preserves loving-kindness and tranquility as Kierkegaard explained.

> But he who loves his neighbour is tranquil. He is made tranquil by being content with the earthly distinction allotted to him, whether it be important or unimportant; moreover he lets earthly distinction retain its significance and be taken for what it is and ought to be worth in this life, for one shall not covet what is his neighbour's,

neither his wife nor his donkey, nor, consequently, the advantages granted to him in life. If they are denied to you, you shall rejoice that they are granted to him. Thus he who loves his neighbour is made tranquil. He neither cravenly shuns those mightier than he, but he loves his neighbour; nor does he proudly shun the less significant, but he loves his neighbour and wishes essentially to be equal to all men, whether he is actually known to many or not. Undeniably this is quite a stretch of one's wings, but this is not a proud flight which soars above the world; it is self-renunciation's humble and difficult flight along the earth. From *Works of Love*.

A stratified society is implicit in the wisdom literature: those qualified for leadership, identified by their prudence, loyalty, competence and fairness, belong to the ruling echelon. Those people not suited to leadership, identified by their sloppy work, subversive attitude, impetuosity and slander, belong to a subservient echelon. It's a type of class-based society, but one based on demonstrated competence, not self-proclaimed merit, mere wealth, privileged birth or intellectual prowess.

People best suited to lower positions of limited responsibility and minor authority should not be promoted, nor should their desire for greater position be encouraged if unmatched by demonstrated competence, loyalty and honesty. Each person has a level of responsibility appropriate for their ability, and any up-ending of this hierarchy is unwarranted.

> It is not fitting for a fool to live in luxury, much less for a slave to rule over princes. 19:10.

> Under three things the earth trembles; under four it cannot bear up: a slave when he becomes king, and a fool when he is filled with food; an unloved woman when she gets a husband, and a maid when she succeeds her mistress. 30:21-23.

> There is an evil which I have seen under the sun, as it were an error proceeding from the ruler: folly is set in many high places, and the rich sit in a low place. I have seen slaves on horses, and princes

walking on foot like slaves. *Ecclesiastes* 10:5-7.

The wisdom literature does not counsel a fixed social hierarchy. People who possess more developed skills and mature attitudes move towards higher responsibility and greater authority, while those with mediocre skills and immature attitudes remain where they're most useful: taking orders, following directions, undertaking simpler tasks and fulfilling necessary but lesser roles. This assumes leaders are wise enough to see and reward proven ability. It isn't an unrealistic assumption except in institutions where nepotism or ideology reigns, but their collapse is likely anyway because of their inherent dysfunction.

> He who troubles his household will inherit wind, and the fool will be servant to the wise. 11:29.
>
> The hand of the diligent will rule, while the slothful will be put to forced labor. 12:24.
>
> In the light of a king's face there is life, and his favor is like the clouds that bring the spring rain. 16:15
>
> He who tends a fig tree will eat its fruit, and he who guards his master will be honored. 27:18.

Again, this wisdom is reflected in Edmund Burke's good political and social sense.

> To avoid therefore the evils of inconstancy and versatility, ten thousand times worse than those of obstinacy and the blindest prejudice, we have consecrated the state, that no man should approach to look at its defects or corruption but with due caution; that he should never dream of beginning its reformation by its subversion; that he should approach to the faults of the state as to the wounds of a father, with pious awe and trembling solicitude. Those who are prompt act rashly to hack that aged parent in pieces, and put him into the kettle of magicians, in hopes that by poisonous weeds and wild incantation, they may regenerate the paternal

constitution, and renovate their father's life.

> Society is indeed a contract. Subordinate contracts for objects of mere occasional interest may be dissolved at pleasure—but the state ought not to be considered as nothing better than a partnership agreement in a trade of pepper and coffee, calico or tobacco, or some other such low concern, to be taken up for a little temporary interest, and to be dissolved by the fancy of the parties. It is to be looked on with reverence; because it is not a partnership in things subservient only to the gross animal existence of a temporary and perishable nature. It is a partnership of all science; a partnership of all art; a partnership of every virtue, and in all perfection. As the ends of such a partnership cannot be obtained in many generations, it becomes a partnership not only between those who are living, but between those who are living, those who are dead, and those who are to be born.

iii. THE FOLLY OF LAZYNESS

Humble ants provide a lesson for humanity, but we overlook the lesson along with the many other lessons animals could teach us simply because we have no expectation of instruction such is our objectification of nature and our sense of superiority. *Proverbs* corrects this supercilious attitude and directs us to learn from the activity, organisation and cunning of the natural world.

> Go to the ant, O sluggard; consider her ways, and be wise. Without having any chief, officer or ruler, she prepares her food in summer, and gathers her sustenance in harvest. How long will you lie there, O sluggard? When will you arise from your sleep? A little sleep, a little slumber, a little folding of the hands to rest, and poverty will come upon you like a vagabond, and want like an armed man. 6:6-11.
>
> Four things on earth are small, but they are exceedingly wise: the ants are a people not strong, yet they provide their food in the

summer; the badgers are a people not mighty, yet they make their homes in the rocks; the locusts have no king, yet all of them march in rank; the lizard you can take in your hands, yet it is in kings' palaces. 30:24-28.

Pascal savoured this injunction because it was a pointed indicator of how astray man's habits and thoughts can be. He enjoyed the irony.

> Scripture sends man to the ant; a clear indication of the corruption of his nature. How splendid it is to see the master of the world sent off to the animals as though to the masters of wisdom! From *Additional Pensees*.

Weak and humble creatures work hard to secure their homes and food; yet some people don't show the good sense of insects. No one aims to defraud themselves and undermine their own welfare; the lazy person desires just a little more sleep, a little more rest and another session of convivial chatter, yet the cumulative effect of this untimely surrender to ease is impoverishment.

It's the timing of rest that's crucial. When work is required to provide necessities for ourself and our family, this work must be a high priority. Ease can be taken later. In agrarian communities, harvest festivals came after the harvest not before or during it. Discerning the seasons of life and applying our energy according to those seasons is evidence of wisdom. Conversely, ignoring important seasons of life, or overlooking opportunities to provide for ourselves, is evidence of lazyness.

> A slack hand causes poverty, but the hand of the diligent makes rich. A son who gathers in summer is prudent, but a son who sleeps in harvest brings shame. 10:4, 5.

> He who tills his land will have plenty of bread, but he who follows worthless pursuits will have plenty of poverty. 28:19.

Timely work is a result of a diligent mind. Shrewd people are active and alert; they're observant; they know what is needed and try to obtain it. They realise the felicitous seasons of life pass and may not come again soon, so opportunities to obtain necessities are precious and must not be wasted.

> He who is slack in his work is a brother to him who destroys. 18:9.
>
> Slothfulness casts into a deep sleep, and an idle person will suffer hunger. 19:15.
>
> Love not sleep, lest you come to poverty; open your eyes, and you will have plenty of bread. 20:13.

Most people know that desire is powerless without action. Yet it's common to hear people express desires, but without planning or making any concerted movement to satisfy them. Lazy people are not insentient—no healthy human being is ever lacking to that degree in consciousness – but they are inactive, poor planners and inattentive to reality.

> A slothful man will not catch his prey, but the diligent man will get precious wealth. 12:27.
>
> The soul of the sluggard craves, and gets nothing, while the soul of the diligent is richly supplied. 13:4.

Reality doesn't allow us to treat it with contempt. The universe has structure, including a moral structure which is at times clear and at other times perplexing; wisdom seeks to act in concert with this structure rather than waste energy and time acting against it. In fact, a characteristic of an immature, unsophisticated and totalitarian mind is that it wants to impose its simplicity on complex reality. Lazyness is a form of arrogance that wants to redraw the universe to suit the narcissistic self.

Lazyness has many guises: relational lazyness that never truly engages with another person; political lazyness that discounts intricacy in human affairs and wants easy answers; vocational lazyness that expects provision or advance without diligence; and educational lazyness that wants its complacent ignorance rewarded. Such arrogance is futile; we cannot remake reality in its entirety to suit ourselves. It resists us, and we are hurt through our inattention.

> The way of a sluggard is overgrown with thorns, but the path of the upright is a level highway. 15:19.

Lazyness is self-defeating; when lazyness becomes habitual, it's self-destructive.

> The sluggard buries his hand in the dish, and will not even bring it back to his mouth. 19:24.

There's no doubt timely work may be difficult or unpleasant, but it must be done to ensure, as far as possible, the best chance of a secure future.

> The sluggard does not plow in the autumn; he will seek at harvest and have nothing. 20:4.

A lazy person denies the connection between their refusal to work in autumn's cold – a time of preparation – and their deprivation during harvest – a time of plenty. Instead, they'll be full of excuses, blaming extraordinary or adverse circumstances for their impoverishment. They'll blame anything, however unlikely, rather than blame themselves. They won't admit their love of immediate ease, or confess the fruitlessness of their endless babble.

> In all toil there is profit, but mere talk tends only to want. 14:23.

> The sluggard says, "There is a lion in the road! There is a lion in the streets!" As a door turns on its hinges, so does a sluggard on his bed. The sluggard buries his hand in the dish; it wears him out to bring it back to his mouth. The sluggard is wiser in his own eyes than seven men who can answer discreetly. 26:13-16.

A lazy person frustrates those dependent on them. Instead of attending to their responsibilities they shun their tasks and roles, harming not only themselves but family members and close neighbours. Children, for example, are exposed to cold and damp in a drafty, leaking house through the sloth of parent. An entire family may find themselves in an incommodious and dangerous dwelling because of the householder or landlord's negligence.

> Through sloth the roof sinks in, and through indolence the house leaks. *Ecclesiastes* 10:18.

Just as the co-operative and expedient activity of ants instructs us in diligence, so wise people learn the obvious lesson provided by the lazy and the lax. It isn't judgmental to note and learn from the errors and failures of others; indeed, if we don't learn from them we're missing a lesson from life. We're given brains and eyes to see, to discern, to discover.

> I passed by the field of a sluggard, by the vineyard of a man without sense; and lo, it was all overgrown with thorns; the ground was covered with nettles, and its stone wall was broken down. Then I saw and considered it; I looked and received instruction. A little sleep, a little slumber, a little folding of the hands to rest, and poverty will come upon you like a robber, and want like an armed man. 24:30-34.

There's a superficial attractiveness to simplicity that appeals to a lazy or lazy-minded person. Ownership of problematic, maintenance-intensive assets, for example, may seem hardly worth the effort but a desire for simplicity may mask an important truth. Assets may be onerous to maintain but the right assets greatly aid productive, profitable work. People who can't tolerate the difficulties of tending to property, equipment, infrastructure or livestock, or of building their skills and knowledge, will miss out on the real benefits that these complicated and sometimes unpleasant tasks bring. People can choose to have an uncluttered, easy life but much potential richness is relinquished. In other words, simplicity has an opportunity cost. *Proverbs* provides an illustration from farming; an opportunity for income is lost simply because a person cannot abide dirt, smell and difficulty.

> Where there are no oxen, there is no grain; but abundant crops come by the strength of the ox. 14:4.

Lazyness squanders opportunities and wastes assets; lazyness invites dependency and limits our freedom. *Proverbs* encourages people to look after themselves through timely, persistent work together with prudent care of the consequent wealth. Looking to charities, churches or government for necessities which we should gain for ourselves is never the first course of action of the sage and the conscientious.

Moreover, a person with an unwarranted dependence on others robs themselves of the privilege of assisting the genuinely poor who through no fault of their own are suffering need. An opportunity to build trust, care and friendliness in a society is forfeited because lazy people are in no position to help meet real needs. Deprivations unnecessarily persist because a sluggard will not – cannot – assist. Lazyness is a threefold failure: a slothful person can't look after themselves, nor can they assist anyone else, and so a sense of living in a consoling community is diminished.

Wisdom teaches us when to work and when to rest; an attentive person will not confuse these two seasons. They'll provide for themselves and for those legitimately dependent on them; they'll seek the dignity and freedom that providing for themselves will bring. They'll avoid the loss of freedom that comes with dependence on others who have the power to determine the level and the conditions of support. A community-minded person will avoid being a burden on anyone else, planning and working to ensure that this happy, independent, compassionate position remains the case.

> Remember the Sabbath day, to keep it holy. Six days you shall labor, and do all your work, but the seventh is a sabbath to the Lord your God; in it you shall not do any work, you, or your son, or your daughter, your manservant or your maidservant, or your cattle, or

> the sojourner who is within your gates, for in six days the Lord made heaven and earth, the sea, and all that is in them, and rested the seventh day; therefore the Lord blessed the seventh day and hallowed it.

The commandment reminds us that we're not crass economic units, but sacred human beings. In contrast, both hard-line Marxism and hyper-capitalism say man is a producer, an exploiter of nature and people, a consumer. The wisdom literature frees us to see ourselves as much more: a creative, resourceful person, a helper, a feaster, a provider, a friend. We're commanded to work, but also commanded to recreate, to play, to pray. After our work we must lay on the lawn with our children and watch clouds; caress our spouse; toot a flute; learn new ukulele chords and compose songs; paint a picture; dance, play chess and cards; give thanks; snooze and relax in the sunshine; drink beer while reading *Proverbs, Ecclesiastes*, Pascal, Burke, Kierkegaard and Chesterton.

There's certainly a season to work, but there's also regular, frequent seasons to explore and enjoy all our other amazingly diverse capabilities.

iv. THE FOLLY OF PRIDE

G.K. Chesterton wrote that if he had just one sermon to preach it would be against the folly of pride.

> Now, one of these very practical and working mysteries in the Christian tradition, and one which the Roman Catholic Church, as I say, has done her best work in singling out, is the conception of the sinfulness of pride. Pride is a weakness in the character; it dries up laughter, it dries up wonder, it dries up chivalry and energy. From *Heretics*.

Chesterton thought pride ruined both the virtues and the vices of humanity. It ruined gratitude, for example, because the egotism of pride, pleased only with itself, was continuously dissatisfied with other people. A proud man does not ask, "Am I good enough for this woman, or this community, or this team?" but "Is this woman, this community, this team good enough for me?" Ingratitude sours the soul of the proud: it's rare to find a proud person who is consistently thankful or content. Chesterton linked contentment with humility, not with pride.

> Human beings are happy so long as they retain the receptive power and the power of reaction in surprise and gratitude to something outside. So long as they have this they have as the greatest minds have always declared, a something that is present in childhood and which can still preserve and invigorate manhood. The moment the self within is consciously felt as something superior to any of the gifts that can be brought to it, or any of the adventures that it may enjoy, there has appeared a sort of self-devouring fastidiousness and a disenchantment in advance, which fulfills all the Tartarean emblems of thirst and of despair. From *The Common Man*.

Not only is humility conducive to contentment, it's also conducive to comedy. One of the delights of life is listening to a witty friend recount their disasters: chaos they caused after badly miscalculating their competence; muddles resulting from their major stuff-ups; indignities they inadvertently brought on themselves; accidents and injuries (hopefully minor) suffered as reality slapped them down. Our failures are often very funny, if we can enjoy being the butt of the joke. Naturally, humility is required to share the comedy. A self-important person robs us of comedy because they won't make fun of themselves. Instead, their humour is snobbish; other people are the bumbling clowns, never them. Pride stands on its over-rated dignity and acts as if this dignity never stumbles. But, of course, it often does; when we don't expect it, the wind whips off our hat and leads us on a merry chase, amusing on-lookers. Not laughing at ourselves is a sure sign of vanity.

Chesterton noticed how pride turned minor vices into appalling vices.

> A man may be naturally slothful and rather irresponsible; he may neglect many duties through carelessness, and his friends may still understand him, so long as it really is careless carelessness. But it is the devil and all when it becomes a careful carelessness. It is the devil and all when he becomes a deliberate and self-conscious Bohemian, sponging on principle, preying on society in the name of his own genius (or rather of his own belief in his own genius) taxing the world like a king on the plea that he himself is a poet, and despising better men than himself who work that he may waste ... It would be easy to point out that even the miser, who is half-ashamed of his madness, is a more human and sympathetic type than the millionaire who brags and boasts of his avarice and calls it sanity and simplicity and the strenuous life. It would be easy to point out that even cowardice, as a mere collapse of the nerves, is better than cowardice as an ideal and theory of the intellect; and that a really imaginative person will have more sympathy with men who, like cattle, yield to what they know is panic, than with a particular type of prig who preaches something that he calls peace. From *The Common Man*.

Pride is also an epistemic liability, just as humility is an epistemic value. Pride blinds a person to realities that may not be conducive to their self-image. Overweening ambition, pretentious ideas and self-centred relationships get their just rebuke from reality, but the proud person rejects the rebuke. He doesn't want his ideas challenged by something as common as mere reality. Chesterton saw this aspect of pride, too.

> Pride consists in a man making his personality the only test rather than making the truth the test. From *The Common Man*.

History, especially military history, is replete with examples of pride blinding people to reality, with horrendous results. Hitler's march on Moscow, confident that the German Army only had to kick in the door and the whole rotten structure of the Soviet Union would collapse; the

German cryptographers assurance that their modern Enigma machines and its codes were unbreakable; France's military arrogance at Dien Ben Phu which led them to underestimate the ingenuity and determination of the Viet Minh; the Argentine junta's belief that Great Britain would not contest the Falkland Islands: these are just some of the military blunders in which pride was a crucial factor.

Financial disasters, particularly in the United States, with a massive loss of wealth, have in large measure been caused by financial experts, the self-proclaimed "Masters of the Universe", who mistakenly believed in their own powers of analysis and prediction. Pride is the attitude that leads directly to this kind of self-delusion. Wittgenstein wrote that the hardest thing of all was not to deceive oneself. It's almost impossible for a proud person to avoid this trap.

Self-deception is a trap for every person; it's an especially common trap for those who imagine they can speak without reflection or self-examination, as if truth and wisdom are always at hand, readily gained without effort, sanctity or self-control. They deceive themselves and anyone else who attends to their advice.

> The wisdom of a prudent man is to discern his way, but the folly of fools is deceiving. 14:8

In a secular setting, it's almost impossible to get a diagnosis of pride as the factor which ruins lives, families and nations. Chesterton was perceptive.

> It is amazing to me that in the modern world, that chatters perpetually about psychology and sociology, about the tyranny with which we are threatened by a few feeble-minded infants, about alcohol poisoning and the treatment of neurotics, about half a hundred things that are near the subject but never on the spot — it is amazing that these moderns really have so little to say about the cause and the cure of a moral condition that poisons nearly every family and

every circle of friends. There is hardly a practical psychologist who has anything to say about it that is half so illuminating as the literal exactitude of the old maxim of the priest; that pride is from hell. From *The Common Man*.

An especially pernicious form of pride is spiritual pride. Jesus judged this form of pride harshly whenever he found it because it's so injurious. It harms other people through hard-heartedness; and it harms the proud person because it blinds them to their need for mercy and forgiveness. *Proverbs* is likewise alert to the spiritual pride that won't admit wrong, even when the wrong committed is serious and unmistakable.

> This is the way of an adulteress: she eats, and wipes her mouth, and says, "I have done no wrong." 30:20.

Chesterton saw that the secular world, far from being in any kind of accord with wisdom on this vital diagnosis, positively condones and encourages spiritual pride; that is, it teaches people to believe in themselves and their activities above all else.

> The practical case against pride, as a mere source of social discomfort and discord, is if possible even more self-evident than the more mystical case against it, as a setting up of the self against the soul of the world. And yet though we see this thing on every side in modern life, we really hear very little about it in modern literature and ethical theory. Indeed, a great deal of modern literature and ethics might be meant specifically for the encouragement of spiritual pride. Scores of scribes and sages are busy writing about the importance of self-culture and self-realisation; about how every child is to be taught to develop his personality (whatever that may be); about how every man must devote himself to developing a magnetic and compelling personality; about how every man may become a superman (by taking Our Correspondence Course) or, in the more sophisticated and artistic type of fiction, how one specially superior superman can learn to look down upon the mere mob of ordinary supermen, who

form the population of that peculiar world. From *The Common Man*.

Kierkegaard identified the peculiar spiritual pride that animates much activism. This pride imagines that truth, justice and equality are weak and crippled, and will languish pitiably without the activists' promotion and enlivening agitation. What pretension and ignorance! Kierkegaard thought. In fact, it's the activist who (like everyone else) needs truth, justice and equality in their heart; we are the weak, beggarly, needy ones, not the dynamic virtues which have God as their guarantor. Jesus said, "The truth will set you free." Clearly, we don't set truth or justice free; they set us free. They don't need our support; we need their support.

> But the secret of the deception, to which in one way or another all the expressions can be traced back, is this: that certainly it is not men that stand in need of the Good, but that it is the Good that stands in need of men. On that account it is men who must be won. For the Good is a poor beggar that is in desperate need, instead of its being men who are in desperate need of the Good, and so much in need of it that it is the one thing necessary to them, that it must be bought at any price, that absolutely all must be given up and sold in order to buy it, but that also, the one who owns it, owns all. Yet it happens that all are naturally fooled by the deception. From *Purity of Heart is to Will One thing*.

In this passage, Kierkegaard alluded to Christ's parables of the pearl of great price and the treasure hidden in the field to emphasise that man needed the Good so desperately that it should be pursued by the individual for his own betterment above anything else. It reverses the common orientation of activists and do-gooders.

Locating the self as the centre of reality is untenable because the self is not self-created; the self is received from the hand of God who created it and instructs it. Kierkegaard provided a diagnosis of the self-frustration of seeking the self without reference to the creator of the self in his book

The Sickness Unto Death. It rewards reading and re-reading over and over.

Wisdom locates the self in relation to the self's creator; acting as if our being and knowledge can be secured without reference to the transcendent is always self-defeating. The impiety of pride is consistently contrasted with humble reverence.

> The LORD's curse is on the house of the wicked, but he blesses the abode of the righteous. Toward the scorners he is scornful, but to the humble he shows favor. The wise will inherit honor, but fools get disgrace. 3:34, 35.

> The fear of the LORD is the beginning of wisdom, and the knowledge of the Holy One is insight. For by me your days will be multiplied, and years will be added to your life. If you are wise, you are wise for yourself; if you scoff, you alone will bear it. 9:10-12.

> Every one who is arrogant is an abomination to the LORD; be assured, he will not go unpunished. 16:5.

A proud person sows the seeds of their own humiliation and demise. The very thing most hateful to them – failure and embarrassment – is the likely outcome of their pride. If they won't admit their own failings and keep blaming other factors and other people for their troubles, then stubborn self-delusion joins the list of their vices.

> Pride goes before destruction, and a haughty spirit before a fall. It is better to be of a lowly spirit with the poor than to divide the spoil with the proud. 16:18, 19.

> Before destruction a man's heart is haughty, but humility goes before honor. 18:12.

> Do not put yourself forward in the king's presence or stand in the place of the great; for it is better to be told, "Come up here," than to be put lower in the presence of the prince. 25:6, 7.

A proud person must be careful in one way at least; he must avoid a variety of opinions, lest he's confronted too directly with reality. Hence, it's common for vain people to surround themselves with toadies and lick-spittles; to prefer an echo-chamber of their own opinions rather than canvass the opinions of many; to limit strictly the breadth and depth of their reading, thinking and counsel. Only a humble modesty about oneself can overcome pride's blinding effect.

> He who is estranged seeks pretexts to break out against all sound judgment. 18:1.
>
> He who trusts in his own mind is a fool; but he who walks in wisdom will be delivered. 28:26.

Spiritual pride is an obvious fault. Intellectual pride is also an obvious fault; it ignores the counsel of experienced people and the sagacity of tradition.

> The wise of heart will heed commandments, but a prating fool will come to ruin. 10:8.
>
> When pride comes, then comes disgrace; but with the humble is wisdom. 11:2.
>
> The way of a fool is right in his own eyes, but a wise man listens to advice. 12:15.
>
> The teaching of the wise is a fountain of life, that one may avoid the snares of death. 13:14.

Spiritual pride is a temptation for both religious people and secular people, but intellectual pride is a particular temptation for secular people. Deeply religious people generally have a lively sense of divine transcendence and the infinite wisdom and power of God. They are, in addition, aware of the effects of sin on man's thinking to the extent that man's ability to know reality independently of God is compromised. Secular people do not generally recognise either of these factors, affirming by faith that, in an impersonal universe, man's intelligence is autonomous. And the concept of sin is an offense, so the possibility and the peril of that limitation are not even considered.

Chesterton was alarmed (and amused) by all that intellectual pride *missed* in its superiority.

> Whatever virtues a triumphant egoism really leads to, no one can reasonably pretend that it leads to knowledge. Turning a beggar from the door may be right enough, but pretending to know all the stories the beggar might have narrated is pure nonsense; and this is practically the claim of the egoism which thinks that self-assertion can obtain knowledge. A beetle may or may not be inferior to me – the matter awaits demonstration; but if it were inferior by ten thousand fathoms, the fact remains that there is probably a beetle view of things of which a man is entirely ignorant. If he wishes to conceive that point of view, he will scarcely reach it by revelling in the fact that he is not a beetle. The most brilliant exponent of the egoistic school, Nietzsche, with deadly and honourable logic, admitted that the philosophy of self-satisfaction led to looking down on the weak, the cowardly, and the ignorant. Looking down on things may be a delightful experience, only there is nothing, from a mountain to a cabbage, that is really *seen* when it is from a balloon. The philosopher of the ego sees everything, no doubt, from a high and rarefied heaven; only he sees everything foreshortened or deformed. From *In Defense of Humility*.

Chesterton also saw that intellectual pride obscured self-knowledge and self-revelation. A clever, person, proud of their intellect, tends to enjoy showing how clever they are – at the cost of revealing *who* they really are.

> One of the thousand objections to the sin of pride lies precisely in this, that self-consciousness of necessity destroys self-revelation. A man who thinks a great deal about himself will try to be many-sided, attempts at theatrical excellence at all points, will try to be an

encyclopedia of culture, and his own real personality will be lost in that false universalism. Thinking about himself will lead to trying to be the universe; trying to be the universe will lead to ceasing to be anything. If, on the other hand, a man is sensible enough to think only about the universe, he will think about it in his own individual way. He will keep virgin the secret of God; he will see the grass as no other man can see it, and will look at a sun that no man has ever known. From *Heretics*.

Chesterton also saw that adventures and surprises belong to the humble person, rather than the proud person. The humble person can be surprised, and is not surprised that he is surprised. A proud person will be surprised – reality often surprises us – but they won't enjoy being surprised because being surprised means they didn't know or didn't foresee something.

> It is the humble man who has the sensational sights vouchsafed to him, and this for three obvious reasons: first, he strains his eyes more than other men to see them; second, that he is more overwhelmed and uplifted with them when they come; third, that he records them more exactly and sincerely and with less adulteration from his more common-place and more conceited everyday self. Adventures are to those to whom they are most unexpected – that is, most romantic. Adventures are to the shy: in this sense adventures are to the unadventurous. From *Heretics*.

The proud man who's right in his own eyes is sometimes an unintelligent fool and sometimes an intelligent fool. Intelligent people – academics, philosophers, intellectuals – may be more prone than ordinary people to trust in their own ability to judge things; because of this disposition, clever people are more likely to argue against the authority of tradition or religion. Pascal noted that pious scholars are rare.

G.K. Chesterton observed the same tendency.

> Cleverness kills wisdom; that is one of the few sad and certain

things. From *What's Wrong with the World*.

Chesterton added that intellectual pride is not only destructive of the proud; worse, it's catastrophic for those impacted, willingly or unwillingly, by this pride.

> To put it briefly; it is now the custom to say that most modern blunders have been due to the Common man. And I should like to point out what appalling blunders have in fact been due to the Uncommon man. It is easy enough to argue that the mob makes mistakes; but as a matter of fact it never has a chance to make mistakes until its superiors have used their superiority to make much worse mistakes. It is easy to weary of democracy and cry out for an intellectual aristocracy. But the trouble is that every intellectual aristocracy seems to have been utterly unintellectual. Anybody might guess beforehand that there would be blunders of the ignorant. What nobody could have guessed, what nobody could have dreamed of in a nightmare, what no morbid mortal imagination could ever have dared to imagine, was the mistakes of the well-informed. It is true, in a sense, to say that the mob has always been led by more educated men. It is more true, in every sense, to say that is has always been misled by educated men. It is easy enough to say the cultured man should be the crowd's guide, philosopher and friend. Unfortunately, he has nearly always been a misguiding guide, a false friend and a very shallow philosopher. And the actual catastrophes we have suffered, including those we are now suffering, have not in historical fact been due to the prosaic practical people who are supposed to know nothing but almost invariably to the highly theoretical people who knew that they knew everything. The world may learn by its mistakes, but they are mostly the mistakes of the learned. From *The Common Man*.

Edmund Burke, too, identified this danger. He saw how the proud assumed their right to guide society, often to the great harm of society. Plus, the intellectually proud were fond of self-promotion, so they liked to foment change because they gained prominence through it. Burke's aphorism is timeless.

> Men of letters, fond of distinguishing themselves, are rarely adverse to innovation.

The innovations they promote aren't the result of deep thought or attention to the wide experience of humanity. The innovations more often originate from self-centred motives such as vanity, license, power or greed. Burke saw this characteristic.

> A spirit of innovation is generally the result of a selfish temper and confined views. People will not look forward to posterity, who never look backward to their ancestors.

Both Chesterton and Burke wanted the freedom to consider other options for society besides the restricted mandate of Progress, the talisman of the conceited, which Chesterton thought had become like a railway-track that locked its passengers in one hurtling direction.

> I shall be completely misunderstood if I am supposed to be calling for a return ticket to Athens or to Eden; because I do not want to go on by the cheap ticket to Utopia. I want to go where I like. I want to stop where I like. I want to know the width as well as the length of the world; and to wander off the railway-track to the ancient plains of liberty. From *The Common Man*.

In its optimistic manifestations, secularism tends to promote straightforward intellectual pride; in its pessimistic manifestations, it tends to promote a perverse form of intellectual pride: nihilistic despair. Albert Camus was an eloquent, almost charming, chronicler of this form of despair. It results when man believes the universe is indifferent to his hopes, suffering, reasoning and being. Camus' book *The Myth of Sisyphus* provides a *precis* of this despair. It's an excellent book to begin, but not to conclude, reading philosophy.

The distance between the wisdom of *Proverbs* and *Ecclesiastes* and the bright pride of secular man or his bleak despair is obvious. Secular thought oscillates between an optimistic view of man's technological competence and a pessimistic vision of man's metaphysical and epistemological absurdity. Both positions issue from the one faith: a dogmatic assertion of autonomy. And a materialistic perspective adds to the distressing conundrum: autonomy has to be dogmatically affirmed because the secular man's scientism tells him he is a spiritless, determined, bio-chemical entity.

Pride is destructive of thought; it's also destructive of personal relationships. Pride is a form of selfishness, a desire to be right at all times, an unwillingness to admit wrong or confess to inadequacy. Pride is unrealistic, and to build relationships or society, a lowly commitment to reality is needed.

Proud people tend to deny inconvenient factors such as the rights or feelings of others, especially those they consider inferior. And they find it hard to apologise, even when they are clearly in the wrong. As a result, harsh words are spoken, disagreements proliferate and arguments intensify. A chattering coxcomb (the phrase courtesy of Jane Austen's *Emma*) doesn't tend to listen carefully and considerately to other people; they prefer to hear themselves speak. *Proverbs* is clear: pride creates and prolongs strife.

> By insolence the heedless make strife, but with those who take advice is wisdom. 13:10.

Pride brings individual and societal calamity, but humility brings a measure of security and contributes to cheerful community.

4

WISDOM AND WEALTH

The wisdom literature offers many instructions about the best way to view and accrue wealth. Wealth is not disparaged; private wealth is encouraged, but with caveats. Wealth helps secure necessities such as warmth, food and shelter; wealth allows a degree of independence and freedom; and it allows us to own beneficial and beautiful possessions. Wealth gained by work and wisdom also expands employment and provides the means to help those in need. Wealth brings a good reputation and esteem for one's family, together with influence in the community. In addition, there's a sense of hope for the future and the happiness of personal fulfillment in the creativity and the commitment to excellence that help create wealth. These are all significant things that contribute to a joyful, satisfied life.

But an unhealthy view of wealth can harm a person. Great wealth can mask vices and lead to fantasies of power. Yearning for wealth can make us greedy, selfish and unjust. It can give us a false sense of security. It may lead us into irreverence. We must limit our desire for wealth to a healthy balance somewhere between bare sufficiency and spirit-occluding opulence.

Moreover, there are limits to what wealth can achieve; it cannot address faults that are intangible. It cannot build virtues, and it cannot correct vices. Wealth is limited in its power. A materialistic culture, eager for easy answers, tends to forget this basic truth. A wise person remembers it.

The Hardest Path is the Easiest

The wisdom literature is intensely practical, that is, it's realistic and therefore measured. It presents the world as complex but the complexity is not chaotic; it's governed by principles – hence wisdom is possible. The fugitive character of wealth is asserted, but it also presents principles to make wealth somewhat easier to gather and relatively more secure, without harmful side-effects.

Wisdom is personified in one *Proverbs* passage and she calls to humanity. Lady Wisdom reminds us that seeking her insights is far better than seeking wealth, although wealth is not scorned.

> I love those who love me, and those who seek me diligently find me. Riches and honor are with me, enduring wealth and prosperity. My fruit is better than gold, even fine gold, and my yield than choice silver. I walk in the way of righteousness, in the paths of justice, endowing with wealth those who love me, and filling their treasuries. 8:17-21.

The last section of *Proverbs* portrays a careful, creative, hard-working woman whose labour brings wealth, and with the wealth there are tremendous benefits for her family, her employees, and her community. Her wealth is a blessing, not a snare.

> A good wife who can find? She is far more precious than jewels. The heart of her husband trusts in her, and he will have no lack of gain. She does him good, and not harm, all the days of her life. She seeks wool and flax, and works with willing hands. She is like the ships of the merchant, she brings her food from afar. She rises while it is yet night and provides food for her household and tasks for her maidens. She considers a field and buys it; with the fruit of her hands she plants a vineyard. She girds her loins with strength and makes her arms strong. She perceives that her merchandise is profitable. Her lamp does not go out at night. She puts her hands to the distaff, and her hands hold the spindle. She opens her hand to the poor, and reaches out her hands to the needy. She is not afraid of

snow for her household, for all her household are clothed in scarlet. She makes herself coverings; her clothing is fine linen and purple. Her husband is known in the gates, when he sits among the elders of the land. She makes linen garments and sells them; she delivers girdles to the merchant. Strength and dignity are her clothing, and she laughs at the time to come. She opens her mouth with wisdom, and the teaching of kindness is on her tongue. She looks well to the ways of her household, and does not eat the bread of idleness. Her children rise up and call her blessed; her husband also, and he praises her: "Many women have done excellently, but you surpass them all." Charm is deceitful, and beauty is vain, but a woman who fears the LORD is to be praised. 31:10-31.

While wealth is desirable, other passages in *Proverbs* address wealth's elusive side: it's unstable and unpredictable. It's needed in life but by itself isn't sufficient for life: tangible things alone never are sufficient satisfaction for humanity's deepest needs. Paradoxically, it's invisible and intangible qualities – in particular, the theological virtues of faith, hope and charity, and the cardinal virtues of prudence, temperance, fortitude and justice – which form the most stable basis for life. Visible and tangible things, while good and necessary, cannot offer anyone guidance, consolation or vision and are therefore an inadequate foundation by themselves on which to build a life, a family, a community, or a nation.

Quality of character is more important than quantity of material. This is often misunderstood by politicians, trade unionists and activists, among others, who imagine all problems can be solved with the allocation of extra money; other people's money, of course, never their own. Despite the demands for ever-increasing funding for schools, for example, no teacher in charge of unruly students can buy 25 kilograms of respect for elders, 45 litres of desire for instruction, 3 cubic metres of quiet self-discipline and distribute it to her class thereby creating an improved learning environment. These qualities are non-physical, spiritual in a sense, and they must be fostered by intangible means including correction, instruction, discipline, and adult example. They cannot be bought by any amount of funding. The poorest people in the meanest setting can provide an abundance of virtue, talent, creativity. Money is close to irrelevant to these qualities. Problems which have their basis in neglected spiritual truths and values can never be fixed by physical expedients. Spiritual destitution cannot be rectified by material means. The impatient and the simple overlook this rule; they demand, and then consequently waste, immense resources.

Adding to the difficulties attendant to any over-dependence on wealth is its inherent instability and uncertainty. It is transient and truant.

> Do not toil to acquire wealth; be wise enough to desist. When your eyes light upon it, it is gone; for suddenly it takes to itself wings, flying like an eagle toward heaven. 23:4, 5.

For this reason, prudence is required; we may seek wealth but shouldn't depend solely upon it. Committing too much time and energy to an absconding thing is foolish: it's seeking what can never be securely possessed nor certainly controlled.

> He who trusts in his riches will wither, but the righteous will flourish like a green leaf. 11:28.

> A faithful man will abound with blessings, but he who hastens to be rich will not go unpunished. 28:20.

It's common in any family, community or nation, for some people – or when the society is really confused, for many people – to base their life on the accumulation of wealth. The common name for this misadventure is greed; it's a vice. Using wealth only as a means to cater for pleasures or crass consumerism is dim-witted. Accumulating wealth for its own sake is madness because it ultimately leads to self-diminishment and to many counter-community attitudes and acts: oppression; the corruption of justice; dishonesty and violence; contempt for neighbours and neglect of our sacred duties. Balance is required to find a wise midpoint between poverty, which has its own set of temptations, and riches which have a different set of temptations.

> Two things I ask of thee; deny them not to me before I die: Remove far from me falsehood and lying; give me neither poverty nor riches; feed me with the food that is needful for me, lest I be full, and deny thee, and say, "Who is the LORD?" or lest I be poor, and steal, and profane the name of my God. 30:7-9.

Great wealth can lead to delusions of wisdom, high status and invulnerability. Wealth can foster grave character faults and mask deep dysfunctions; it can't make anyone a better person, but it can ruin an immature person.

> A gracious woman gets honor, and violent men get riches. 11:16.

> A rich man's wealth is his strong city, and like a high wall protecting him. 18:11.

> A rich man is wise in his own eyes, but a poor man who has understanding will find him out. 28:11.

The difficulties of managing wealth are compounded if, in the very unpredictability of the financial world, wealth is acquired quickly. Sudden riches become a trap for many people; a windfall doesn't bring with it the experience necessary for shrewd use. It's better if time and effort have done their disciplining work in the heart and mind, gradually teaching us how to manage wealth. Gaining wealth over time through work brings discernment and vital knowledge, minimising the possibility of turmoil.

> Wealth hastily gotten will dwindle, but he who gathers little by little will increase it. 13:11

> An inheritance gotten hastily in the beginning will in the end not be blessed. 20:21.

> A miserly man hastens after wealth, and does not know that want will come upon him. 28:22.

We must question the wisdom of overly-generous welfare programs that give people money but cannot provide the lessons that are only learned by toiling for pay over significant periods of time. Giving money to a person who hasn't gained the experience to use it sensibly can be a counter-productive exercise even when the intentions are charitable. In ancient Israel, the poor were assisted by rules directing farmers to leave the corners of fields unharvested, and the vineyard owners were not to gather every last bunch of grapes. The poor could glean; they had their immediate needs met but they had to work for sustenance. They were not idle and passive. They did not burden their community. Ancient Israel understood that a person's most basic needs motivated them to find and stay at work.

> A worker's appetite works for him; his mouth urges him on. 16:26.

There is one group of people to whom we should give our money, and promptly: our employees; the contractors and professionals, the tradesmen and women who have done work for us; and the utilities that provide us with services. If we have the money at hand, then payment on-time is our responsibility and their due. Any delay in payment is unjust, and harms the goodwill and faith that are necessary to a peaceful, functional community. Resentment and contention are unnecessarily aroused by delayed payment. The same principle pertains to items we may have borrowed, or promises we have made.

> Do not say to your neighbor, "Go, and come again, tomorrow I will give it" – when you have it with you. Do not plan evil against your neighbor who dwells trustingly beside you. Do not contend with a man for no reason, when he has done you no harm. 3:28-30.

Any shortcut to wealth usually involves something either overly risky or underhanded: an unstable basis for acquiring an errant commodity. If a choice must be made between wealth or honesty, money or integrity, riches or justice, then always the wisest choice is to value righteousness, truth and fairness. In the long run, these values bring the greatest satisfaction. *Proverbs* is emphatic about this order of priorities and repeatedly affirms it. We are easily duped by money, so the lesson needs reinforcement.

> Treasures gained by wickedness do not profit, but righteousness delivers from death. The LORD does not let the righteous go hungry, but he thwarts the craving of the wicked. 10:2, 3.
>
> Riches do not profit in the day of wrath, but righteousness delivers from death. 11:4
>
> A man is not established by wickedness, but the root of the righteous will never be moved. 12:3.
>
> He who is greedy for unjust gain makes trouble for his household, but he who hates bribes will live. 15:27.
>
> Bread gained by deceit is sweet to a man, but afterward his mouth will be full of gravel. 20:17.
>
> Diverse weights are an abomination to the LORD, and false scales are not good. 20:23.
>
> The getting of treasures by a lying tongue is a fleeting vapor and a snare of death. 21:6.
>
> A good name is to be chosen rather than great riches, and favor is better than silver or gold. The rich and the poor meet together; the LORD is the maker of them all. 22:1, 2.
>
> Better is a poor man who walks in his integrity than a rich man who is perverse in his ways. 28:6.
>
> He who augments his wealth by interest and increase gathers it for him who is kind to the poor. 28:8.

Once we have the right perspective on wealth so it's an aid to us and not a stumbling-block, we need to manage what we have accrued, or what has been entrusted to us. A wise view of wealth and appropriate care of our assets are, of course, closely related.

5

WISDOM AND ASSET MANAGEMENT

Most people want more wealth; many have imagined how riches could change their life. Money – any asset – can be used with wisdom or it can be wasted. How can we manage our wealth and use it in a way that truly benefits ourselves and those around us? The wisdom literature answers that question.

Of course, our use of wealth will reflect the quality of our character: our prudence or our selfishness. And our decisions will affect others, for better or worse, especially the people near and dear to us.

> In the house of the righteous there is much treasure, but trouble befalls the income of the wicked. 15:6.

As previously noted, *Proverbs* commends wealth primarily as a means of providing for our family: allowing for a comfortable home where there is warmth, nutritious food, beauty, and the valuable accoutrements for life. Our home allows us to show hospitality; it's a shelter of security, fruitfulness, instruction, recreation. Often our home is a base for business. This is the first and most important use of wealth: to look after ourself and our family.

> By wisdom a house is built, and by understanding it is established; by knowledge the rooms are filled with all precious and pleasant riches. 24:3, 4.

Leaving an inheritance is affirmed. A careful manager of wealth can be bountiful to more than one generation, whereas someone who has squandered their wealth is unable to leave much, if anything, to his children, let alone his grandchildren. There are benefits when wealth accumulates or at least remains in the family through generations; it aids an on-going sturdy independence. This is a good thing, not a bad thing. Inheritance taxes and death duties are contrary to this valuable practice.

> A good man leaves an inheritance to his children's children, but the sinner's wealth is laid up for the righteous. 13:22.

The degree of bounty in an inheritance may be determined by the relative merits of those who are to receive it, with allowances for faithful and diligent people who are not family members in preference to one's own profligate, aberrant children.

> A slave who deals wisely will rule over a son who acts shamefully, and will share the inheritance as one of the brothers. 17:2.

Wealth brings the opportunity to provide for the poor. Obviously, when deciding the time and extent of the charity, the virtue of prudence is crucial. In particular, financial aid should be withheld if it's likely to encourage harmful or lazy behaviour. At an international level, for example, the history of foreign aid is blighted with the misuse of funds provided by well-meaning donors to corrupt regimes and disorganised states. At a national level, the growth of massive welfare programs has the potential to weaken the financial health of the nation while subsidising irresponsible behaviour among many welfare recipients.

Our support of the poor must be judicious. Each case is different and needs individual evaluation. This is something government programs never do; they may be generous, but lack critical discernment. Fearing accusations of discrimination, they become indiscriminate. Our gifts to the poor are unwise in proportion to the extent they encourage on-going dependency. Gifts should be appropriate to the circumstances; they should never undermine the recipient's initiative or sense of responsibility. There is a season to give, and a season withhold. All people, rich or poor, are equally capable of grasping, manipulative attitudes. Welfare recipients and pensioners as well as the CEOs of global conglomerates are all capable of demanding more than their fair share. The shirker, the labouring man and the well-paid executive are all vulnerable to the temptations of self-seeking. *Proverbs* is realistic about this side of human nature.

> A poor man who oppresses the poor is a beating rain that leaves no food. 28:3.

> The leech has two daughters; "Give, give," they cry. 30:15.

All this said, our individual support of the genuinely poor and distressed should be bountiful and habitual, rather than parsimonious and rare. The exhortation to generosity is repeated.

> Honor the LORD with your substance and with the first fruits of all your produce; then your barns will be filled with plenty, and your vats will be bursting with wine. 3:9, 10.

> One man gives freely, yet grows all the richer; another withholds what he should give, and only suffers want. A liberal man will be enriched, and one who waters will himself be watered. The people curse him who holds back grain, but a blessing is on the head of him who sells it. 11:24-26.

The wisdom literature doesn't see generous giving as a loss; rather, giving to the poor is seen as a sort of faith-filled investment. Charity can be an expression of reverence, a form of worship, and God will honour the generosity of the giver. Here, paradoxically, is one of the safest and most profitable uses of wealth: by giving it away, we secure it in eternity. But it takes belief in the worldview presented by the wisdom literature, or at least a preparedness to experiment existentially and see if the result is as promised, to view generous giving in this way. It's a very long term experiment! But we are assured that giving to the poor in a timely, appropriate manner is a blessing that leads to blessing.

> He who oppresses a poor man insults his Maker, but he who is kind to the needy honors him. 14:31.
>
> He who is kind to the poor lends to the LORD, and he will repay him for his deed. 19:17.
>
> He who has a bountiful eye will be blessed, for he shares his bread with the poor. 22:9.
>
> He who gives to the poor will not want, but he who hides his eyes will get many a curse. 28:27.

The reverse is also affirmed: hard-hearted parsimony is self-defeating. A merciless heart reflects a shrunken soul. No blessing will be forthcoming.

> He who closes his ear to the cry of the poor will himself cry out and not be heard. 21:13.
>
> He who oppresses the poor to increase his own wealth, or gives to the rich, will only come to want. 22:16.

Prudent generosity must not be feigned; integrity is hugely important. Advertising our bounty when in fact we are miserly is a two-fold lie; we mislead others, and contradict our reason and conscience. Boasting of virtues one doesn't possess is a common form of self-aggrandisement.

> Like clouds and wind without rain is a man who boasts of a gift he does not give. 25:14.
>
> Like the glaze covering an earthen vessel are smooth lips with an evil heart. 26:23.

> Let another praise you, and not your own mouth; a stranger, and not your own lips. 27:2.

Generosity to those who through no fault of their own lack necessities is a good use of wealth. A poor use of wealth is to spend it endlessly on luxurious consumables. It's good to celebrate special occasions with excellent food and drink, but it's a thoughtless, incapacitating habit if poverty is the guest that stays after the party.

> He who loves pleasure will be a poor man; he who loves wine and oil will not be rich. 21:17.

Another misuse of wealth is to spend it on illegitimate pleasures: prostitutes, drugs, entertaining drunks and gluttons. It's even worse when the money belongs to the family estate, the taxpayer, a charity organisation or a company; in other words, misusing money that belongs to others.

> Precious treasure remains in a wise man's dwelling, but a foolish man devours it. 21:20.

> He who loves wisdom makes his father glad, but one who keeps company with harlots squanders his substance. 29:3.

Every week we hear about bureaucrats or business executives, members of parliament or union officials spending money entrusted to them on call-girls, lavish parties or expensive holidays. It's a double folly: the waste is bad enough; it's worse when the money has been given to us for safe-keeping.

Spending money at the wrong time can be as damaging as spending money on the wrong things. For example, spending money on a house or pleasure boat when the means of paying for these expenses hasn't yet been secured is extravagant. Far better first to cultivate the asset or enterprise generating the wealth, and only when that's robust may other expenses be incurred.

> Prepare your work outside, get everything ready for you in the field;

and after that build your house. 24:27.

It's disturbing to see how often this obvious principle is ignored. In business, executives are given bonuses or pay rises despite the fact that the company they are overseeing is not yet profitable, efficient, debt-free or has significant reserves of cash for unforeseen problems. And many people borrow large amounts of money to build and extensively furnish their house before they have finished their training or learned to perform their job with expertise.

Luxuries aren't evidence of greed; the possession of luxuries may be the result of wise living and a legitimate appreciation of high quality goods, but building one's life around pleasures based only on luxuries is witless in two ways. First, material things can never fulfill us in a deep, permanent way; second, it's negligent spending significant amounts of money on items that are quickly consumed – such as exotic food and expensive wine – with no appreciable benefit to anyone. As Jesus said to the food-obsessives of his day, it goes into the stomach and soon after goes into the sewer.

> Hear, my son, and be wise, and direct your mind in the way. Be not among winebibbers, or among gluttonous eaters of meat; for the drunkard and the glutton will come to poverty, and drowsiness will clothe a man with rags. 23:19-21.

The commercial world is filled with cunning people who make their living by depriving us of our wealth. A wise person is alert to the tricks of those with something to sell. Avarice is buried deep in the human heart and the marketplace is thick with those in its thrall, both sellers and buyers. Prudence, investigation and a sense of caution are required to avoid rip-offs. The common phrase, "Buyer, beware!" applies not just to shoddy goods but to dodgy deals.

> "It is bad, it is bad," says the buyer; but when he goes away, then he boasts. 20:14.

An obvious principle of financial management is that expenditure should be appropriate to the circumstances. Profligacy of expenditure in conditions when frugality is warranted is short-sighted. The acumen that discerns what may be ahead and prepares for it is praised. Of course, what happens may be completely unexpected, but there are still ways to prepare for the unforeseen: stockpiling, minimising debt, ensuring multiple streams of income, exploring diversification and building redundancies. In particular, savings allow us to take advantage of unanticipated opportunities, and provide a buffer against difficulties that surprise us.

> A prudent man sees danger and hides himself; but the simple go on, and suffer for it. 22:3.

> Do not boast about tomorrow, for you do not know what a day may bring forth. 27:1.

One danger a cautious man foresees and avoids is going guarantor for another person's debts. There are strong warnings against this precarious commitment because it can lead to the guarantor's destitution. Too much is out of our control, too much is staked. And people are unlikely to cherish the resources of another. Escaping from this risk is an urgent matter.

> My son, if you have become surety for your neighbor, have given your pledge for a stranger; if you are snared in the utterance of your lips, caught in the words of your mouth; then do this, my son, and save yourself, for you have come into your neighbor's power: go, hasten, and importune your neighbor. Give your eyes no sleep and your eyelids no slumber; save yourself like a gazelle from the hunter, like a bird from the hand of the fowler. 6:1-5.

> He who gives surety for a stranger will smart for it, but he who hates suretyship is secure. 11:15.

Those close to us might assume they have a greater claim on our loyalty and support, and pressure us to act as guarantor. Of course, families should assist one another; there are many ways to help those dear to us, and measured help should be given whenever possible. But this does not include jeopardising our critical assets by acting as guarantor, even for a close friend or family member.

> A man without sense gives a pledge, and becomes surety in the presence of his neighbor. 17:18.
>
> Take a man's garment when he has given surety for a stranger, and hold him in pledge when he gives surety for foreigners. 20:16.
>
> Be not one of those who give pledges, who become surety for debts. If you have nothing with which to pay, why should your bed be taken from under you? 22:26, 27.

Given the repeated and dire warnings about being guarantor, one sees the risk accepted often enough, unfortunately, at personal and national level. For example, governments use taxpayers' money to guarantee the solvency of banks and to rescue struggling big businesses, which is foolishness writ large because the risks are unknown and the potential losses are immense. It's a form of surety that makes the tax-payer the loser.

Our wealth may create the expectation that we are able to provide for people who are fully capable of providing for themselves. Ostentatious spending, for instance, attracts people and often enough they're insincere people. Caution is needed because many of those attracted to us are attracted by our wealth and would abandon us if it disappeared. This is common in life: obvious abundance attracts inconstant people.

> The poor is disliked even by his neighbor, but the rich has many friends. 14:20.
>
> Wealth brings many new friends, but a poor man is deserted by his friend. 19:4.

> Many seek the favor of a generous man, and every one is a friend to a man who gives gifts. All a poor man's brothers hate him; how much more do his friends go far from him! He pursues them with words, but does not have them. 19:6, 7.

Proverbs counsels a conservative approach to debt. It doesn't condemn borrowing money outright, although it makes the obvious point that if spending large amounts of one's own money on luxuries and consumables is block-headed, then borrowing money for these things compounds the error. The sober reality is that debts reduce our security and freedom. Debts must be paid back and the lender will insist on this happening. We place ourselves in servitude when we borrow money. We are not our own masters; someone else controls us to some extent and often for many long years.

> The rich rules over the poor, and the borrower is the slave of the lender. 22:7.

We may be able to renegotiate our debts if repayment becomes difficult, but this is an uncertain venture because we're in a position of weakness, dependent on the patience of others who will want their money and may be inclined to severity.

> The poor use entreaties, but the rich answer roughly. 18:23.

Despite the loss of freedom that comes with debt, there are whole industries that encourage people to embrace debt, including banks and retailers. They make their money by the thralldom of others; the larger the debt and the longer it takes to pay it back, the greater their profit. Sometimes it's necessary to borrow money for a home, for example, but the debt should always be as small as possible and paid back as quickly as possible. Further, debts should not be multiplied, nor is it wise to loan money for things that are neither necessary nor wealth-creating. Borrowing money for items that depreciate is a common but very costly way to add things to our lives. It should be avoided unless the items are for profitable work: a tradesman's tools and equipment, for instance.

> Better is a man of humble standing who works for himself than one who plays the great man but lacks bread. 12:9.

Again, despite the burdens that debt imposes, one sees indebtedness everywhere, often to satisfy greed, from a desire to gain acceptance through conspicuous consumption, or as a way to deal with previous wealth mismanagement. It's bad enough when this bondage through debt limits individuals, it's much worse when governments incur massive debts and then exacerbate the situation by borrowing more funds to service the original debt. The result is diminished self-determination, social unrest, unemployment, the neglect of essential infrastructure, and vulnerability to enemies. In addition, deliberate misinformation to mask the debt, and frequent changes of government under the pressure of recurrent financial crises are common consequences of massive government debt. Both governments and individuals confuse assets with liabilities: a lamentable, impoverishing confusion. Oddly, government treasurers seem to assume that high levels of consumer spending indicate a robust economy without considering if the spending and the consumption are fuelled by debt. It's another common but inexcusable confusion.

Once wealth-creating assets have been acquired, they must be continuously managed. It's naive to expect assets to look after themselves, especially given the slippery nature of wealth. It's equally naive expecting other people – managers, agents, stewards, financial advisors – to look after our assets with the diligent care required. The enterprises and activities that bring our income and secure us against need are too important to neglect or manage at arm's length.

It's better to look after our own assets, or if time or distance makes this impossible, at the very least to scrutinise closely those commissioned to manage them. Again, this is an obvious principle but one too often neglected. Our savings, our superannuation, our investments are given into the care of others – bankers, investment gurus, financial functionaries – who have little or no accountability and who may have dubious expertise. They might take risks with our money that we do not know about and would not countenance if we did know, and they will not suffer the consequences we will suffer if they make poor decisions. Their decisions on our behalf could be compromised by self-interest generated by commissions, rewards or productivity targets. Yet we readily trust them. *Proverbs* counsels close, constant supervision of the assets and investments fundamental to our livelihood.

> Know well the condition of your flocks, and give attention to your herds; for riches do not last for ever; and does a crown endure to all generations? When the grass is gone, and the new growth appears, and the herbage of the mountains is gathered, the lambs will provide your clothing, and the goats the price of a field; there will be enough goats' milk for your food, for the food of your household and maintenance for your maidens. 27:23-27.

Here, there are two principles of good management. The manager is exhorted to develop expertise through close observation. The manager is also exhorted to be alert to changes, opportunities and dangers. A rural Chinese proverb recommends observation and constant attention as the basis for good management: *Fertility follows in the footsteps of the farmer.*

If animals are involved in our work – in farming, for example – then proper care of the animals is essential. Animal cruelty is condemned; in fact, caring for animals is a characteristic of righteous people while cruelty is evidence of a wicked heart.

> A righteous man has regard for the life of his beast, but the mercy of the wicked is cruel. 12:10.

Related to diligent care of assets, is the need to employ skilled, honest people. Most of the problems that come with employing people would not arise if the right people were employed in the first place. We'll have endless frustrations through wasted time, lost opportunities and mismanaged resources if we employ unskilled or lazy people. The opposite is also true: we will be assisted with our difficulties and refreshed in our enterprises if we employ the right people.

> Like vinegar to the teeth, and smoke to the eyes, so is the sluggard to those who send him. 10:26.

> A bad messenger plunges men into trouble, but a faithful envoy brings healing. 13:17.

> Like the cold of snow in the time of harvest is a faithful messenger to those who send him, he refreshes the spirit of his masters. 25:13.

> He who sends a message by the hand of a fool cuts off his own feet and drinks violence. 26:6.

It's especially important to employ good people during times of change or turmoil. When circumstances are confusing, there is less room for errors in appointment. People may clamour and jostle for key roles, but those roles should go to those people who have a history of fidelity, diligence and discretion.

> Trust in a faithless man in time of trouble is like a bad tooth or a foot that slips. 25:19.

> Like one who binds the stone in the sling is he who gives honor to a fool. 26:8.

We should employ people who possess skills appropriate for the task and are prepared to learn; who can receive correction and are patient with complexity; who are loyal and honest. We should not employ people who won't receive instruction; who are stubbornly content with their current knowledge and make excuses for poor performance; who are gluttons or drunks, loose with money, disloyal, dishonest, angry, and impatient with difficulties.

> A man is commended according to his good sense, but one of perverse mind is despised. 12:8.
>
> What is desired in a man is loyalty, and a poor man is better than a liar. 19:22.

The greater the responsibilities, the more important it is that mature people are given those responsibilities. Political leaders have an especially onerous task; they have great power to encourage that which is good or encourage that which is calamitous. They influence the spread and liveliness of virtues or vices in a city, state or nation. The ramifications are wide and deep and felt throughout society. It's no surprise that *Proverbs* and *Ecclesiastes* describe the fundamental requirements of those in government.

6

WISDOM AND GOVERNMENT

Proverbs and *Ecclesiastes* are rich with principles for sound leadership and good government. They attest that good individual self-government is the foundation of good communal government. Each person is responsible to act with justice, kindness and friendliness in their daily life. The cumulative effect is a large measure of stable amity. In other words, justice, stability and dignity are the products of the population first and foremost rather than a creation of government. A society will only ever be as good as the moral wisdom of the constituency's individuals. A nation whose people are inept at self-government will always be unstable, dysfunctional.

> When wickedness comes, contempt comes also; and with dishonor comes disgrace. 18:3.
>
> An evil man is ensnared in his transgression, but a righteous man sings and rejoices. 29:16.

The maturity to limit our desires is crucial; Chesterton posited this as the basis of good self-government.

> Self-denial is the test and definition of self-government. From *Alarms and Discursions*.

Chesterton understood that if we do not control ourselves, the state will try to control us with wild flurries of prohibitions as passing scientific, psychological and social conjectures about what is causing the ills of the individual and of society gain acceptance, before being superseded by other conjectures that result in further prohibitions.

> In short, so long as we combine ceaseless and often reckless scientific speculation with rapid and often very random social reform, the result must inevitably be not anarchy but ever-increasing tyranny. There must be a ceaseless and almost mechanical multiplication of things forbidden. The resolution to cure all the ills that flesh is heir to, combined with the guesswork about all possible ills that flesh and nerve and brain-cell may be heir to—these two things conducted simultaneously must inevitably spread a sort of panic of prohibition. Scientific imagination and social reform between them will quite logically and almost legitimately have made us slaves. From *The Fear of the Film*.

Edmund Burke and Soren Kierkegaard (especially in his book *Works of Love*) focused on the vital connection between reverence, self-control and social stability. Here is Burke's assessment.

> We know, and it is our pride to know, that man is by his constitution a religious animal; that atheism is against, not only our reason but our instincts; and that it cannot prevail long. But if, in the moment of riot, and in a drunken delirium from the hot spirit drawn out of the alembick of hell ... we should uncover our nakedness by throwing off the Christian religion which has hitherto been our boast and comfort, and one great source of civilization amongst us, and among many other nations, we are apprehensive (being well aware that the mind will not endure a void) that some uncouth, pernicious, and degrading superstition, might take place of it.

Pascal knew that the state's laws and regulations, no matter how many or severe, could not make people *want* to act with kindness and justice. Although it may be unconsciously-held, a heart-felt sacred sense of the dignity of other people is necessary, leading people to self-less courtesy. There's an economy to such inwardly-oriented, spiritually-developed reverence and neighbourly love: less externally-imposed governance is required because those individuals who've made this commitment to love govern themselves in good ways, building polity without creating polarities. As the apostle Paul said, and Kierkegaard enlarges on this precise idea in *Works of Love*: "Owe no one anything except to love one another, for he who loves another has fulfilled the law."

Blaise Pascal expressed the effectiveness of reverence-based love in an aphorism.

> Two laws suffice to rule the whole Christian republic better than all the laws of statecraft. 484.

Pascal was referring to the great commandments of Judeo-Christian ethics: "Love the Lord your God with all your body, mind, soul and strength; and, Love your neighbour as yourself." When these two laws are embraced by a significant proportion of the population the result is probity and graciousness, which will never be matched by the busiest parliament producing reams of legislation backed legions of police. A further efficiency pertains because these two commandments are so simple to understand they can be practiced by anyone of any ability, status or age, however little they know about jurisprudence, sociology, psychology, moral philosophy or politics. Pascal expressed this idea with lively precision.

> This religion taught her children what men have only been able to discover by their greatest knowledge. 444.

Kierkegaard, too, advocated the individual in relation with the personal Eternal as the best basis for society. This sacred love prescribes humility because the proper response to mercy and grace is to govern oneself in reverence (that is challenge enough), rather than trying to govern other people. This may seem like too little to people who want to change the world – in other words change external conditions – but governing oneself in love does change the world, albeit in silence and obscurity. Kierkegaard understood humility's effectiveness.

> Christianity's divine meaning is to say in confidence to every man, "Do not busy yourself with changing the shape of the world or your conditions in life, as if you… instead of being a poor scrub-woman, perhaps could manage to be called *Madam*. No, make Christianity your own, and it will show you a point outside of the world by the help of which you shall move heaven and earth so quietly, so easily, that no one notices it." From *Works of Love*.

Firm faith in God is the best motivation to a kind, wise life. Secularism, especially an aggressive atheism, cannot provide an equivalent motivation because in the absence of sacred values many people quickly make pleasure, power or consumption their ultimate value, often harming themselves and other people. *Proverbs* makes this exact point.

> Where there is no prophecy the people cast off restraint, but blessed is he who keeps the law. 29:18.

Pascal highlighted the anti-community nature of aggressive atheism, which is for many people merely a fashionable pose devoid of the sort of tough thinking that would follow things through to their logical conclusion.

> There must be a strange confusion in the nature of man, that he should boast of being in that state in which it seems incredible that a single individual should be. However, experience has shown me so great a number of such persons that the fact would be surprising, if we did not know that the greater part of those who trouble themselves about the matter are disingenuous, and not in fact what they say. They are people who have heard it said that it is the fashion to be thus daring. It is what they call shaking off the yoke, and they try to imitate this. But it would not be difficult to make them understand how greatly they deceive themselves in thus seeking esteem. This is not the way to gain it, even I say among those men of the world who take a healthy view of things, and who

know that the only way to succeed in this life is to make ourselves appear honourable, faithful, judicious, and capable of useful service to a friend; because naturally men love only what may be useful to them. Now, what do we gain by hearing it said of a man that he has now thrown off the yoke, that he does not believe there is a God who watches our actions, that he considers himself the sole master of his conduct, and that he thinks he is accountable for it only to himself? Does he think that he has thus brought us to have henceforth complete confidence in him, and to look to him for consolation, advice, and help in every need of life? Do they profess to have delighted us by telling us that they hold our soul to be only a little wind and smoke, especially by telling us this in a haughty and self-satisfied tone of voice? Is this a thing to say gaily? Is it not, on the contrary, a thing to say sadly, as the saddest thing in the world?

If they thought of it seriously, they would see that this is so bad a mistake, so contrary to good sense, so opposed to decency and so removed in every respect from that good breeding which they seek, that they would be more likely to correct than to pervert those who had an inclination to follow them. And indeed, make them give an account of their opinions, and of the reasons which they have for doubting religion, and they will say to you things so feeble and so petty, that they will persuade you of the contrary. The following is what a person one day said to such a one very appositely: "If you continue to talk in this manner, you will really make me religious." And he was right, for who would not have a horror of holding opinions in which he would have such contemptible persons as companions! 194.

Burke, observing the antagonism of the French revolutionaries towards religion, noticed that their optimism about their own ability to reform society was based on faith – the very quality they despised in religion.

> These gentlemen perhaps do not believe a great deal in the miracles of piety; but it cannot be questioned, that have an undoubting faith in the prodigies of sacrilege.

Both Pascal and *Proverbs* insist that true justice is not something that can be known outside revelation, and in the absence of revelation, or when it is discounted, then a variety of other principles determine what is regarded as justice. *Proverbs* says the further from sacred rectitude someone strays, the less they understand justice.

> Evil men do not understand justice, but those who seek the LORD understand it completely. 28:5.

The communist regimes of the Soviet Union, Maoist China and Kampuchea provide obvious examples of this principle. These regimes were atheist by design and force, executing large numbers of people who questioned communist leaders, loyalty or dogma. There was a near-complete absence of legal process, legal representation, weighing of evidence, hearing of testimony or rights of appeal. The State accused and guilt was assumed in that accusation. Torture was common, followed by murder. There was no justice, and in many cases no attempt to mimic a system of justice for appearances' sake. There was no *understanding* of justice; the concept was twisted to conform to the will of the state's malignant rulers and their apparatchiks.

When revealed law is ignored – and here the Decalogue would be at the forefront of the *Proverb* compilers' minds – then self-interest, custom and fashion become prominent alternative principles of law. Pascal was especially alert to this tendency; in several passages he considered the contingent nature of human law.

> On what shall man found the order of the world which he would govern? Shall it be on the caprice of each individual? What confusion! Shall it be on justice? Man is ignorant of it. Certainly had he known it, he would not have established this maxim, the most general of all that obtain among men, that each should follow the custom of his own country. The glory of true equity would have brought all nations under subjection, and legislators would not have taken

as their model the fancies and caprice of Persians and Germans instead of this unchanging justice. We should have seen it set up in all the States on earth and in all times; whereas we see neither justice nor injustice which does not change its nature with change in climate. Three degrees of latitude reverse all jurisprudence; a meridian decides the truth. Fundamental laws change after a few years of possession; right has its epochs; the entry of Saturn into the Lion marks to us the origin of such and such a crime. A strange justice that is bounded by a river! Truth on this side of the Pyrenees, error on the other side.

Men admit that justice does not consist in these customs, but that it resides in natural laws, common to every country. They would certainly maintain it obstinately, if reckless chance which has distributed human laws had encountered even one which was universal; but the farce is that the caprice of men has so many vagaries that there is no such law ...

The result of this confusion is that one affirms the essence of justice to be the authority of the legislator; another, the interest of the sovereign; another, present custom, and this is the most sure. Nothing, according to reason alone, is just in itself; all changes with time. Custom creates the whole of equity, for the simple reason that it is accepted. It is the mystical foundation of its authority; whoever carries it back to first principles destroys it. Nothing is so faulty as those laws which correct faults. He who obeys them because they are just, obeys a justice which is imaginary, and not the essence of law; it is quite self-contained, it is law and nothing more. He who will examine its motive will find it so feeble and so trifling that if he be not accustomed to contemplate the wonders of human imagination, he will marvel that one century has gained for it so much pomp and reverence. The art of opposition and of revolution is to unsettle established customs, sounding them even to their source, to point out their want of authority and justice. We must, it is said, get back to the natural and fundamental laws of the State, which an unjust custom has abolished. It is a game certain to result in the loss of all;

nothing will be just on the balance. Yet people readily lend their ear to such arguments. They shake off the yoke as soon as they recognise it; and the great profit by their ruin, and by that of these curious investigators of accepted customs. But from a contrary mistake men sometimes think they can justly do everything which is not without an example. That is why the wisest of legislators said that it was necessary to deceive men for their own good; and another, a good politician, *Cum veritatem qua liberetur ignoret, expedit quod fallatur.* [When he doesn't know the truth by which he is freed, it is a good thing that he should be deceived]. We must not see the fact of usurpation; law was once introduced without reason, and has become reasonable. We must make it regarded as authoritative, eternal, and conceal its origin, if we do not wish that it should soon come to an end. 294.

Justice. – As custom determines what is agreeable, so also does it determine justice. 309.

Proverbs everywhere presupposes that the great majority of people are adequate to provide for themselves, make good decisions for themselves, and can be left alone to get on with their lives. It likewise presupposes that when people make bad decisions, then they can – in most circumstances – be left to suffer the consequences of those bad decisions so they learn to make better decisions in future. The consequences should not be borne by someone else; a family member, the tax-payer or shareholder, for example.

Most modern people regard themselves as free and even bold in their opinions and attitudes, but this bravado often masks fear: fear of isolation; fear of independence; fear of fending for oneself economically, intellectually, spiritually. We often want the government to provide for us because we don't want to take too much burdensome responsibility for ourselves. Chesterton saw how this fear, prevalent among the socialists of his day, motivated demands for extensive and intrusive government agencies.

Now most modern freedom is at root fear. It is not so much that we are too bold to endure rules; it is rather that we are too timid to endure responsibilities. And Mr. [Bernard] Shaw and such people are especially shrinking from that ancient and ancestral responsibility to which our fathers committed us when they took the wild step of becoming men. From *What's Wrong with the World*.

The wisdom literature does not assume, unlike many well-intentioned but patronising government agencies, that people are too childish or foolish to make good decisions and must be guided by experts or welfare workers and that under no circumstances must people suffer the consequences of their own behaviour. This is government as if adults were infants who are unable to learn and can't handle responsibility; who are unable to endure a setback or provide for themselves.

This paternalism encourages dependency, immaturity, irresponsibility and passiveness; it handicaps people and robs them of the joy and dignity of self-determination. It lessens the wealth of a nation through large bureaucracies and costly welfare programs. But more importantly, it diminishes the nation's human capital – the skills, expertise and creativity of its people.

A nation's real wealth is not measured by the extent of its oil fields, agricultural land, or mineral deposits; the wealth of a nation is ultimately found in the mature decency of its people. When the great majority of people govern themselves with prudence and common sense, then society functions with relative prosperity and peace, and government doesn't need to become intrusive. But when too many people live in a mindless, selfish manner, then instability, violence and waste begin to emerge and government tends to become more regulatory – and society becomes more dysfunctional.

> When it goes well with the righteous, the city rejoices; and when the wicked perish there are shouts of gladness. By the blessing of the upright a city is exalted, but it is overthrown by the mouth of the

wicked. 11:10, 11.

When a land transgresses it has many rulers; but with men of understanding and knowledge its stability will long continue. 28:2.

When the righteous triumph, there is great glory; but when the wicked rise, men hide themselves. 28:12.

When the wicked rise, men hide themselves, but when they perish, the righteous increase. 28:28.

Scoffers set a city aflame, but wise men turn away wrath. 29:8.

Proverbs further presupposes that every human being is so creative, intelligent, capable and so rich with potential that population growth is a good thing rather than, as is increasingly urged by misanthropic environmentalists, a bad thing. A decline in population is a portent of weakness and possible ruin.

> In a multitude of people is the glory of a king, but without people a prince is ruined. 14:28.

As previously noted, the wisdom literature declares a world created and sustained by God: a present, generous and wise creator who richly furnished the world for man and all other creatures. There's no lack of life-sustaining resources; there's a plenitude to be discovered, harnessed and enjoyed. If there is a shortage of anything necessary for life, it does not result from creation's inadequacy, but from a lack of wisdom in harnessing or distributing the plenitude. Lazyness, frivolity and waste have already been identified as delinquencies that result in deprivation, but injustice is perhaps the main cause of want.

Throughout history, destitution has affected large numbers of people. Droughts, floods and locust plagues are common natural causes of misery, yet too often injustice is overlooked as a factor. Media reports of famines highlight drought, for example, as the immediate reason for failed crops;

less often identified are the scourging activities of armed rebels, jihadists or corrupt governments who all massively exacerbate the grief of natural disasters. Human failings, especially selfish ambition expressed in violent ideologies or a desire for conquest, often prevent the extravagance of the earth from reaching people. This point is often missed by mass media news services whose reportage very frequently has all the depth of a puddle.

There's a readiness to blame God rather than man for hardship. A discerning person knows war, greed and mismanagement are behind many ordeals.

> The fallow ground of the poor yields much food, but it is swept away through injustice. 13:23.
>
> Like a roaring lion or a charging bear is a wicked ruler over a poor people. A ruler who lacks understanding is a cruel oppressor; but he who hates unjust gain will prolong his days. 28:15, 16.
>
> When the righteous are in authority, the people rejoice; but when the wicked rule, the people groan. 29:2.

This is a fundamental point that both *Proverbs* and *Ecclesiastes*, and Edmund Burke make: keeping the wrong people from government is imperative. The host of bumbling mediocrities in the parliaments of Western democracies may on occasion do some good, but more importantly they don't cause the massive catastrophic harm to the nation that one evil ruler will quickly cause: Hitler, Mussolini, Lenin, Stalin, Mao Tse Tung, Pol Pot, Robert Mugabe, Idi Amin, etc. As we will see, many of the injunctions about rulers and government warn against bad characters getting influence and power because of their efficient destructiveness. The contrast between wisdom and wickedness is most dramatic at this point because of the huge number of people affected by one wretched ruler's propensity for violence. But the principle applies to all areas of life: minimise the impact of wanton, selfish people and much suffering is avoided. Good people can be relied on to contribute benignly more often than not; they won't cause much widespread harm, unlike vice-ridden people who rapidly unleash cruel afflictions.

> Wisdom is better than weapons of war, but one sinner destroys much good. *Ecclesiastes* 9:18.

> Dead flies make the perfumer's ointment give off an evil odor; so a little folly outweighs wisdom and honor. *Ecclesiastes* 10:1.

Chesterton noted that original sin – the self-centredness lurking in each one of us – is the only Christian doctrine that is always and everywhere supported by volumes of evidence. It's imperative that wicked acts are identified and confronted. This is one of the government's main roles: to protect the innocent against the acts of trouble-makers, and then to punish obvious crimes.

> A wise king winnows the wicked, and drives the wheel over them. 20:26.

> The violence of the wicked will sweep them away, because they refuse to do what is just. 21:7.

> When justice is done, it is a joy to the righteous, but dismay to evildoers. 21:15.

The poorest people are the most vulnerable; they are easy targets for the greedy and violent. Diligent, caring rulers will protect those who are weak and easily oppressed.

> Do not rob the poor, because he is poor, or crush the afflicted at the gate; for the LORD will plead their cause and despoil of life those who despoil them. 22:22.

> A righteous man knows the rights of the poor; a wicked man does not understand such knowledge. 29:7.

> Open your mouth for the dumb, for the rights of all who are left

desolate. Open your mouth, judge righteously, maintain the rights of the poor and needy. 31:8, 9.

Long-term stability in a nation is not achieved through government oppression since this leads to an impoverished nation and a widely disgruntled population. Rather, stability is achieved through the efficient implementation of justice. A leader desiring to establish his rule won't achieve it by multiplying bodyguards or secret police, although these may be necessary. He'll rule in safety and stability by providing the security and justice that people want and the opportunities for a good life that are subsequent to these two qualities. In this sense, the government must be the servant of the people, actively working to fulfill the peoples' natural desire for fair judgments and just laws. Common people, the strugglers and battlers, have greater need for good government because they're more exposed to the knocks of life. Their troubles were expressed by Pascal.

> The great and the humble have the same misfortunes, the same griefs, the same passions; but the one is at the top of the wheel, and the other near the centre, and so less disturbed by the same revolutions. 180.

Chesterton too noted that the poorest people have the greatest desire for stable, fair government, and for the same reason: they don't have the cushions against hardship that wealth provides.

> The poor have been rebels, but they have never been anarchists; they have more interest than anyone else in there being some form of decent government. The poor man really has a stake in the country. The rich man hasn't; he can go away to New Guinea in a yacht. The poor have sometimes objected to being governed badly; the rich have always objected to being governed at all. From *The Man Who was Thursday.*

Chesterton noted that even in a state or organisation with good laws, the mere existence of these laws isn't enough. There are always some people, favouring the powerful and wealthy, who want to bend the rules.

> Above all, if we wish to protect the poor we shall be in favour of fixed rules and clear dogmas. The *rules* of a club occasionally favour the poor member. The drift of the club is always in favour of a rich one. From *Orthodoxy*.

This emphasis on justice for the most vulnerable is ratified in *Proverbs*.

> He who mocks the poor insults his Maker; he who is glad at calamity will not go unpunished. 17:5.

> If a king judges the poor with equity his throne will be established for ever. 29:14.

To restrain evil, *Proverbs* affirms the value of corporal punishment in some situations because bodily pain is a powerful inducement to change. This isn't a popular principle today, but it's true nonetheless. We want to avoid pain, especially after we have experienced it (or have seen others experience it), so we quickly learn to behave in a manner that doesn't invite the punishment. It is, moreover, a means of justice that avoids the negative consequences – for both the perpetrator and society – of locking people away in gaol. *Proverbs* also recommends, among the tools of justice, restitution to victims of crime by the perpetrator and the restriction of the malefactor's community privileges.

> Condemnation is ready for scoffers, and flogging for the backs of fools. 19:29.

> Blows that wound cleanse away evil; strokes make clean the innermost parts. 20:30.

> A whip for the horse, a bridle for the ass, and a rod for the back of fools. 26:3.

Proverbs and *Ecclesiastes* acknowledge that those who primary role is to punish evil may themselves grow evil. This is one of the deepest frustrations in life. It's yet more evidence for the potential for sin present in every person. But surrender to this selfishness is never acceptable; nor is there any end to the battle within ourselves and within society between right and wrong, good and evil. The two principles are implacably opposed. Indeed, good and evil form an admixture battling for supremacy in the human heart; another aspect of man's complicated, contradictory nature.

> Bloodthirsty men hate one who is blameless, and the wicked seek his life. 29:10.
>
> An unjust man is an abomination to the righteous, but he whose way is straight is an abomination to the wicked. 29:27.

Of course, no one is wholly unjust, or wholly upright. Nor do people necessarily follow the path of folly or wisdom with predictable consistency. An immature person might wake up to himself and begin seeking sense, and a mature man turn aside to licentiousness. The fall of a just and compassionate person into injustice and apathy is lamentable; the reorientation of the immature person towards truth and kindness is delightful.

> Like a muddied spring or a polluted fountain is a righteous man who gives way before the wicked. 25:26.
>
> Better is a poor and wise youth than an old and foolish king, who will no longer take advice, even though he had gone from prison to the throne or in his own kingdom had been born poor. *Ecclesiastes* 4:13, 14.

To govern with justice and wisdom, a leader must have an inquisitive mind and a sense of the detective. He must investigate and sift evidence, he should not be gulled by fashionable theories, he must quickly spot falsifiers and their propaganda. Grotesqueries spread if a ruler is hasty, naive or easily manipulated.

> An intelligent mind acquires knowledge, and the ear of the wise seeks knowledge. 18:15.
>
> He who states his case first seems right, until the other comes and examines him. 18:17.
>
> It is the glory of God to conceal things, but the glory of kings is to search things out. 25:2.

We live in time and it takes time for us to process information, to discern worth and value, to determine pros and cons, risks and rewards, to arrive at a good decision. Solomon, ruler of an extensive kingdom, knew that prudent judgments and wise decisions should not be rushed even if people were in distress. This doesn't suit the activist's impatience, or their absolutising of compassion, or their demand for intervention for their favoured groups. Pressure is brought on decision-makers to take action *now*. Wisdom says, wait and watch, test and discern before any decision is made so the best way and means is chosen, even if the delay means that some people continue to suffer. Pressure to act is profound if lives are at stake, but even in crisis situations it's best to take time to ask hard questions, to examine, to weigh evidence. Precipitant action may make the situation worse; it may harm the innocent and foster the opportunities of the selfish; it may result in greater disasters in the future.

> He who obeys a command will meet no harm, and the mind of a wise man will know the time and way. For every matter has its time and way, although man's trouble lies heavy upon him. For he does not know what is to be, for who can tell him how it will be? *Ecclesiastes* 8:5-7.

Proverbs is alert to the value of reflection and patience; it is also alert to the destructiveness of impetuosity. Nearly every decision will benefit from a thorough examination of the relevant issues, together with the issues that at first glance may not seem so relevant. Life is intricate and a rushed decision is often a bad decision.

> A wise man is cautious and turns away from evil, but a fool throws off restraint and is careless. A man of quick temper acts foolishly, but a man of discretion is patient. 14:16, 17.
>
> The plans of the diligent lead surely to abundance, but every one who is hasty comes only to want. 21:5.
>
> It is not good for a man to be without knowledge, and he who makes haste with his feet misses his way. 19:2.

Attempting to impose simplicity on a complex reality is misguided. Ambitious people whose ideas are arrogantly at odds with the fine embroidery of society are utterly unsuited to positions of power. The twentieth century is replete with examples of governments guided by simple beliefs – which had the attraction of providing one answer to multiple difficulties (which often appeals to the torpid) – but these simple beliefs lead to massive tragedies. Nazism espoused the twin ideas of *Blut und Volk*, with the corollaries that the Jewish people and international communism were to blame for Germany's troubles. Communist despots believed that class struggle was the energising principle of social and economic history and that revolution would dismantle the inequalities between labour and capital. The Khmer Rouge believed that a return to peasant agrarianism would restore Kampuchea's glory. All these simple notions failed in the face of stubborn, intricate reality.

Any society that is functional to any satisfactory extent is the result of hundreds, and often thousands of years of gradual development and realistic accommodation to the puzzles of the human and natural world. And this development and adaptation is subtle and sophisticated; it has to be so people can live together. It cannot be dismantled with impunity, or constructed with ease. Burke wrote about this principle.

> The science of constructing a commonwealth, or renovating it, or reforming it, is, like every other experimental science, not to be

taught *a priori*. Nor is it a short experience that can teach us in that practical science; because the real causes of moral causes are not always immediate; but that which is in the first instance prejudicial may be excellent in its remoter operation; and its excellence may arise even from the ill effects it produces in the beginning. The reverse also happens; and very plausible schemes, with very pleasing commencements, have often shameful and lamentable conclusions. In states there are often some obscure and almost latent causes, things which appear at first view of little moment, on which a very great part of its prosperity or adversity may most essentially depend. The science of government being therefore so practical in itself, and intended for such practical purposes, a matter which requires experience, and more experience than a person can gain in his whole life, however sagacious and observing he may be, it is with infinite caution that any man ought to venture upon pulling down an edifice which has answered in any tolerable degree for ages the common purposes of society, or on building it up again, without having models and patterns of approved utility before his eyes…

The nature of man is intricate; the objects of society are of the greatest possible complexity; and therefore no simple disposition or direction of power can be suitable either to man's nature, or to the quality of his affairs. When I hear the simplicity of contrivance aimed at and boasted of in any new political constitutions, I am at no loss to decide that the artificers are grossly ignorant of their trade, or totally negligent of their duty. The simple governments are fundamentally defective, to say no worse of them. If you were to contemplate society in but one point of view, all these simple modes of polity are infinitely captivating. In effect each would answer its single end much more perfectly than the more complex is able to attain all its complex purposes. But it is better that the whole should be imperfectly and anomalously answered, than that, while some parts are totally neglected, or perhaps materially injured, by the over-care of a favourite member.

The particular circumstances of any situation requiring correction must be ascertained before taking action. A thorough and specific investigation must be undertaken; not from a distance, and not in a cursory manner. Individual problems need tailored solutions to be effective, otherwise we may create problems more pernicious than the original issue. And because we are so ignorant about so many things, we need to proceed gradually and note the ramifications of our actions, which may not be immediately obvious.

Burke knew that context was everything, whether advocating certain values or making a weighty decision. He knew liberty, for example, was worthy of efforts to promote it, but it too was bound by circumstances. Indeed, liberty can't exist in the abstract: always and everywhere it has a setting that should be acknowledged and respected.

> But I cannot stand forward, and give praise to any thing which relates to human concerns, on a simple view of the object, as it stands stripped of every relation, in all the nakedness and solitude of metaphysical abstraction. Circumstances (which with some gentlemen pass for nothing) give in reality to every political principle its distinguishing colour, and discriminating effect. The circumstances are what render every civil and political scheme beneficial or noxious to mankind… Is it because liberty in the abstract may be classed amongst the blessings of mankind, that I am seriously to felicitate a madman, who has escaped from the protecting restraint and wholesome darkness of his cell, on his restoration to the enjoyment of the liberty of light and freedom? Am I to congratulate an highwayman and murderer, who has broke prison, upon the recovery of his natural rights? …I must be tolerably sure, before I venture to congratulate men on a blessing, that they have really received one.

We shouldn't be frustrated with complicated policies, with the nuances of legislation, or the time needed to discuss changes to any important law. Only simpletons insist on speed and simplicity in politics. And those are the very people who should never be in politics.

Such is the ruler's example and power, for good or evil, that what the ruler models becomes the norm. People see what is acceptable, what is rewarded, and they tend to align themselves to that standard. This is as old as society. The principle should not be forgotten.

> If a ruler listens to falsehood, all his officials will be wicked. 29:12.

Self-indulgence is a perennial temptation for those in power, cossetted as they are with privileges. Rulers should be particularly careful to avoid over-eating and heavy drinking which will lead to neglected duties. Binge drinking has no place in life, and particularly no place in public life. Members of parliament, councillors, bureaucrats, administrators and judges must not be drunkards, and if they are, they should either change their habits or be removed from office.

> It is not for kings, O Lemuel [an ancient king], it is not for kings to drink wine, or for rulers to desire strong drink; lest they drink and forget what has been decreed, and pervert the rights of all the afflicted. 31:4, 5.

Rulers with extravagant, impulsive habits tend to make extravagant, impulsive decisions. In other words, a lack of self-control in eating and drinking indicates a lack of qualification for leadership. A mind fuddled with alcohol is in no state to judge, to advise, to allocate resources or to formulate policy.

> Woe to you, O land, when your king is a child, and your princes feast in the morning! Happy are you, O land, when your king is the son of free men, and your princes feast at the proper time, for strength, and not for drunkenness! *Ecclesiastes* 10:16, 17.

Any good enterprise requires energy and persistence; none more than fighting the pressures exerted by the selfish to advance their cause, especially if one has decisive power. *Proverbs* is unequivocal about the need for courage during a time of testing. If a person fails when tempted or when facing adversity, that person lacks fortitude and perseverance. It's a harsh assessment, but the goal is to encourage moral resilience.

> If you faint in the day of adversity, your strength is small. 24:10.

Because of the tragedy that follows moral collapse, there are frequent warnings against corrupt practices. These injunctions apply to everyone since the responsibility to act justly rests upon each of us, but they are particularly directed to those in authority.

> Inspired decisions are on the lips of a king; his mouth does not sin in judgment. 16:10.

> Fine speech is not becoming to a fool; still less is false speech to a prince. 17:7.

> If a man returns evil for good, evil will not depart from his house. 17:13.

> He who justifies the wicked and he who condemns the righteous are both alike an abomination to the LORD. 17:15.

> To impose a fine on a righteous man is not good; to flog noble men is wrong. 17:26.

> It is not good to be partial to a wicked man, or to deprive a righteous man of justice. 18:5.

> A king who sits on the throne of judgment winnows all evil with his eyes. 20:8.

Corruption is recognised as a common temptation associated with power. People who want favours from judges or politicians know a gift can influence decisions.

> A bribe is like a magic stone in the eyes of him who gives it; wherever he turns he prospers. 17:8.

> A man's gift makes room for him and brings him before great men. 18:16.
>
> A gift in secret averts anger; and a bribe in the bosom, strong wrath. 21:14.
>
> To show partiality is not good; but for a piece of bread a man will do wrong. 28:21.

Bribery is a common temptation; constant scrutiny is necessary to prevent it becoming pervasive. Corrupt officials must be exposed and removed from office without hesitation: the stability and integrity of government is too important to trifle with miscreants.

> By justice a king gives stability to the land, but one who exacts gifts ruins it. 29:4.

The same principle applies to businesses, organisations and agencies. Corruption can flourish wherever power and privilege meet. Companies that give or receive kick-backs; union representatives getting cash for their co-operation; police protecting criminals: corruption is possible in any enterprise, and credibility is always forfeited by it. The result is broken trust and organisational dereliction. A few unworthy individuals become wealthier, but society suffers. Those offering bribes and those accepting them are both guilty of perverting justice: a serious crime that undermines support for any government.

> A wicked man accepts a bribe from the bosom to pervert the ways of justice. 17:23.
>
> A worthless witness mocks at justice, and the mouth of the wicked devours iniquity. 19:28.

Throughout the wisdom literature there's the sense that God is invisibly but constantly active in his creation. He moves in inscrutable ways to guard the precepts he has established in creation and revealed through scripture. A person who constantly disregards his own reason and conscience, the good moral guidance of others, and the guidelines of religion places himself at odds with reality. Sometimes the recalcitrant experience ruin in this life, sometimes they don't, but even if there is continued prosperity, *Proverbs* foresees eventual overthrow.

> The righteous observes the house of the wicked; the wicked are cast down to ruin. 21:12.

> The eyes of the LORD keep watch over knowledge, but he overthrows the words of the faithless. 22:12.

> These also are sayings of the wise. Partiality in judging is not good. He who says to the wicked, "You are innocent," will be cursed by peoples, abhorred by nations; but those who rebuke the wicked will have delight, and a good blessing will be upon them. 24:23-25.

As well as being honest and just, leaders must also be compassionate because true justice and good administration are allied to mercy and benevolence. A kind ruler will aid his people rather than burden his people, particularly during times of turmoil; for example, in the aftermath of disasters such as cyclones or floods.

> Loyalty and faithfulness preserve the king, and his throne is upheld by righteousness. 20:28.

> He who pursues righteousness and kindness will find life and honor. 21:21.

Even a good government that implements justice as its first priority will not succeed in achieving this goal in every case. Grievances will remain and the aggrieved will seek to have the injustices they've suffered addressed. But this correction will not always happen, and here a firm faith in the ultimate justice of God rather than in the relative justice of man is consoling. Those who suffer injustice not addressed by man's courts should remind themselves that God's justice will not fail, although it may not be fully evident in this life.

> The fear of the LORD prolongs life, but the years of the wicked

will be short. The hope of the righteous ends in gladness, but the expectation of the wicked comes to nought. The LORD is a stronghold to him whose way is upright, but destruction to evildoers.10:27-29.

Do not say, "I will repay evil"; wait for the LORD, and he will help you. 20:22.

Many seek the favor of a ruler, but from the LORD a man gets justice. 29:26.

A reverent person acts justly and wants justice in return. But he won't succumb to resentment, vengefully taking the law into his own hands if others continue to treat him unjustly. Patient hope will be his comfort; peace in his community will be his goal.

7

WISDOM AND RELATIONSHIPS

If *Ecclesiastes* is primarily a meditation about our life in a familiar but still enigmatic reality, *Proverbs* is overwhelmingly about our relationships with other people. The natural social inclinations of man are affirmed; humanity was created to live in communities of family, friends, neighbours, tribe, faith and nation. In every sphere of life, a right relationship with other people is based on a right relationship with one's self. Man is able to speak to himself, tell stories to himself, correct himself or destroy himself, so effective self-management is the first and most important responsibility of our life. One indicator of mature self-management is the peaceful beauty of our relationships with other people; our family first, and then our friends and neighbours. A desire to live with gentle trust radiates outwards from those committed to wisdom.

> Deceit is in the heart of those who devise evil, but those who plan good have joy. 12:20.

The wisdom literature reinforces the fundamental qualities of personal integrity: kindness, a dependable honesty, a laudable transparency. A person without integrity is both unreliable and unreasonable; their fractured character will result in fractured relationships. They harm other people as well as themselves. Their dysfunctions will become obvious.

> He who walks in integrity walks securely, but he who perverts his ways will be found out. 10:9.

Integrity protects a person from many difficulties – by directing them towards honesty and fairness. Wisdom entails both choosing goodness and avoiding vices; constant, life-long selection and rejection is required to maintain integrity. It is a foundational requirement, so multiple sayings emphasise it.

> Keep your heart with all vigilance; for from it flow the springs of life. 4:23.

> Let your eyes look directly forward, and your gaze be straight before you. Take heed to the path of your feet, then all your ways will be sure. Do not swerve to the right or to the left; turn your foot away from evil. 4:25-27.

> The integrity of the upright guides them, but the crookedness of the treacherous destroys them. 11:3.

> The righteousness of the blameless keeps his way straight, but the wicked falls by his own wickedness. The righteousness of the upright delivers them, but the treacherous are taken captive by their lust. 11:5,6.

> Righteousness guards him whose way is upright, but sin overthrows the wicked. 13:6.

> He who walks in integrity will be delivered, but he who is perverse in his ways will fall into a pit. 28:18.

Inward integrity is much more important than outward beauty, talent or wealth. Spiritual and moral qualities aren't spectacular, but they have an attractiveness a mature person will appreciate. A shrewd person will recognise that someone may look pleasant, talk eloquently and dress with style, yet lack the qualities of prudence, humility and sanctity that are truly beautiful. We must be alert to inconsistency between inner reality and outer show.

> Like a gold ring in a swine's snout is a beautiful woman without discretion. 11:22.

Every person is capable of evil: the short-sighted perception that we'll benefit by serving our desires, despite the harm our actions causes others.

It's a temptation each person must resist. Conversely, acting in a prudent, gracious manner – which enriches our life and other people's lives – is the privilege we've all been given. We begin good or evil by what we say to ourselves; by cultivating or correcting our heart's thoughts and intents. Our relationships will prosper or falter, as much as depends on us, according to our thoughts because they will energise our acts. Wisdom warns us to correct spiteful, selfish attitudes because they result in spiteful, selfish words and actions.

> He who belittles his neighbor lacks sense, but a man of understanding remains silent. 11:12.

> The soul of the wicked desires evil; his neighbor finds no mercy in his eyes. 21:10.

Sagacity decrees that we correct our heart's thoughts and intents so we don't construct an imaginary, belittling picture of anyone, leading us to treat them with contempt.

> Do they not err that devise evil? Those who devise good meet loyalty and faithfulness. 14:22.

We monitor and correct the impulses of our own heart to protect us from our own worst proclivities; this correction also protects other people from our worst proclivities. Self-control frees us from pride and selfish grasping; self-control also protects the freedom and dignity of other people because we will not tempt them into foolish activities.

> A man of violence entices his neighbor and leads him in a way that is not good. 16:29.

Other people, not exercising self-control themselves, might tempt us to join their nonsense by appealing to our greed, our sense of adventure or our desire for pleasure. In the absence of their self-control, we must exercise our self-control and reject their enticements. This rejection shields our life and dignifies other people's lives.

> My son, if sinners entice you, do not consent. If they say, "Come with us, let us lie in wait for blood, let us wantonly ambush the innocent; like Sheol let us swallow them alive and whole, like those who go down to the Pit; we shall find all precious goods, we shall fill our houses with spoil; throw in your lot among us, we will all have one purse" – my son, do not walk in the way with them, hold back your foot from their paths; for their feet run to evil, and they make haste to shed blood. For in vain is a net spread in the sight of any bird; but these men lie in wait for their own blood, they set an ambush for their own lives. Such are the ways of all who get gain by violence; it takes away the life of its possessors. 1:10-19.

Our hearts are particularly disposed to treat a poor person with disdain. While *Proverbs* does teach that wisdom tends towards a degree of material wealth, it never says material success only results from wisdom. Wealth might equally result from chance or dishonesty. In other words, a poor person is not necessarily lazy or foolish; they might be the victim of dreadful government, injustice or misfortune. Nobody is justified viewing them with contempt while praising themselves.

> He who despises his neighbor is a sinner, but happy is he who is kind to the poor. 14:21.

> All a poor man's brothers hate him; how much more do his friends go far from him! He pursues them with words, but does not have them. 19:7.

Correcting the stories we tell ourselves so we don't prejudge another person, especially someone down and out, is one obvious area of self-control. In addition, we need to correct the stories we tell other people. Duplicity is tempting: fibbing to our family, misrepresenting ourselves to our neighbour, pretending we're honest and generous when we're not. This deception causes chaos in every setting.

> Put away from you crooked speech, and put devious talk far from you. 4:24.

> The lips of the righteous know what is acceptable, but the mouth of the wicked what is perverse. 10:32.
>
> With his mouth the godless man would destroy his neighbor, but by knowledge the righteous are delivered. 11:9.
>
> Better is a poor man who walks in his integrity than a man who is perverse in speech, and is a fool. 19:1.
>
> He who hates, dissembles with his lips and harbors deceit in his heart; when he speaks graciously, believe him not, for there are seven abominations in his heart; though his hatred be covered with guile, his wickedness will be exposed in the assembly. 26:24-26.
>
> A lying tongue hates its victims, and a flattering mouth works ruin. 26:28.

Allied to the dishonour of lying to our neighbour is its complement: telling lies about our neighbour. Slander and gossip are everywhere condemned in the wisdom literature. There's nothing merely mischievous or incidentally harmful about calumny: it's destructive of people and relationships. A kind person will resist spreading damaging stories about other people. An astute person will note gossipers and slanderers, (and those lapping it up), and avoid their example and intimacy.

> He who conceals hatred has lying lips, and he who utters slander is a fool 10:18.
>
> The words of a whisperer are like delicious morsels; they go down into the inner parts of the body. 18:8.

An employer or a leader of any organisation will reprove a gossiper and if they don't change their behavior, demote or remove them. They undermine the unity, morale and effectiveness of the whole group, so unequivocal action must be taken to restore trust and peace. Innuendo and lies are not peccadilloes.

> An evildoer listens to wicked lips; and a liar gives heed to a mischievous tongue. He who mocks the poor insults his Maker; he

who is glad at calamity will not go unpunished. 17:4, 5.

For lack of wood the fire goes out; and where there is no whisperer, quarreling ceases. As charcoal to hot embers and wood to fire, so is a quarrelsome man for kindling strife. 26:20, 21.

Drive out a scoffer, and strife will go out, and quarreling and abuse will cease. 22:10.

Slander takes an especially pernicious turn in courts, where truth is supposed to prevail so justice is served. The wisdom literature abominates perjury: innocent people face the fearsome consequences of the law so some vain, callous person gets some gain. Meanwhile, confidence in justice erodes, undermining faith in important institutions and processes. Any lying is bad; perjury is inexcusable. There are many warnings about it.

He who speaks the truth gives honest evidence, but a false witness utters deceit. There is one whose rash words are like sword thrusts, but the tongue of the wise brings healing. Truthful lips endure for ever, but a lying tongue is but for a moment. Deceit is in the heart of those who devise evil, but those who plan good have joy. No ill befalls the righteous, but the wicked are filled with trouble. Lying lips are an abomination to the LORD, but those who act faithfully are his delight. 12:17-22.

From the fruit of his mouth a good man eats good, but the desire of the treacherous is for violence. 13:2.

A faithful witness does not lie, but a false witness breathes out lies. 14:5.

A gentle tongue is a tree of life, but perverseness in it breaks the spirit. 15:4.

A false witness will not go unpunished, and he who utters lies will not escape. 19:5.

A worthless witness mocks at justice, and the mouth of the wicked devours iniquity. 19:28.

Be not a witness against your neighbor without cause, and do not deceive with your lips. Do not say, "I will do to him as he has done to me; I will pay the man back for what he has done." 24:28, 29.

A man who bears false witness against his neighbor is like a war club, or a sword, or a sharp arrow. 25:18.

Proverbs lists seven attitudes and actions that offend the creator whose good character sets the moral boundaries for mankind. All seven contradict the gentle care we're commanded to show.

There are six things which the LORD hates, seven which are an abomination to him: haughty eyes, a lying tongue, and hands that shed innocent blood, a heart that devises wicked plans, feet that make haste to run to evil, a false witness who breathes out lies, and a man who sows discord among brothers. 6:16-19.

Wisdom teaches that good attitudes and kind behavior bring their own reward; likewise selfish actions will bring harm and grief.

He who diligently seeks good seeks favor, but evil comes to him who searches for it. 11:27.

A good man obtains favor from the LORD, but a man of evil devices he condemns. 12:2.

Death and life are in the power of the tongue, and those who love it will eat its fruits. 18:21.

This isn't karma because the wisdom literature doesn't posit an impersonal universe or reincarnation. Rather, it posits a personal creator who will bring his creation to a just culmination at a time of his choosing when devious deeds and benevolent acts will be sifted.

In the path of righteousness is life, but the way of error leads to death. 12:28.

The partner of a thief hates his own life; he hears the curse, but discloses nothing. 29:24.

People with good values and excellent life-skills make the best friends. Or, negatively, immature or immoral people don't warrant close connection. This might seem obvious, but the obvious isn't sufficient for many people. Every day we see business ventures and romances entered by people with meagre qualifications for such important ventures beyond the superficiality of availability, glamour, or the gift of the gab. Discernment is an obvious need.

> A righteous man turns away from evil, but the way of the wicked leads them astray. 12:26.

Pascal wrote about choosing companions who will help us build virtues rather than vices; companions who will encourage us towards sanctity rather than towards mischief.

> Just as we harm the understanding, we harm the feelings also.

> The understanding and the feelings are moulded by intercourse; the understanding and feelings are corrupted by intercourse. Thus good or bad society improves or corrupts them. It is, then, all-important to know how to choose in order to improve and not to corrupt them; and we cannot make this choice, if they be not already improved and not corrupted. Thus a circle is formed, and those are fortunate who escape it. 6.

Proverbs and *Ecclesiastes* never assume that once we have made good decisions, our path is set. At any time we can change direction, ignore all we've learned and choose degradation. Our free-will can point us in a good or bad direction as time and opportunity allow. A righteous person can fail on any occasion to act uprightly, and being linked to unworthy people is one way we're seduced away from dulcet life.

> He who walks with wise men becomes wise, but the companion of fools will suffer harm. 13:20.

> The highway of the upright turns aside from evil; he who guards his way preserves his life. 16:17.

Proverbs places great value on the right choice of friends; it also places great value on the right use of words. Like friends, words are powerful to harm or to encourage; to instruct or to deceive. A tactful person ponders before they speak because they know that their words are conveyors of good or evil, truth or falsehoods. Words build friendships, marriages, families, communities, and nations; words can also destroy these good things. Words are a common yet important resource that everyone possesses, and yet we waste them in profligate and unconsidered ways.

The facility of speech is another example of how generous and democratic our creator is: he has given the overwhelming majority of people the near miraculous gift of speech. The wisdom literature guides our use of this dynamic facility. The instructions and warnings about speech are repeated, indicating their importance. There's particular praise for the person who thinks before they speak and then speaks sparingly.

> When words are many, transgression is not lacking, but he who restrains his lips is prudent. 10:19.
>
> He who guards his mouth preserves his life; he who opens wide his lips comes to ruin. 13:3.
>
> The tongue of the wise dispenses knowledge, but the mouths of fools pour out folly. 15:2.
>
> A man of crooked mind does not prosper, and one with a perverse tongue falls into calamity. 17:20.
>
> He who restrains his words has knowledge, and he who has a cool spirit is a man of understanding. Even a fool who keeps silent is considered wise; when he closes his lips, he is deemed intelligent. 17:27, 28.
>
> He who keeps his mouth and his tongue keeps himself out of trouble. 21:23.
>
> A fool gives full vent to his anger, but a wise man quietly holds it back. 29:11.
>
> Do you see a man who is hasty in his words? There is more hope for a fool than for him. 29:20.

Kierkegaard commented on the necessity of a foolish person (that is, every one of us) exercising temperance in speech: staying silent far more often.

> And this is so, not merely because then he would not betray his foolishness, but also because his self-control would help him to become conscious of himself as an individual, and would prevent him from adopting the crowd's opinion. Or if he had an opinion of his own, it would prevent him from hastening to get the crowd to adopt it. From *Purity of Heart is to Will One Thing*.

In delicate, tense or important situations, there's greater need for forethought and sensitivity. For example, when dealing with a person lacking self-control or when raising difficult matters, it's crucial the right person speaks at the right time. In some cases, not speaking to a foolish person is best to avoid making troublesome situations more eruptive.

Choosing the right time to speak is as important as what we say; we need to ensure, if we can, propitious circumstances so our message is considered. It might be best to speak in private or in a relaxed setting, to initiate a conversation during a long car trip, while enjoying a meal together, or before or after a meeting, for example.

> A scoffer does not like to be reproved; he will not go to the wise. 15:12.

> Do not speak in the hearing of a fool, for he will despise the wisdom of your words. 23:9.

Well-chosen words minimise strife and argument. Ill-considered, insulting words cause and prolong disputes. A sober person will reflect before a difficult conversation, determine what he hopes to achieve, choose kind words, and avoid inflammatory or tactless references that escalate contention.

> The beginning of strife is like letting out water; so quit before the quarrel breaks out. 17:14.

> A fool's lips bring strife, and his mouth invites a flogging. A fool's mouth is his ruin, and his lips are a snare to himself. 18:6, 7.
>
> It is an honor for a man to keep aloof from strife; but every fool will be quarreling. 20:3.

Discretion is another crucial aspect of any relationship. A prudent man or woman will speak privately, maintaining confidentiality when required. In many situations in business, among family or between friends, it's entirely proper to keep sensitive, embarrassing or intimate matters private. No one likes their follies or failures broadcast, or their personal business made public knowledge. Divulging delicate matters beyond the circle of those who strictly need to know will damage mutual trust: the very basis of all relationships. The discreet person is commended; a talebearer is condemned.

> He who goes about as a talebearer reveals secrets, but he who is trustworthy in spirit keeps a thing hidden. 11:13.
>
> He who forgives an offense seeks love, but he who repeats a matter alienates a friend. 17:9.
>
> He who goes about gossiping reveals secrets; therefore do not associate with one who speaks foolishly. 20:19.

Discretion during contentions is advised for an additional reason: we may not have the whole story. Each of us is skilled at presenting ourself favourably. Knowing this, a shrewd person will withhold judgment or action on the first report of any matter. Reports from anyone, especially mass media journalists, should be viewed with caution pending further information. Believing everything we hear, and then reacting in haste without thorough investigation, is stupid. It's embarrassing when the truth emerges and proves we've been blockheads. We must allow time to do its work.

Too often governments and organisations react to frenzied media reports, to the concerns of so-called panels of experts, or social media teacup storms without taking the time to dig deeper, to think, to allow the fashionable concerns to pass and the truth to emerge. Bad legislation, unnecessary and fussy regulations, and a huge amount of money, time and resources are wasted when action occurs in a panicked manner.

One of the great benefits of parliament is to put decision-makers at a prudent distance from whims and ephemeral issues. This distance is needed so emotion doesn't overwhelm judgment. But it's being eroded by digital communication and broadcasting which elevates the sentimental response, the fashionable opinion, the quick reaction. Public figures are under pressure to act, with little encouragement to think deeply before they act. This pressure must be resisted by everyone. There are very few matters that are so urgent that no time can be spared for a more complete investigation. This pertains to large national matters and to personal relationships. *Proverbs* is blunt.

> If one gives answer before he hears, it is his folly and shame. 18:13.

Committing time to investigation has the benefit of allowing truth to correct a skewed perspective and to expose outright falsehoods. We're prey to emotional responses, to a natural empathy that may not be entirely merited after close examination, and an unwitting bias toward those we love. All these things may cloud our thinking and dull our discernment unless we spend time seeking the facts.

Acting with senseless haste also exposes us to the machinations of the devious and the manipulations of the unstable. Because of these hazards, we're told to investigate before a making a decision. First impressions may be false impressions, and may lead to waste and injustice.

> He who states his case first seems right, until the other comes and examines him. 18:17.

Impetuous people oppose prudent deliberation; in their minds, they already know the facts so investigation is a waste of time. They ignore the reality of their own limits, and the possibility of other people's self-interest, and become agents of stupidity and injustice rather than reason and justice. A vigilant person values knowledge, a foolish person values self-proclamation. It's a waste of time expecting those quick to express their opinion to become sage; it's best to leave them alone. Instead, treasure the company and counsel of prudent, patient and knowledgeable people.

> A prudent man conceals his knowledge, but fools proclaim their folly. 12:23.
>
> A fool takes no pleasure in understanding, but only in expressing his opinion. 18:2.
>
> Wisdom abides in the mind of a man of understanding, but it is not known in the heart of fools. 14:33.

We can't manufacture our emotions, we can't make ourselves feel happy or sad or angry, but we can manage the expression of feelings. In an age when emotional incontinence is considered a virtue and self-restraint is viewed as unhealthy repression, the wisdom literature provides the necessary corrective to the distortions and excesses of our silly culture which tries to build a gentle society but without any metaphysical foundation. We're endlessly exhorted to be respectful and sensitive in our language, especially when speaking about select minorities, but all these exhortations have not produced a more polite culture. Impatience, abrasiveness and rudeness are as widespread as ever. Indeed, they seem to be getting worse.

> He who is slow to anger is better than the mighty, and he who rules his spirit than he who takes a city. 16:32.
>
> A man without self-control is like a city broken into and left without walls. 25:28.

Warm emotions help keep relationships from becoming arid and merely practical, but destructive emotions upend relationships. Unjustified anger and cruel spite, in particular, will always be harmful.

> A soft answer turns away wrath, but a harsh word stirs up anger. 15:1.

> The north wind brings forth rain; and a backbiting tongue, angry looks. 25:23.

We should steer clear of any irascible man or woman, boy or girl. Angry people get themselves in trouble, dragging those associated with them into their fracas. Anger is particularly hard on intimate relationships; it vandalises marriages, families and friendships. Rage is a destroyer; there are stern warnings about it.

> A hot-tempered man stirs up strife, but he who is slow to anger quiets contention. 15:18.

> Let a man meet a she-bear robbed of her cubs, rather than a fool in his folly. 17:12.

> Make no friendship with a man given to anger, nor go with a wrathful man, lest you learn his ways and entangle yourself in a snare. 22:24, 25.

> If you have been foolish, exalting yourself, or if you have been devising evil, put your hand on your mouth. For pressing milk produces curds, pressing the nose produces blood, and pressing anger produces strife. 30:32, 33.

> Be not quick to anger, for anger lodges in the bosom of fools. *Ecclesiastes* 7:9.

An ill-tempered person has ignored the divine summons to develop maturity; spiritually and psychologically, they're childish. Little children must be taught to control their emotions but some people don't seem to have learned the lesson as children, bringing a lack of self-control into adulthood. Unlike infancy, when a temper tantrum doesn't harm much apart from one's eardrums, adult rage can result in murder, injury, financial loss, divorce, estrangement and gaol.

> A man of wrath stirs up strife, and a man given to anger causes much transgression. 29:22.

Anger is a red flag, identifying a person to avoid if possible and to keep from positions of responsibility. A man or woman, young or old, who cannot rule their emotions isn't ready to rule anything else; they will only cause mayhem for everyone around them.

> He who is slow to anger has great understanding, but he who has a hasty temper exalts folly. 14:29.

There are many irritations in life, from the common rudeness on the roads and the freely-flowing insults of online interactions to deliberate provocations. In all these, it's much better to ignore offense rather than respond with matching rudeness. A thick skin protecting a gentle heart is best. Unfortunately, the opposite – thin skin over an unforgiving heart – is being encouraged by various government tribunals, courts and agencies. They facilitate complaints of inequality and charges of discrimination, but with no or minor consequences for the accuser if their charges prove false. This is a sure recipe for rash, trivial complaints. These agencies don't encourage the good sense of overlooking an offense, even if it's grievous and deliberate; instead they privilege quick anger, a desire for revenge and possible mercenary gain. Rather than developing social harmony, these government bodies dismantle it and create deeper, enduring animosities between people. In contrast, wisdom recommends graciousness and forbearance in our interactions with others.

> Good sense makes a man slow to anger, and it is his glory to overlook an offense. 19:11.

> What your eyes have seen do not hastily bring into court; for what will you do in the end, when your neighbor puts you to shame?

> Argue your case with your neighbor himself, and do not disclose another's secret; lest he who hears you bring shame upon you, and your ill repute have no end. 25:8-10.

Proverbs counsels against rescuing an angry person from the results of their rages. It's better to let them suffer the painful consequences; perhaps the hurt will encourage a gentler attitude. Perhaps they'll learn nothing and remain hot-headed, but if some do-gooder rescues them from the consequences they'll have sabotaged a lesson. A concerned onlooker may want to help, but non-interference is right.

> A man of great wrath will pay the penalty; for if you deliver him, you will only have to do it again. 19:19.

The most serious consequence of anger is violence inflicted on other people. Again, a busy-body may want to rescue the attacker from the consequences of their actions, to intercede on their behalf and allow sentiment and excuse to prevail over justice, but wisdom absolutely rejects this meddling.

> If a man is burdened with the blood of another, let him be a fugitive until death; let no one help him. 28:17.

Always it's necessary to control strong, destructive emotions. Restraint is especially important in intimate, long-term relationships: marriage, family ties and friendships. It's precisely where love, energy and emotion have been invested over years that spiteful words and callous actions cause the most pain. Men and women, of all ages, are directed to gentleness, love and loyalty especially towards those who share our life.

> A wise son makes a glad father, but a foolish son is a sorrow to his mother. 10:1.
>
> Hatred stirs up strife, but love covers all offenses. 10:12.
>
> A brother helped is like a strong city, but quarreling is like the bars of a castle. 18:19.

> There are friends who pretend to be friends, but there is a friend who sticks closer than a brother. 18:24.

Privation is preferable to persistent contention; each of the proverbs offering this counsel has the household as the place of irritation. This alerts husbands and wives, children and extended family to treat the closest people with special loving-kindness. Constant anger and provocation are so distressing that lonely poverty is preferable to hurt amid riches. Money and luxuries are no consolation for broken relationships.

> Better is a dinner of herbs where love is than a fatted ox and hatred with it. 15:17.
>
> Better is a dry morsel with quiet than a house full of feasting with strife. 17:1.
>
> It is better to live in a corner of the housetop than in a house shared with a contentious woman. 21:9.

Furious words provoke trouble; gracious words bring peace, encouragement and hope. They help to restore relationships.

> The tongue of the righteous is choice silver; the mind of the wicked is of little worth. The lips of the righteous feed many, but fools die for lack of sense. 10:20, 21.
>
> Pleasant words are like a honeycomb, sweetness to the soul and health to the body. 16:24.
>
> He who gives a right answer kisses the lips. 24:26.
>
> A word fitly spoken is like apples of gold in a setting of silver. 25:11.

The ability to provide perspective, hope, encouragement and consolation is based on the possession of wisdom and integrity; the mouth speaks only what the heart and mind give. In dramatic circumstances a volatile, opinionated person will certainly want to be heard, being full of themselves, but what they say will reflect their shallow mind and pitiful heart. The words of a mature friend, in contrast, may be spoken with hesitation, they may express basic concepts and cause some discomfort, but they will be sincere, full of truth and realistic.

> The mind of the righteous ponders how to answer, but the mouth of the wicked pours out evil things. 15:28.

> As in water face answers to face, so the mind of man reflects the man. 27:19.

The wisdom literature equates truthful words with righteousness, security and stable love. Moreover, truthful words are a sacred delight – a measure of how important it is to speak less but well.

> Lying lips are an abomination to the LORD, but those who act faithfully are his delight. 12:22.

Keeping clear of indiscreet and irascible people also applies to gluttons and thieves. It isn't fashionable to identify over-eating and heavy drinking as gluttony; but *Proverbs* is unambiguous. The obesity prevalent in many societies isn't in the first place a medical or physical condition; in the first place it's a spiritual condition. Addressing the dysfunctions of a person's spirit, heart and mind is the key to dealing with behaviours that harm the body. Discipline of the mind will lead to increased discipline of the body. Appetites can be trained through frequent fasting, for example, to accept more readily the direction of conscience and reason.

Again, avoiding gluttons and drunks is an obvious aid to keep these faults from developing in, or hurting, our life. Nobody should risk injury or death, for instance, because of a friend's drunk-driving. It's crazy getting involved in the fighting and lawlessness of drinking parties. It's self-defeating constantly wasting money on excessive food and grog that's soon vomited, or which leads to diabetes, cancers, heart failure, or liver disease.

> Wine is a mocker, strong drink a brawler; and whoever is led astray by it is not wise. 20:1.

> Who has woe? Who has sorrow? Who has strife? Who has complaining? Who has wounds without cause? Who has redness of eyes? Those who tarry long over wine, those who go to try mixed wine. Do not look at wine when it is red, when it sparkles in the cup and goes down smoothly. At the last it bites like a serpent, and stings like an adder. Your eyes will see strange things, and your mind utter perverse things. You will be like one who lies down in the midst of the sea, like one who lies on the top of a mast. "They struck me," you will say, "but I was not hurt; they beat me, but I did not feel it. When shall I awake? I will seek another drink." 23:29-35.

Quite apart from the substantial expense, the ill-health and shame associated with gluttony and heavy drinking may result in job loss, in legal imbroglios, in divorce. Gluttony is bad enough for a single person, but it's especially bad habit for a husband or wife because the negative consequences directly impact loved ones; humiliation and hardship affects people who should be dearest to us.

> He who keeps the law is a wise son, but a companion of gluttons shames his father. 28:7.

A person serving a superior should be careful to demonstrate self-control at social occasions because a shrewd superior will note the behaviour.

> When you sit down to eat with a ruler, observe carefully what is before you; and put a knife to your throat if you are a man given to appetite. 23:1, 2.

In many Mediterranean cultures, drinking wine and beer is a common part of everyday life; it's part of the rich social life of the people, yet drunkenness is not common and is frowned upon. Parents teach their children to enjoy wine and beer, to reap the benefits of taste, relaxation and festiveness without over-indulging. The real answer to the ugly misuse of alcohol is not prohibition, heavy taxes and stiff penalties, although these may help restrain the worst excesses of public drunkenness. The answer lies with parents teaching children to drink in a moderate way, with alcohol an adjunct to the enjoyment of conversation, dancing and food. Temperance is another of the virtues that parents must teach their children so the children prosper as they mature. It can't be left to chance.

> The rod and reproof give wisdom, but a child left to himself brings shame to his mother. 29:15.

Chesterton, a great lover of beer and wine, but no abuser of these wondrous things, often spoke against the prohibitionists of his day and all others proposing only bans and restrictions to correct social problems.

> In all these problems I should urge the solution which is positive, or, as the silly people say, "optimistic." I should set my face, that is, against most of the solutions that are solely negative and abolitionist. Most educators of the poor seem to think that they have to teach the poor man not to drink. I should be quite content if they teach him to drink; for it is mere ignorance about how to drink and when to drink that is accountable for most of his tragedies. From *What's Wrong with the World*.

Prudent teaching from loving adults establishes good patterns of behavior far more effectively than restrictions, sentencing, and tedious public policy slogans.

Although unexpected, *Proverbs* advises strong drink for the dying to alleviate suffering. In an age when effective medicines and pain-killers were not especially advanced, strong drink was one tool of palliative care. Today, opiates are (perhaps unfortunately) more common but there's still a place for the dulling effects of alcohol during the difficult final days of life.

> Give strong drink to him who is perishing, and wine to those in

bitter distress; let them drink and forget their poverty and remember their misery no more. 31:6.

On this basis, there's a case for medical use of marijuana, for example, to lessen the turmoil of terminal disease. No doubt there's a plethora of other drugs and medicines in the natural world waiting discovery. An immense, generous wisdom is the very basis of creation, so we can expect a wealth of potentialities, resources and options for human needs. Science and technology can proceed with confident hope. We've only scratched the surface of what God has placed in creation for us. As Pascal noted, we will tire of imagining wonders before nature tires of producing them. We can explore these wonders, but with humility rather than arrogant presumption.

> The whole visible world is only an imperceptible atom in the ample bosom of nature. No idea approaches it. We may enlarge our conceptions beyond all imaginable space; we only produce atoms in comparison with the reality of things. It is an infinite sphere, the centre of which is everywhere, the circumference nowhere. In short it is the greatest sensible mark of the almighty power of God, that imagination loses itself in that thought. 199.

Good companions are among God's gifts to us. The wisdom literature extols the value and joy of good friends. Equally, it cautions us to avoid traps that harm these friendships. Two common traps develop out of the very joy of friendship: one, seeking to spend too much time with the friend; and, second, spending the wrong time with the friend. Friendships, like any relationship, need the investment of thought as well as emotion. Friendships fueled only by the emotions tend to be neurotic and short-lived; friendships that are dominated by the intellect tend to be dry; they may be fruitful but not richly enjoyable. And humans are made to enjoy friendship and festivity.

Friendships are ruined by demanding too much of someone's time.

Functional, friendly people tend to be reasonably busy because they are committed to the good of themselves, their families, work and communities – and their time has to be considered precious and fleeting. A prudent person will recognise this reality and manage their expectation of friendship so that they don't demand more time and attention than is reasonable. Better if friends wish they saw more of us than wishing they saw less of us!

> Let your foot be seldom in your neighbor's house, lest he become weary of you and hate you. 25:17.

Clearly, some times are simply not suitable for demanding attention from friends: including late at night or early in the morning. The intent may be convivial, but the result will not match the intent.

> He who blesses his neighbour with a loud voice, rising early in the morning, will be counted as cursing. 27:14.

There are seasons in friendships; a season to grieve with the grieving and to celebrate with the joyful, for example. A good friend will not mixed them up.

> To make an apt answer is a joy to a man, and a word in season, how good it is! 15:23.

> He who sings songs to a heavy heart is like one who takes off a garment on a cold day, and like vinegar on a wound. 25:20.

Far from speaking without regard to the seasons a loyal friend will discern what needs to be said, especially to encourage a mate towards wise decisions. The emphasis is not on flattery but on maturity. Sometimes there is a need for hard truths, albeit subtly delivered. This is much better than an easy but false sentiment. However, it takes courage to say and to heed earnest counsel.

> Better is open rebuke than hidden love. Faithful are the wounds of

> a friend; profuse are the kisses of an enemy. 27:5, 6.
>
> Iron sharpens iron, and one man sharpens another. 27:17.
>
> It is better for a man to hear the rebuke of the wise than to hear the song of fools. For as the crackling of thorns under a pot, so is the laughter of the fools; this also is vanity. *Ecclesiastes* 7:5, 6.

One benefit of maintaining friendships – and of honouring the good friends of one's parents and treating them with especial respect – is the potential for mutual support in difficult circumstances. Friends and neighbours nearby can provide immediate assistance and comfort, and we can provide for them in their need. This ready assistance may be more valuable when family is distant. Obviously, we don't cultivate friendships because of their usefulness, but the co-operation of friends builds lives and communities.

> A friend loves at all times, and a brother is born for adversity. 17:17.

Burke noted that one of the worst aspects of the French Revolution was the dismantling of trust, friendship and neighbourly help as suspicion, the prevalence of informers and the threat of denunciation became obvious. This is always the case in revolutionary societies – usually the revolution is imposed on the common people by a smarter-than-the-rest-of-you elite – with mistrust, disengagement and withdrawal of compassion the sure result.

There's incredible value in the informal, spontaneous and free associations that people form. Often they form for a specific purpose, but the additional benefit is that they're effective at building friendly rapport. Town bands, sport and hobby groups, book clubs, service clubs, men's sheds, churches, the people who host soirees and organise fetes and farmers' markets must be celebrated. Burke knew these "little platoons" were not incidental to society but the life and breath of society which the presence of revolutionary zealots disrupted and suffocated.

In modern times, under Soviet rule, these community groups were quickly undermined, when not banned outright, because of the presence or just the *possible* presence of informers. They destroyed trust and the free exchange of perspectives and honest opinions. Behind the iron Curtain, the KGB, East Germany's *Stasi*, Poland's vicious MSW, Hungary's malign AVH and Czechoslovakia's StB infiltrated society and destroyed the possibility of communities enlivened by affection and common interest.

Burke wrote that an over-looked basis for friendship and neighbourly assistance was the love a person naturally has for their immediate social class, village, town or region. He noted that those who despised these local loyalties seemed keen to despoil their immediate, familiar society in the forlorn hope of a better, more 'equal' society of their own inflamed imagination.

> To squander away the objects which made the happiness of their fellows, would be to them no sacrifice at all. Turbulent, discontented men of quality, in proportion as they are puffed up with personal pride and arrogance, generally despise their own order. One of the first symptoms they discover of a selfish and mischievous ambition, is a profligate disregard of a dignity which they partake with others. To be attached to the subdivision, to love the little platoon we belong to in society, is the first principle (the germ as it were) of public affections. It is the first link in the series by which we proceed towards a love to our country, and to mankind. The interest in that portion of social arrangement is a trust in the hands of all those who compose it; and none but bad men would justify it in abuse, none but traitors would barter it away for their own personal advantage.

Proverbs and *Ecclesiastes* counsel realism. A specific, known and immediate, albeit limited, situation is the arena for contentment, not grandiose but largely fantastical dreams and desires. Better by far to learn to love family, home, friends, neighbours, town and place in society than to imagine we would be better, happier people if only we had a different – somehow magically improved – family, home, or place in society.

> A man of understanding sets his face toward wisdom, but the eyes of a fool are on the ends of the earth. 17:24.

> Better is the sight of the eyes than the wandering of desire; this also is vanity and a striving after wind. *Ecclesiastes* 6:9.

Chesterton wrote that discontentment – and then striving for what another person has got – causes much unhappiness.

> But though the creed of content is unsuited for certain special riddles and wrongs, it remains true for the normal of mortal life. We speak of divine discontent; discontent may sometimes be a divine thing, but content must always be the human thing. It may be true that a particular man, in his relation to his master or his neighbour, to his country or his enemies, will do well to be fiercely unsatisfied or thirsting for an angry justice. But it is not true, no sane person can call it true, that man as a whole in his general attitude towards the world, in his posture towards death or green fields, towards the weather or the baby, will be wise to cultivate dissatisfaction. In a broad estimate of our earthly experience, the great truism of the tablet remains: he must not covet his neighbour's ox nor his ass nor anything that is his. From *The Contented Man*.

Discontent and coveting will always bring disputes, but if we're not involved in these disputes we should not get involved. *Proverbs* counsels keeping aloof from other people's arguments. Electronic social networks almost invite this sort of meddling: increased nastiness is the usual result. International alliances also invite bungling interference: nations go to war, taking sides or obligated to take sides over distant matters, despite the fact that the nation's own interests are not directly or remotely threatened. Interfering in arguments is futile; it wastes energy, time and resources. There is enough work to do managing our own lives without trying to superintend the lives of others or solve their problems.

> He who meddles in a quarrel not his own is like one who takes a passing dog by the ears. 26:17.

In the same vein, there's no point arguing with someone sure of their own opinion, despite the wealth of contrary facts or their own evident failures. It's better to walk away without comment.

> The talk of a fool is a rod for his back, but the lips of the wise will preserve them. 14:3.

> Leave the presence of a fool, for there you do not meet words of knowledge. 14:7.

If someone isn't open to reason and polite discussion; if they respond with anger, mockery or scorn, there will be no peaceful resolution or fair compromise. Discussion will be an unnecessary aggravation. Again, it's best to walk away without comment, avoiding ensnarement in fruitless contentions.

> If a wise man has an argument with a fool, the fool only rages and laughs, and there is no quiet. 29:9.

Sometimes contending with a scoffer is unavoidable, in which case *Proverbs* provides two strategies. First, avoid imitating their ranting and mockery. While they rage, the wise person stays calm, patient and gentle while explaining his position. Second, argue in a manner consistent with their own convictions so they can see the inconsistency of their thought.

> Answer not a fool according to his folly, lest you be like him yourself. Answer a fool according to his folly, lest he be wise in his own eyes. 26:4, 5.

Chesterton argued in this way throughout his long career. For example, he used the arguments of obstructionism, traditionalism, and backwardness hurled at opponents of the progressive agenda *against* the progressives themselves. That is, he argued with the fool according to his folly. He reasoned in this way with a liberated woman who was sceptical about the need for modesty in dress.

> Now, as a matter of fact, every thinking person wants to stop the tide of evolution at some particular mark in his own mind. If I were to propose that people should wear no clothes, the lady might be shocked. But I should have as much right as any one else to say that she was obviously an individual with an unprogressive mind. If I were to propose that this reform should be imposed on people by force, she would be justly indignant. But I could answer her with her own argument—that there had always been unprogressive people and there would be until Doomsday. If I then proposed that people should be not only stripped but skinned alive, she might, perhaps, see several moral objections. But her own argument would still hold good, or as good as it held in her own case; and I could say that evolution would not stop and the skinning would go on. The argument is quite as good on my side as on hers; and it is worthless on both. From *The Pagoda of Progress*.

Pascal and Kierkegaard also knew that arguing in a direct manner was not often effective. It's psychologically naïve to expect a person, fond of their own opinion, to embrace a different opinion merely through rational argument. People are not logic machines whose settings are easy to change. Imagination, pride, emotion and self-esteem are as important as reason. Pascal advised the following strategy.

> When we wish to correct with advantage, and to show another that he errs, we must notice from what side he views the matter, for on that side it is usually true, and admit that truth to him, but reveal to him the side on which it is false. He is satisfied with that, for he sees that he was not mistaken, and that he only failed to see all sides. Now, no one is offended at not seeing everything; but one does not like to be mistaken, and that perhaps arises from the fact that man naturally cannot see everything, and that naturally he cannot err in the side he looks at, since the perceptions of our senses are always true. 9.

Acknowledging the dignity of people is important because each person's sense of their own dignity is usually vibrant. It's best to work with this sense of dignity rather than against it. Pascal was realistic.

> People are generally better persuaded by the reasons which they have discovered themselves than by those which have come into the mind of others. 10.

Kierkegaard also understood the benefits gained by a gentle approach, correcting a mistaken view in a shrewd, indirect manner. Kierkegaard wrote under many pseudonyms, adopting personas whose opinions were sometimes contrary to his own to facilitate this indirect communication. He often used alternative designations for God and the incarnation, such as the Eternal, the Moment, to help people look at familiar ideas in new ways. And he wrote with skill and beauty – "as an aesthetic writer" – to make his convictions and conjectures as pleasing as possible. He explained his method.

> A direct attack only strengthens a person in his illusion and, at the same time, embitters him. There is nothing that requires such gentle handling as an illusion, if one wishes to dispel it. If anything prompts the prospective captive to set his will in opposition, all is lost. And this is what a direct attack achieves, and it implies moreover the presumption of requiring a man to make to another person, or in his presence, an admission which he can make most profitably to himself, privately. This is what is achieved by the indirect method which, loving and serving the truth, arranges everything dialectically for the prospective captive, and then shyly withdraws (for love is always shy), so as not to witness the admission which he makes to himself alone before God – that he has lived hitherto in an illusion....

> If real success is to attend the effort to bring a man to a definite position, one must first of all take pains to find him where he is and begin there. This is the secret of the art of helping others. Anyone who has not mastered this is himself deluded when he proposes to

help others. In order to help another effectively I must understand more than he – yet first of all surely I must understand what he understands. If I do not know that my greater understanding will be of no help to him. If, however, I am disposed to plume myself on my greater understanding, it is because I am vain or proud, so that at bottom, instead of benefitting him, I want to be admired. But all true effort must begin with self-humiliation: the helper first must humble himself under him he would help, and therewith must understand that to help does not mean to be a sovereign but a servant, that to help does not mean to be ambitious but to be patient, that to help means to endure for the time being the imputation that one is in the wrong and does not understand what the other understands.

Take the case of a man who is passionately angry, and let us assume that he is really in the wrong. Unless you can begin with him by making it seem as if it were he that had to instruct you, and unless you can do it in such a way that the angry man, who was too impatient to listen to a word of yours, is glad to discover in you a complaisant and attentive listener—if you cannot do that, you cannot help him at all ... From *The Point of View for my Work as an Author*.

A person is more likely to listen if conversation and debate is good-humoured and eloquently expressed, appealing to their imagination and emotions as well as to reason. Anybody with any semblance of sense prefers pleasant, reasonable conversation. And when the people we argue with become friends, although the arguments continue, life is enriched.

The wise of heart is called a man of discernment, and pleasant speech increases persuasiveness. 16:21.

We are commanded in the Judeo-Christian scriptures: *You shall love your neighbour as yourself.* No one always feels like loving their neighbour, or even family members. The commandment exists to provide resolution, correcting aberrant and fleeting feelings. Kierkegaard regarded obeying the commandment, no matter what our circumstances or emotional state, as eternity's guarantee of resilient love. *Act with prudent love* is the best possible advice to give or receive.

> You have no right to harden yourself against this emotion, for you *ought* to love; but neither do you have the right to love despairingly, for you *ought* to love; just as little do you have the right to misuse this emotion in you, for you *ought* to love. You ought to preserve the love and you ought to preserve yourself in and by preserving yourself to preserve the love. There where the merely human wants to storm forth, the command still holds; there where the merely human would lose courage, the command strengthens; there where the merely human would become tired and clever, the command flames up and gives wisdom. The command consumes and burns out what is unsound in your love, but through the command you shall be able to kindle it again when humanly considered it would cease. When you think you can easily give counsel take the command as your counsel; but when you do not know how to counsel, the command shall prevail so that everything nevertheless turns out well. From *Works of Love*.

8

WISDOM AND REVERENCE

Blaise Pascal made this observation:

> Experience makes us see an enormous difference between piety and goodness. 496.

It's possible to attain a significant level of temporal wisdom without reverence for the personal creator. Anyone could follow the practical principles of the wisdom literature and live with good sense: faithful in their relationships, prudent in their decisions, measured in their responses and appetites, conservative yet generous with their resources. Thankfully, there are plenty of people with these lovely qualities. Nevertheless, *Proverbs* and *Ecclesiastes* join the rest of the Judeo-Christian scriptures commanding reverence for the creator and sustainer of all. Personal goodness is valuable, but by itself it's incomplete: piety completes humanity.

Ancient Israel had seen, whatever the ambiguities and conceptual difficulties that surround the events to the modern mind, the creator acting unmistakably in their history. They hadn't sought this favour. Sometimes they did not welcome it, and often wished they could be like the other nations with their more comprehensible local gods. But they understood that they interacted with a personal, moral, unimaginably wise and sovereign spirit who had revealed something of his character, activity and purposes in the world, sometimes directly, but more often through the intermediaries of prophets who did not speak without a clear inner compulsion and a publicly-acknowledged gift. What the prophets had to say wasn't always heeded, but that they had a right to speak wasn't often disputed in ancient Israel.

One consistent message conveyed by the prophets was that wisdom preceded and guided the acts of creation. Nothing was brought into existence without deliberation. And the wisdom that brought everything into being was focused on expressing beauty, generosity, love, intricacy, provision and order; all with a particular delight in humanity. This personal expression of wisdom is not merely a poetic conceit; a loving, just Person is the ultimate reality presented by the wisdom literature.

Wisdom and beneficence are not alien to us, rather they envelope and nurture us, especially if we respond with grateful acceptance. Here, personified Wisdom speaks of her participation in creation.

> The LORD created me at the beginning of his work, the first of his acts of old. Ages ago I was set up, at the first, before the beginning of the earth. When there were no depths I was brought forth, when there were no springs abounding with water. Before the mountains had been shaped, before the hills, I was brought forth; before he had made the earth with its fields, or the first of the dust of the world. When he established the heavens, I was there, when he drew a circle on the face of the deep, when he made firm the skies above, when he established the fountains of the deep, when he assigned to the sea its limit, so that the waters might not transgress his command, when he marked out the foundations of the earth, then I was beside him, like a master workman; and I was daily his delight, rejoicing before him always, rejoicing in his inhabited world and delighting in the sons of men. And now, my sons, listen to me: happy are those who keep my ways. 8:22-32.

If we decide to explore these ways, we must accept that it will not be an easy path. There are many diversions, many stumbling-blocks to avoid and comparatively few fellow-travellers. And puzzles about ourselves and puzzles about God abound, but the puzzles provide a subtle sort of guidance.

Kierkegaard prefaced *The Sickness unto Death* with an epigram, a prayer. It's appropriate to remember it at this point.

> Lord, give us poor vision for things of no account, but clear vision for all your truth.

Happiness is the reward for reverence, says Wisdom, but wisdom is required to pursue reverence, and then more wisdom is needed to grow in reverence.

i. REVERENCE AND THE PUZZLE OF MAN.

Pascal knew that knowledge of God, knowledge of observable reality and knowledge of humanity couldn't be attained separately, but this is the self-defeating task many thinkers have set themselves. The truths they arrive at will be half-truths at best with an inevitable oscillation between hope and despair, pride and self-loathing, dogma and scepticism. This dizzying oscillation operates within philosophy, culture and indeed within the individual. It fascinated Pascal who sought an explanation.

> Man's true nature, his true good, true virtue, and true religion are things of which the knowledge is inseparable. 442.

> No other religion has recognised that man is the most excellent creature. Some, which have quite recognised the reality of his excellence, have considered as mean and ungrateful the low opinions which men naturally have of themselves; and others, which have thoroughly recognised how real is this vileness, have treated with proud ridicule those feelings of greatness, which are equally natural to man.

> "Lift your eyes to God," say the first; "see Him whom you resemble,

and who has created you to worship Him. You can make yourselves like unto Him; wisdom will make you equal to Him, if you will follow it." "Raise your heads, free men," says Epictetus. And others say, "Bend your eyes to the earth, wretched worm that you are, and consider the brutes whose companion you are."

What, then, will man become? Will he be equal to God or the brutes? What a frightful difference! What, then, shall we be? Who does not see from all this that man has gone astray, that he has fallen from his place, that he anxiously seeks it, that he cannot find it again? And who shall then direct him to it? The greatest men have failed. 431.

Man is obviously made to think. It is his whole dignity and his whole merit; and his whole duty is to think as he ought. Now, the order of thought is to begin with self, and with its Author and its end. Now, of what does the world think? Never of this, but of dancing, playing the lute, singing, making verses, running at the ring, etc., fighting, making oneself king, without thinking what it is to be a king and what to be a man. 146.

Kierkegaard, like Pascal, also saw the puzzles of man. Like Pascal, he observed that these puzzles don't seem to command the attention of too many people. Kierkegaard saw what society commonly thinks about – the ephemeral and the vain – and realised that a degree of disinterestedness towards society's passing interests was required to find truth, transcendent wisdom, and therefore ourself. Temporal concerns obscure these vital things; crucial aspects of our being are only revealed, and then partially, through contemplation of the eternal.

Orientating life around the temporal brings a self-frustrating twist: the person who neglects the eternal has to convince himself that the passing temporal has significance and meaning. This is impossible if there is no eternal to guarantee that the passing temporal has these or any other enduring qualities. Kierkegaard knew that when the eternal was neglected, the temporal would be inflated to preposterous importance. This is the signature characteristic of the news media, for example, and it's one more reason why their coverage is often so exaggerated, unbalanced and packed with platitudes.

> How necessary disinterestedness is in these times when everything is done to make everything momentary and the momentary is regarded as everything! – Is not everything done to make the present moment as supreme as possible, supreme over the eternal, over the truth, is not everything done to make the present moment self-sufficient in almost proud ignorance of God and the eternal, so conceited in presumed possession of all truth, so presumptuous in the idea of itself being the discoverer of truth! How many of the better ones have not bowed down before the power of the present moment and thereby made the moment even worse; for the very one who is superior, when weakly or selfishly he gives in, must in the very noise of the present moment seek to forget his downfall and now work with all his might to make the present moment even more puffed up. From *Works of Love*.

Pascal expressed a similar thought. Man's imagination, when it was orientated towards temporal things, judged in a vastly distorted manner, inflating the minute and ephemeral, but minimising the essential.

> The imagination enlarges little objects so as to fill our souls with a fantastic estimate; and with rash insolence, it belittles the great to its own size, as when talking of God. 84.

Wisdom requires that man, the world and the Eternal are considered together; wisdom could be defined as their proper relation. The temporal and the eternal, the physical and the spiritual all need to be admitted. *Proverbs* and *Ecclesiastes* certainly address spiritual matters, but they don't contain much that would pass for spirituality in its popular forms today. In contemporary culture, spirituality is widely accepted – especially in esoteric Asian forms which have an exotic appeal – and has even suffered the ultimate indignity of becoming somewhat fashionable. But a credible spirituality always results in sanctity: in honest, diligent, caring, faithful character and actions.

Proverbs is not filled with therapies, with good reason. Most personal problems will not be resolved through consciousness-raising, psycho-pharmaceuticals, meditation, counselling sessions or psychotherapy (although these may help); they'll have their most effective solution in sanctity. This is unlikely to grow fashionable, especially since Western scientism has promoted the idea that man is a bio-chemical entity devoid of spirit, said to possess soul only as a metaphor for the immense complication of human biology.

It's no surprise that therapeutic interventions for troubling symptoms and dysfunctional behaviour have become common. These treatments don't require acknowledging the profound primacy of the spirit or any fundamental re-orientation of the soul, attitudes, and perspectives. A cocktail of pills, hours of conversation or a meditative routine are prescribed. This, of course, also conforms to, and reinforces, the *acedia* that lingers in every heart. But it neglects the gifts of God that can restore man to substantial spiritual and psychological health. This approximate, but not perfect, wholeness is not a prize one must struggle to gain; it grows from graces a devout person receives and cultivates; together, they energise joy.

> My son, do not forget my teaching, but let your heart keep my commandments; for length of days and years of life and abundant welfare will they give you. 3:1, 2

> There is nothing better for a man than that he should eat and drink, and find enjoyment in his toil. This also, I saw, is from the hand of God; for apart from him who can eat or who can have enjoyment? For to the man who pleases him God gives wisdom and knowledge and joy; but to the sinner he gives the work of gathering and heaping, only to give to one who pleases God. This also is vanity

and a striving after wind. *Ecclesiastes* 2:24-26.

Some cultures assume that spirituality without sanctity is possible; this fatuity is common in contemporary Western culture. Other more worthy ancient cultures detailed duties that had an appearance of sanctity but fell short of prescribing love for God and love for neighbour. Instead, they championed nobility in war, stoicism in difficulties, fasting, feast days, pilgrimages, sexual abstinence or the sexual license of fertility cults, extinguishing desire (an impossible task) or the annihilation of self (a contradictory task). Such is man's confusion that anything and everything can be permitted by labelling it spiritual. Pascal saw how muddled people can become when left to make their own rules.

> Man is neither angel nor brute, and the unfortunate thing is that he who would act the angel acts the brute. 358.

> True nature being lost, everything became its own nature; as the true good being lost, everything becomes its own true good. 426.

> All men seek happiness. This is without exception. Whatever different means they employ, they all tend to this end. The cause of some going to war, and of others avoiding it, is the same desire in both, attended with different views. The will never takes the least step but to this object. This is the motive of every action of every man, even of those who hang themselves.

> And yet after such a great number of years, no one without faith has reached the point to which all continually look. All complain, princes and subjects, noblemen and commoners, old and young, strong and weak, learned and ignorant, healthy and sick, of all countries, all times, all ages, and all conditions.

> A trial so long, so continuous, and so uniform, should certainly convince us of our inability to reach the good by our own efforts. But example teaches us little. No resemblance is ever so perfect that there is not some slight difference; and hence we expect that

our hope will not be deceived on this occasion as before. And thus, while the present never satisfies us, experience dupes us, and from misfortune to misfortune leads us to death, their eternal crown.

What is it then that this desire and this inability proclaim to us, but that there was once in man a true happiness of which there now remain to him only the mark and empty trace, which he in vain tries to fill from all his surroundings, seeking from things absent the help he does not obtain in things present? But these are all inadequate, because the infinite abyss can only be filled by an infinite and immutable object, that is to say, only by God Himself.

He only is our true good, and since we have forsaken Him, it is a strange thing that there is nothing in nature which has not been serviceable in taking His place; the stars, the heavens, earth, the elements, plants, cabbages, leeks, animals, insects, calves, serpents, fever, pestilence, war, famine, vices, adultery, incest. And since man has lost the true good, everything can appear equally good to him, even his own destruction, though so opposed to God, to reason, and to the whole course of nature.

Some seek good in authority, others in scientific research, others in pleasure. Others, who are in fact nearer the truth, have considered it necessary that the universal good, which all men desire, should not consist in any of the particular things which can only be possessed by one man, and which, when shared, afflict their possessor more by the want of the part he has not, than they please him by the possession of what he has. They have learned that the true good should be such as all can possess at once, without diminution and without envy, and which no one can lose against his will. And their reason is that this desire being natural to man, since it is necessarily in all, and that it is impossible not to have it, they infer from it ... 425.

It's no surprise that a variety of religions and a multitude of religious practices have evolved: man has a desire to plumb his own being and a desire to plumb eternity but both are beyond man's unaided grasp. Man gropes but he gropes without success because the Eternal has ordered creation so man, using his natural faculties, cannot understand himself or comprehend the Eternal with surety.

Pascal was especially alert to the confusion man faced when confronted by contradictions in his own being. On one hand, man shared biological life with animals; on the other, he was unlike the animals in his self-consciousness, his language and ethics, his religiosity, his cultural and technical aspirations. The Church's doctrine of man's creation in the image of God, and the complementary doctrine that the individual suffers abasement when he rebels against this image, provided Pascal with the unique framework necessary to understand the disparities of man's nature.

> Man does not know in what rank to place himself. He has plainly gone astray, and fallen from his true place without being able to find it again. He seeks it anxiously and unsuccessfully everywhere in impenetrable darkness. 427.

> For myself, I confess that so soon as the Christian religion reveals the principle that human nature is corrupt and fallen from God, that opens my eyes to see everywhere the mark of this truth: for nature is such that she testifies everywhere, both within man and without him, to a lost God and a corrupt nature. 441.

Pascal noticed the irony that those who disdained man and emphasised his correlation with animals still wanted man's esteem for this belittling observation. We can see the same desire for man's esteem, for degrading man, among intellectuals and some scientists today.

> The greatest baseness of man is the pursuit of glory. But it is also the greatest mark of his excellence; for whatever possessions he may have on earth, whatever health and essential comfort, he is not satisfied if he has not the esteem of men. He values human reason so highly that, whatever advantages he may have on earth, he is not

content if he is not also ranked highly in the judgment of man. This is the finest position in the world. Nothing can turn him from that desire, which is the most indelible quality of man's heart.

And those who most despise men, and put them on a level with the brutes, yet wish to be admired and believed by men, and contradict themselves by their own feelings; their nature, which is stronger than all, convincing them of the greatness of man more forcibly than reason convinces them of their baseness. 404.

The greatness of man. – We have so great an idea of the soul of man that we cannot endure being despised, or not being esteemed by any soul; and all the happiness of men consists in this esteem. 400.

Chesterton also saw the freakishness of man; not because man was a very smart animal, but because he was, in a sense, *un*natural, an anomaly.

Man is an exception, whatever else he is. If he is not the image of God, then he is a disease of the dust. If it is not true that a divine being fell, then we can only say that one of the animals went entirely off its head. In neither case can we really argue very much from the body of man simply considered as the body of an innocent and healthy animal. His body has too much mixed up with his soul, as we see in the supreme instance of sex... Man is always something worse or something better than an animal; and an mere argument from animal perfection never touches him at all. Thus, in sex no animal is either chivalrous or obscene. And thus no animal ever invented anything so bad as drunkenness — or so good as drink. From *Wine When it is Red*.

This admixture of the animal and the spiritual in humanity is a perpetual difficulty for monists who deny either man's flesh or his spirit. This is common in sexual studies, for example. Chesterton observed that researchers tended to simplify humanity for the sake of finding a scientific explanation – but the explanation left out half of everyone's humanity.

> No man could say exactly how much his sexuality was coloured by a clean love of beauty, or the mere boyish itch for adventure, like running away to sea. No man could say how much his animal dread of the end was mixed up with mystical traditions touching morals and religion. It is exactly because these things are animal, but not quite animal, that the dance of all the difficulties begins. The materialists analyze the easy part, deny the hard part and go home to their tea. From *What's Wrong with the World*.

Pascal thought that showing man either his exalted spiritual status or his bestial condition in isolation from its complementary truth was distorting. Both truths were necessary to know, but the two truths – taken together – are not what any philosopher would entertain or even imagine. Scholars and philosophers tended to affirm one or the other, hence the different sects among thinkers. They tend to be materialistic or idealistic, dogmatists or sceptics, and since none of these positions is entirely tenable, they hop from one to the other on different issues.

> This twofold nature of man is so evident that some have thought that we had two souls. A single subject seemed to them incapable of such sudden variations from unmeasured presumption to a dreadful dejection of heart. 417.
>
> It is dangerous to make man see too clearly his equality with the brutes without showing him his greatness. It is also dangerous to make him see his greatness too clearly, apart from his vileness. It is still more dangerous to leave him in ignorance of both. But it is very advantageous to show him both. Man must not think that he is on a level either with the brutes or with the angels, nor must he be ignorant of both sides of his nature; but he must know both. 418
>
> Christianity is strange. It bids man recognise that he is vile, even abominable, and bids him desire to be like God. Without such a counterpoise, this dignity would make him horribly vain, or this humiliation would make him terribly abject. 536.

> With how little pride does a Christian believe himself united to God! With how little humiliation does he place himself on a level with the worms of earth! A glorious manner to welcome life and death, good and evil! 537.

Pascal, noting the vacillations of man's nature, said the teaching best adapted to man's real needs had to correct both his pride and despair.

> There is no doctrine more appropriate to man than this, which teaches him his double capacity of receiving and of losing grace, because of the double peril to which he is exposed, of despair or of pride. 523.
>
> All these same miseries prove man's greatness. They are the miseries of a great lord, of a deposed king. 398.
>
> *Contraries. After having shown the vileness and the greatness of man.*—Let man now know his value. Let him love himself, for there is in him a nature capable of good; but let him not for this reason love the vileness which is in him. Let him despise himself, for this capacity is barren; but let him not therefore despise this natural capacity. Let him hate himself, let him love himself; he has within him the capacity of knowing the truth and of being happy, but he possesses no truth, either constant or satisfactory.
>
> I would then lead man to the desire of finding truth; to be free from passions, and ready to follow it where he may find it, knowing how much his knowledge is obscured by the passions. I would indeed that he should hate in himself the lust which determined his will by itself, so that it may not blind him in making his choice, and may not hinder him when he has chosen. 423.
>
> All these contradictions, which seem most to keep me from the knowledge of religion, have led me most quickly to the true one. 424.

Pascal's method was to highlight the contradictions in mankind, which are evident to everyone since we all embody them. Then he presented the "knot in our condition" that considered the contradictions in a richer, (but for the proud possibly more offensive), perspective.

> If he exalts himself, I humble him; if he humble himself, I exalt him; and I always contradict him, till he understands that he is an incomprehensible monster. 420.
>
> What a chimera then is man! What a novelty! What a monster, what a chaos, what a contradiction, what a prodigy! Judge of all things, imbecile worm of the earth; depositary of truth, a sink of uncertainty and error; the pride and refuse of the universe!
>
> Who will unravel this tangle? Nature confutes the sceptics, and reason confutes the dogmatists. What then will you become, O men! who try to find out by your natural reason what is your true condition? You cannot avoid one of these sects, nor adhere to one of them.
>
> Know then, proud man, what a paradox you are to yourself. Humble yourself, weak reason; be silent, foolish nature; learn that man infinitely transcends man, and learn from your Master your true condition, of which you are ignorant. Hear God.
>
> For in fact, if man had never been corrupt, he would enjoy in his innocence both truth and happiness with assurance; and if man had always been corrupt, he would have no idea of truth or bliss. But, wretched as we are, and more so than if there were no greatness in our condition, we have an idea of happiness, and cannot reach it. We perceive an image of truth, and possess only a lie. Incapable of absolute ignorance and of certain knowledge, we have thus been manifestly in a degree of perfection from which we have unhappily fallen.
>
> It is, however, an astonishing thing that the mystery furthest removed from our knowledge, namely, that of the transmission of sin, should be a fact without which we can have no knowledge of ourselves. For it is beyond doubt that there is nothing which more shocks our reason than to say that the sin of the first man

has rendered guilty those, who, being so removed from this source, seem incapable of participation in it. This transmission does not only seem to us impossible, it seems also very unjust. For what is more contrary to the rules of our miserable justice than to damn eternally an infant incapable of will, for a sin wherein he seems to have so little a share, that it was committed six thousand years before he was in existence? Certainly nothing offends us more rudely than this doctrine; and yet, without this mystery, the most incomprehensible of all, we are incomprehensible to ourselves. The knot of our condition takes its twists and turns in this abyss, so that man is more inconceivable without this mystery than this mystery is inconceivable to man.

Whence it seems that God, willing to render the difficulty of our existence unintelligible to ourselves, has concealed the knot so high, or, better speaking, so low, that we are quite incapable of reaching it; so that it is not by the proud exertions of our reason, but by the simple submissions of reason, that we can truly know ourselves.

These foundations, solidly established on the inviolable authority of religion, make us know that there are two truths of faith equally certain: the one, that man, in the state of creation, or in that of grace, is raised above all nature, made like unto God and sharing in His divinity; the other, that in the state of corruption and sin, he is fallen from this state and made like unto the beasts.

These two propositions are equally sound and certain. Scripture manifestly declares this to us, when it says in some places: *Deliciæ meæ esse cum filiis hominum.* [My delights were with the sons of men]. *Effundam spiritum meum super omnem carnem.* [I will pour out my spirit on all flesh]. *Dii estis* [Ye are gods], etc.; and in other places, *Omnis caro fœnum.* [All flesh is as grass]. *Homo assimilatus est jumentis insipientibus, et similis factus est illis. Dixi in corde meo de filsis hominum. Ecclesiastes* 3. [Man is like the beasts that perish – I said in my heart concerning the estate of the sons of men].

Whence it clearly seems that man by grace is made like unto God, and a partaker in His divinity and that without grace he is like unto the brute beasts. 434.

Without this divine knowledge what could men do but either become elated by the inner feeling of their past greatness which still remains to them, or become despondent at the sight of their present weakness? For, not seeing the whole truth, they could not attain to perfect virtue. Some considering nature as incorrupt, others as incurable, they could not escape either pride or sloth, the two sources of all vice; since they cannot but either abandon themselves to it through cowardice, or escape it by pride. For if they knew the excellence of man, they were ignorant of his corruption; so that they easily avoided sloth, but fell into pride. And if they recognised the infirmity of nature, they were ignorant of its dignity; so that they could easily avoid vanity, but it was to fall into despair. Thence arise the different schools of the Stoics and Epicureans, the Dogmatists, Academicians, etc.

The Christian religion alone has been able to cure these two vices, not by expelling the one through means of the other according to the wisdom of the world, but by expelling both according to the simplicity of the Gospel. For it teaches the righteous that it raises them even to a participation in divinity itself; that in this lofty state they still carry the source of all corruption, which renders them during all their life subject to error, misery, death, and sin; and it proclaims to the most ungodly that they are capable of the grace of their Redeemer. So making those tremble whom it justifies, and consoling those whom it condemns, religion so justly tempers fear with hope through that double capacity of grace and of sin, common to all, that it humbles infinitely more than reason alone can do, but without despair; and it exalts infinitely more than natural pride, but without inflating; thus making it evident that alone being exempt from error and vice, it alone fulfils the duty of instructing and correcting men.

Who then can refuse to believe and adore this heavenly light? For is

> it not clearer than day that we perceive within ourselves ineffaceable marks of excellence? And is it not equally true that we experience every hour the results of our deplorable condition? What does this chaos and monstrous confusion proclaim to us but the truth of these two states, with a voice so powerful that it is impossible to resist it? 435.

Pascal accepted the doctrine that man had altered from his original position; it made the best sense of all the evidence, especially the hiddenness of God and the puzzle of man's concurrent nobility and degradation. But it was a doctrine that has long caused offense because it said man was, in his altered state, incapable of seeing the reason for his alteration; that is, man couldn't comprehend himself by himself.

> Original sin is foolishness to men, but it is admitted to be such. You must not then reproach me for the want of reason in this doctrine, since I admit it to be without reason. But this foolishness is wiser than all the wisdom of men, *sapientius est hominibus*. [It is wiser than men]. For without this, what can we say that man is? His whole state depends on this imperceptible point. And how should it be perceived by his reason, since it is a thing against reason, and since reason, far from finding it out by her own ways, is averse to it when it is presented to her? 445.

Chesterton discovered that knowing he was altered was liberating because it explained himself. He knew he wasn't whole and wholly good nor was he totally fragmented and utterly bad, but he didn't know why, and the philosophers had been no help by insisting he was normal as he was – a dispiriting thought.

> I had often called myself an optimist, to avoid the too evident blasphemy of pessimism. But all the optimism of the age had been false and disheartening for this reason, that it had always been trying to prove that we fit in to the world. The Christian optimism is based on the fact that we do *not* fit in to the world. I had tried to be happy

by telling myself that man is an animal, like any other which sought its meat from God. But now I was really happy, for I had learnt that man is a monstrosity. I had been right in feeling all things as odd, for I myself was at once worse and better than all things. The optimist's pleasure was prosaic, for it dwelt on the naturalness of everything; the Christian pleasure was poetic, for it dwelt on the unnaturalness of everything in the light of the supernatural. The modern philosopher had told me again and again that I was in the right place, and I had still felt depressed even in acquiescence. But I had learned that I was in the *wrong* place, and my soul sang for joy, like a bird in spring. From *Orthodoxy*.

Creation was of the Creator and declared as good; the power in it could be praised by the angels and by the sons of God shouting for joy. If we were ourselves only occasionally overheard in the act of shouting for joy, it was because we were only partially or imperfectly the sons of God; not indeed wholly disinherited, but not wholly domesticated. From *The Common Man*.

All the real argument about religion turns on the question of whether a man who was born upside down can tell when he comes right way up. The primary paradox of Christianity is that the ordinary condition of man is not his sane or sensible condition; that the normal itself is an abnormality. That is the inmost philosophy of the Fall. From *Orthodoxy*.

The sense that apparently ordinary things might be hinting at mystery stirs in us delight and poetic wonder. Chesterton believed we experienced this strange grasp of primeval rightness most fully when we were children.

There was a time when you and I and all of us were all very close to God; so that even now the colour of a pebble (or a paint), the smell of a flower (or a firework), comes to our hearts with a kind of authority and certainty; as if they were fragments of a muddled message, or features of a forgotten face. From *What's Wrong with the World*.

Chesterton recorded that he and a friend once caught a train in rural Belgium; but it was the wrong train that took them farther from their intended destination. He enjoyed the adventure once he realised they'd made a mistake. He lifted the mundane sense of being in the wrong place into a cosmic and anthropological meditation in *Ballade of a Strange Town*.

> We did not speak again until we had left Lierre, in its sacred cloud of rain, and were coming again to Mechlin, under a clearer sky, that even made one think of stars. Then I leant forward and said to my friend in a low voice:
>
> "I have found out everything. We have come to the wrong star."
>
> He stared his query, and I went on eagerly:
>
> "That is what makes life at once so splendid and so strange. We are in the wrong world. When I thought that was the right town, it bored me; when I knew I was wrong, I was happy. So the false optimism, the modern happiness, tires us because it tells us we fit into this world. The true happiness is that we don't fit. We come from somewhere else. We have lost our way."

The search for the truth about man's contradictory nature is a frustrating one, yet the thoroughness of the agonised search, conducted now over thousands of years, makes the humble person ready for reverence because only the Divine can explain the evidence. Pascal found hope and comfort after exploring so deeply the discomfort of the human condition.

> We desire truth, and find within ourselves only uncertainty.
>
> We seek happiness, and find only misery and death.
>
> We cannot but desire truth and happiness, and are incapable of certainty or happiness. This desire is left to us, partly to punish us, partly to make us perceive wherefrom we are fallen. 437.
>
> It is good to be tired and wearied by the vain search after the true good, that way we stretch out our arms to the Redeemer. 422.

> Comfort yourselves. It is not from yourself that you should expect grace; but on the contrary, it is in expecting nothing from yourselves, that you must hope for it. 516.
>
> The God of the Christians is a God who makes the soul feel that He is her only good, that her only rest is in Him, that her only delight is in loving Him; and who makes her at the same time abhor the obstacles which keep her back, and prevent her from loving God with all her strength. Self-love and lust, which hinder us, are unbearable to her. Thus God makes her feel that she has this root of self-love which destroys her, and which He alone can cure. 543.

Kierkegaard had the same perspective as Pascal: when an individual despaired of making sense of his life, his being, his nature and worth, then he *might* be ready to hear the sacred speak and provide the required perspective.

> Only when a man has become so unhappy, or has grasped the misery of his existence so profoundly that he can truly say, 'For me life is worthless'—only then can he make a bid for Christianity. And then life can have worth in the highest degree. From *The Last Years, Journals, 1853-55*.

ii. REVERENCE AND THE PUZZLE OF GOD.

Adding to the perplexity of humanity is the equivocal evidence about God. Pascal made this ambiguity a distinguishing feature of his argument for the validity of Christianity which professes and explains the divine dissonance. He expressed the predicament of man who wants clarity, but sees a puzzle.

> This is what I see and what troubles me. I look on all sides, and I see only darkness everywhere. Nature presents to me nothing which is not matter of doubt and concern. If I saw nothing there which revealed a Divinity, I would come to a negative conclusion; if I saw

> everywhere the signs of a Creator, I would remain peacefully in faith. But, seeing too much to deny and too little to be sure, I am in a state to be pitied; wherefore I have a hundred time wished that if a God maintains nature, she should testify to Him unequivocally, and that, if the signs she gives are deceptive, she should suppress them altogether; that she should say everything or nothing, that I might see which cause I ought to follow. Whereas in my present state, ignorant of what I am or of what I ought to do, I know neither my condition nor my duty. My heart inclines wholly to know where is the true good, in order to follow it; nothing would be too dear to me for eternity.
>
> I envy those whom I see living in the faith with such carelessness, and who make such a bad use of a gift of which it seems to me I would make such a different use. 229.

Pascal thought God's obscurity was fundamental; any religion that didn't acknowledge it was inadequate and couldn't teach man what was necessary to know.

> That God has willed to hide Himself. – If there were only one religion, God would indeed be manifest. The same would be the case, if there were no martyrs but in our religion.
>
> God being thus hidden, every religion which does not affirm that God is hidden, is not true; and every religion which does not give the reason of it, is not instructive. Our religion does, all this: *Vere tu es Deus absconditus*. [Truly you are a hidden God]. 584.
>
> Instead of complaining that God had hidden Himself, you will give Him thanks for having revealed so much of Himself; and you will also give Him thanks for not having revealed Himself to haughty sages, unworthy to know so holy a God.
>
> Two kinds of persons know Him: those who have a humble heart, and who love lowliness, whatever kind of intellect they may have, high or low; and those who have sufficient understanding to see the

truth, whatever opposition they may have to it. 288.

In his *Pensees*, Pascal confronted the claims of sceptics who say God's existence is not obvious. Pascal replied, of course, it's not obvious. Human apprehension of God is problematic: that's a Christian teaching, and a reason to accept Christianity rather than a reason to reject it. But one must make the effort to explore the matter. Those who didn't exasperated him.

> Let them at least learn what is the religion they attack, before attacking it. If this religion boasted of having a clear view of God, and of possessing it open and unveiled, it would be attacking it to say that we see nothing in the world which shows it with this clearness. But since, on the contrary, it says that men are in darkness and estranged from God, that He has hidden Himself from their knowledge, that this is in fact the name which He gives Himself in the Scriptures, *Deus absconditus*, [the absconding God] and finally, if it endeavours equally to establish these two things: that God has set up in the Church visible signs to make Himself known to those who should seek Him sincerely, and that He has nevertheless so disguised them that He will only be perceived by those who seek Him with all their heart; what advantage can they obtain, when, in the negligence with which they make profession of being in search of the truth, they cry out that nothing reveals it to them; and since that darkness in which they are, and with which they upbraid the Church, establishes only one of the things which she affirms, without touching the other, and, very far from destroying, proves her doctrine?
>
> In order to attack it, they should have protested that they had made every effort to seek Him everywhere, and even in that which the Church proposes for their instruction, but without satisfaction. If they talked in this manner, they would in truth be attacking one of her pretensions. But I hope here to show that no reasonable person can speak thus, and I venture even to say that no one has ever done so. We know well enough how those who are of this mind behave. They believe they have made great efforts for their instruction, when they have spent a few hours in reading some book of Scripture, and

have questioned some priest on the truths of the faith. After that, they boast of having made vain search in books and among men. But, verily, I will tell them what I have often said, that this negligence is insufferable. We are not here concerned with the trifling interests of some stranger, that we should treat it in this fashion; the matter concerns ourselves and our all.

The immortality of the soul is a matter which is of so great consequence to us, and which touches us so profoundly, that we must have lost all feeling to be indifferent as to knowing what it is. All our actions and thoughts must take such different courses, according as there are or are not eternal joys to hope for, that it is impossible to take one step with sense and judgment, unless we regulate our course by our view of this point which ought to be our ultimate end.

Thus our first interest and our first duty is to enlighten ourselves on this subject, whereon depends all our conduct. Therefore among those who do not believe, I make a vast difference between those who strive with all their power to inform themselves, and those who live without troubling or thinking about it.

I can have only compassion for those who sincerely bewail their doubt, who regard it as the greatest of misfortunes, and who, sparing no effort to escape it, make of this inquiry their principal and most serious occupations.

But as for those who pass their life without thinking of this ultimate end of life, and who, for this sole reason that they do not find within themselves the lights which convince them of it, neglect to seek them elsewhere, and to examine thoroughly whether this opinion is one of those which people receive with credulous simplicity, or one of those which, although obscure in themselves, have nevertheless a solid and immovable foundation, I look upon them in a manner quite different.

This carelessness in a matter which concerns themselves, their eternity, their all, moves me more to anger than pity; it astonishes and shocks me; it is to me monstrous. I do not say this out of the pious zeal of a spiritual devotion. I expect, on the contrary, that we ought to have this feeling from principles of human interest and self-love; for this we need only see what the least enlightened persons see.

We do not require great education of the mind to understand that here is no real and lasting satisfaction; that our pleasures are only vanity; that our evils are infinite; and, lastly, that death, which threatens us every moment, must infallibly place us within a few years under the dreadful necessity of being for ever either annihilated or unhappy.

There is nothing more real than this, nothing more terrible. Be we as heroic as we like, that is the end which awaits the noblest life in the world. Let us reflect on this, and then say whether it is not beyond doubt that there is no good in this life but in the hope of another; that we are happy only in proportion as we draw near it; and that, as there are no more woes for those who have complete assurance of eternity, so there is no more happiness for those who have no insight into it.

Surely then it is a great evil thus to be in doubt, but it is at least an indispensable duty to seek when we are in such doubt; and thus the doubter who does not seek is altogether completely unhappy and completely wrong. And if besides this he is easy and content, professes to be so, and indeed boasts of it; if it is this state itself which is the subject of his joy and vanity, I have no words to describe so silly a creature.

How can people hold these opinions? What joy can we find in the expectation of nothing but hopeless misery? What reason for boasting that we are in impenetrable darkness? And how can it happen that the following argument occurs to a reasonable man?

"I know not who put me into the world, nor what the world is, nor what I myself am. I am in terrible ignorance of everything. I know not what my body is, nor my senses, nor my soul, not even that part of me which thinks what I say, which reflects on all and on itself, and knows itself no more than the rest. I see those frightful spaces of the universe which surround me, and I find myself tied to one corner of this vast expanse, without knowing why I am put in this place rather than in another, nor why the short time which is given me to live is assigned to me at this point rather than at another of the whole eternity which was before me or which shall come after me. I see nothing but infinities on all sides, which surround me as an atom, and as a shadow which endures only for an instant and returns no more. All I know is that I must soon die, but what I know least is this very death which I cannot escape.

As I know not whence I come, so I know not whither I go. I know only that, in leaving this world, I fall for ever either into annihilation or into the hands of an angry God, without knowing to which of these two states I shall be for ever assigned. Such is my state, full of weakness and uncertainty. And from all this I conclude that I ought to spend all the days of my life without caring to inquire into what must happen to me. Perhaps I might find some solution to my doubts, but I will not take the trouble, nor take a step to seek it; and after treating with scorn those who are concerned with this care, I will go without foresight and without fear to try the great event, and let myself be led carelessly to death, uncertain of the eternity of my future state."

Who would desire to have for a friend a man who talks in this fashion? Who would choose him out from others to tell him of his affairs? Who would have recourse to him in affliction? And indeed to what use in life could one put him?

In truth, it is the glory of religion to have for enemies men so unreasonable: and their opposition to it is so little dangerous that it serves on the contrary to establish its truths. For the Christian faith goes mainly to establish these two facts, the corruption of nature, and redemption by Jesus Christ. Now I contend that if these men do not serve to prove the truth of the redemption by the holiness of their behaviour, they at least serve admirably to show the corruption of nature by sentiments so unnatural.

Nothing is so important to man as his own state, nothing is so formidable to him as eternity; and thus it is not natural that there should be men indifferent to the loss of their existence, and to the perils of everlasting suffering. They are quite different with regard to all other things. They are afraid of mere trifles; they foresee them; they feel them. And this same man who spends so many days and nights in rage and despair for the loss of office, or for some imaginary insult to his honour, is the very one who knows without anxiety and without emotion that he will lose all by death. It is a monstrous thing to see in the same heart and at the same time this sensibility to trifles and this strange insensibility to the greatest objects. It is an incomprehensible enchantment, and a supernatural slumber, which indicates as its cause an all-powerful force ...

As for those who live without knowing Him and without seeking Him, they judge themselves so little worthy of their own care, that they are not worthy of the care of others; and it needs all the charity of the religion which they despise, not to despise them even to the point of leaving them to their folly. But because this religion obliges us always to regard them, so long as they are in this life, as capable of the grace which can enlighten them, and to believe that they may, in a little time, be more replenished with faith than we are, and that, on the other hand, we may fall into the blindness wherein they are, we must do for them what we would they should do for us if we were in their place, and call upon them to have pity upon themselves, and to take at least some steps in the endeavour to find light. Let them give to reading this some of the hours which they otherwise employ so uselessly; whatever aversion they may bring to the task, they will perhaps gain something, and at least will not lose much. But as for those who bring to the task perfect sincerity and a real desire to meet with truth, those I hope will be satisfied and convinced of the proofs of a religion so divine, which I have here collected, and in which I have followed somewhat after this order. 194.

Wise people see the chasm between the spiritual infinite and the physical finite, and know it can't be bridged from the finite to the infinite. Even wiser people know this chasm can be bridged from the infinite to the finite, but this bridge will appear forbiddingly strange. If the world we live in is weird and puzzling, how much more when the transcendent, even briefly, appears!

> And I applied my mind to seek and to search out by wisdom all that is done under heaven; it is an unhappy business that God has given to the sons of men to be busy with. I have seen everything that is done under the sun; and behold, all is vanity and a striving after wind. What is crooked cannot be made straight, and what is lacking cannot be numbered. *Ecclesiastes* 1:13-15.

The initiative in bridging this infinite chasm lies with the Infinite. Hence the need for revelation, and this revelation, because of the difference between the eternal spiritual and the temporal physical-spiritual, will look strange, unlikely and therefore offensive to many people. Jesus made this exact point, speaking of himself as the strange bridge between the infinite and the finite.

> He who comes from above is above all; he who is of he earth belongs to the earth, and of the earth he speaks; he who comes from heaven is above all. He bear witness to what he has seen and heard, yet no one receives his testimony; he who receives his testimony sets his seal on this, that God is true. For he whom God has sent utters the words of God, for it is not by measure he gives the Spirit; the father loves the Son, and has given all things into his hand. John 3:31-35.

The writer of *Ecclesiastes* saw the mad behaviour of mankind: we run after money or fame, curse others, envy our neighbours, love those who please us but hate those who oppose us, get drunk, act recklessly, waste time, money and resources. And all this while turning a blind eye to the certainty of our death and physical decay.

> This is an evil in all that is done under the sun, that one fate comes to all; also the hearts of men are full of evil, and madness is in their hearts while they live, and after that they go to the dead. But he who is joined with all the living has hope, for a living dog is better than a dead lion. For the living know that they will die, but the dead know nothing, and they have no more reward; but the memory of them is lost. Their love and their hate and their envy have already perished, and they have no more for ever any share in all that is done under the sun. *Ecclesiastes* 9:3-7.

We poor humans make relative values like pleasure, wealth, power, grievance and ease into absolute values and we treat absolute values like kindness, reverence, love and forgiveness as if they were merely relative values. And then we die. It looks like, because it is, craziness.

The message of sanity – embodied in the actions and teaching of Jesus – comes to a planet filled with partial-lunatics. And then some of the more academically-inclined lunatics try to pigeon-hole Jesus as a teaching exemplar or an ancient world proto-humanitarian, but these categorisations do not admit all the truly odd evidence. Jesus was strange in the time of Tiberius; he would be equally strange if he appeared today. But the real strangeness lies in humanity, not in the Divine. Chesterton wanted all the riddles properly addressed.

> If I take it for granted (as most modern people do) that Jesus of Nazareth was one of the ordinary teachers of men, then I find him splendid and suggestive indeed, but full of riddles and outrageous demands… But suppose the Divine really did walk and talk upon the earth, what would we be likely to think of it? I think we should see in such a being exactly the perplexities that we see in the central figure of the Gospels: I think he would seem to us extreme and violent; because he would see… the virtue which would be for us untried.

> I think he would seem to us to contradict himself; because, looking down on life like a map, he would see a connection between things which to us are disconnected. I think, however, that he would always ring true to our own sense of right, but ring (so to speak) too loud and too clear. He would be too good but never too bad for us ... I think there would be, in the nature of things, some tragic collision between him and the humanity he had created, culminating in something that would be at once a crime and an expiation. I think he would be blamed as a hard prophet for dragging down the haughty, and blamed also as a weak sentimentalist for loving the things that cling to corners, children or beggars. I think, in short, that he would give us the sensation that he was turning all our standards upside down, and yet also a suggestion that he had undeniably put them the right way up. From *Hibbert Journal*, 1909.

Kierkegaard summarised the two possible attitudes to this strange revelation: he who is not offended, worships. Wisdom warns against taking offense and thereby neglecting revelation.

> Trust in the LORD with all your heart, and do not rely on your own insight. In all your ways acknowledge him, and he will make straight your paths. Be not wise in your own eyes; fear the LORD, and turn away from evil. It will be healing to your flesh and refreshment to your bones. 3:5-8.

> He who despises the word brings destruction on himself, but he who respects the commandment will be rewarded. 13:13.

Like Kierkegaard and Chesterton, Pascal was alert to the strangeness of divine appearance. Kierkegaard focused on the chasm of difference between the infinite Spirit and the finite spirit/flesh composite that was man. Pascal saw there was a similar disproportion between God's justice and man's justice; another source of constant offense. We are limited to a temporal, finite, altered existence and we struggle to lend credence to anything we can't comprehend within those narrow limits, especially the vast expanses of divine mercy and justice.

> *Infinite – nothing.* – Our soul is cast into a body, where it finds number, time, dimension. Thereupon it reasons, and calls this nature, necessity, and can believe nothing else.
>
> Unity joined to infinity adds nothing to it, no more than one foot to an infinite measure. The finite is annihilated in the presence of the infinite, and becomes a pure nothing. So our spirit before God, so our justice before divine justice. There is not so great a disproportion between our justice and that of God, as between unity and infinity.
>
> The justice of God must be vast like His compassion. Now justice to the outcast is less vast, and ought less to offend our feelings than mercy towards the elect. 233.

Our altered imagination, feverish with pride, leads us to think we can evaluate divine things. But it's arrogant for us to judge God's existence, justice or mercy. Not only is there a disparity in being and morality; there is also a disparity in time. God dwells in eternity; we live for only a few decades. This further skews our perspective, making the divine even stranger. Put simply, we are incompetent judges. *Ecclesiastes* reminds us that both the brevity and the mysteries of our life should lead to humility.

> I said in my heart, God will judge the righteous and the wicked, for he has appointed a time for every matter, and for every work. I said in my heart with regard to the sons of men that God is testing them to show them that they are but beasts. For the fate of the sons of men and the fate of beasts is the same; as one dies, so dies the other. They all have the same breath, and man has no advantage over the beasts; for all is vanity. All go to one place; all are from the dust, and all turn to dust again. *Ecclesiastes* 3:17-20.
>
> As you do not know how the spirit comes to the bones in the womb of a woman with child, so you do not know the work of God who makes everything. *Ecclesiastes* 11:5.

Proverbs emphasises the transcendent wisdom of God which infinitely surpasses our comprehension. We see something of this majesty in nature, and we know it isn't limited by our circumference of knowledge or experience.

> Surely I am too stupid to be a man. I have not the understanding of a man. I have not learned wisdom, nor have I knowledge of the Holy One. Who has ascended to heaven and come down? Who has gathered the wind in his fists? Who has wrapped up the waters in a garment? Who has established all the ends of the earth? What is his name, and what is his son's name? Surely you know! Every word of God proves true; he is a shield to those who take refuge in him. Do not add to his words, lest he rebuke you, and you be found a liar. 30:2-6.

Pascal knew that the two-fold purposes of God, to reveal Himself to some but obscure Himself from others, didn't create difficulties for God – for whom all things are possible – but it did create difficulties for man because it means God is substantially hidden, leading to a degree of divinely-purposed confusion. Jesus embodied this two-fold purpose: he provided many positive signs of his divinity, yet he also did and said things that created perplexity and offense, especially among the proud and self-righteous. He said he taught in parables specifically to teach some but blind others. He announced on several occasions, speaking of illuminating grace, "To those who have, more will be given; to those who have not, the little they have shall be taken from them."

Jesus explained the principle that unlocked the difficulties of his actions and words: acceptance or rejection of the truth about the state of one's own heart determined whether a person received insight or obfuscation. Humility and honesty were prerequisites to understanding unfavourable teaching, while pride and self-righteousness predisposed a person towards offense and prevented that person from understanding the teaching.

Pascal meditated often about this principle and the life of Jesus.

> What do the [Old Testament] prophets say of Jesus Christ? That he will clearly be God? No; but that He is a God truly hidden; that He will be slighted; that none will think that it is He; that He will be a stone of stumbling upon which many will stumble, etc. Let people then reproach us no longer for want of clearness, since we make profession of it. But, it is said, there are obscurities. And without that, no one would have stumbled over Jesus Christ, and this is one of the formal intentions of the prophets: 'Shut their eyes.' 750.
>
> We understand nothing of the works of God, if we do not take as a principle that He has willed to blind some, and enlighten others. 565.
>
> Sceptic, for obstinate. 51.
>
> The prophecies, the very miracles and proofs of our religion, are not of such a nature that they can be said to be absolutely convincing. But they are also of such a kind that it cannot be said that it is unreasonable to believe them. Thus there is both evidence and obscurity to enlighten some and confuse others. But the evidence is such that it surpasses, or at least equals, the evidence to the contrary; so that it is not reason which can determine men not to follow it, and thus it can only be lust or malice of heart. And by this means there is sufficient evidence to condemn, and insufficient to convince; so that it appears in those who follow it, that it is grace, and not reason, which makes them follow it; and in those who shun it, that it is lust, not reason, which makes them shun it. 563.
>
> God has willed to redeem men, and to open salvation to those who seek it. But men render themselves so unworthy of it, that it is right that God should refuse to some, because of their obduracy, what He grants to others from a compassion which is not due to them. If He had willed to overcome the obstinacy of the most hardened, He could have done so by revealing Himself so manifestly to them that they could not have doubted of the truth of His essence; as it will appear at the last day, with such thunders and such a convulsion of

nature, that the dead will rise again, and the blindest will see Him.

It is not in this manner that He has willed to appear in His advent of mercy, because, as so many make themselves unworthy of His mercy, He has willed to leave them in the loss of the good which they do not want. It was not then right that He should appear in a manner manifestly divine, and completely capable of convincing all men; but it was also not right that He should come in so hidden a manner that He could not be known by those who should sincerely seek Him. He has willed to make Himself quite recognisable by those; and thus, willing to appear openly to those who seek Him with all their heart, and to be hidden from those who flee from Him with all their heart, He so regulates the knowledge of Himself that He has given signs of Himself, visible to those who seek Him, and not to those who seek Him not. There is enough light for those who only desire to see, and enough obscurity for those who have a contrary disposition. 430.

It is then true that everything teaches man his condition, but he must understand this well. For it is not true that all reveals God, and it is not true that all conceals God. But it is at the same time true that He hides Himself from those who tempt Him, and that He reveals Himself to those who seek Him, because men are both unworthy and capable of God; unworthy by their corruption capable by their original nature. 556.

If there were no obscurity, man would not be sensible of his corruption; if there were no light, man would not hope for a remedy. Thus, it is not only fair, but advantageous to us, that God be partly hidden and partly revealed; since it is equally dangerous to man to know God without knowing his own wretchedness, and to know his own wretchedness without knowing God. 585.

According to the doctrine of chance, you ought to put yourself to the trouble of searching for the truth; for if you die without worshipping the True Cause, you are lost. – "But," say you, "if He had wished me to worship Him, He would have left me signs of His

> will." – He has done so; but you neglect them. Seek them, therefore; it is well worth it. 236.
>
> Man is not worthy of God, but he is not incapable of being made worthy. It is unworthy of God to unite Himself to wretched man; but it is not unworthy of God to pull him out of his misery. 510.

There's an additional reason why reverence is a challenging puzzle – or appears absurd – to many people, especially in a secular culture: there is a widespread tendency to see oneself, and to compare oneself, only in relation to other people with the same worldview. The result is complacency and self-satisfaction; and the Eternal is further obscured. Kierkegaard was alert to the misplaced comparison with our peers, many of whom are distracted, complacent, self-seeking and indifferent to eternity.

> The quiet patience, the humble and obedient monotony, the magnanimous abandonment of momentary influence, the infinite distance from the momentary, the love devoted to his thought and to his God, which is necessary to think one thought: this seems to disappear; it is almost on the way to be a laughing-stock to men. "Man" has again become "the measure of everything thing" and completely in the understanding of the moment. All communications must be contrived opportunely into a light pamphlet and be supported by untruth upon untruth. Yes, it is as if all communication must finally be so contrived that it can be presented in at most an hour before a gathering which spends half an hour for noises of approval or disapproval and for the other half-hour is too confused to gather the ideas. And yet this is considered to be the highest! Children are brought up to regard this as the highest: to be heard and admired for an hour. In this way the coinage standard of being a human is debased. Nothing is said anymore of the highest, of being acceptable to God, as the apostle says, or of pleasing the noble men who lived in the past, or of pleasing a few of excellence who are contemporary; no, to satisfy for an hour a haphazard gathering of men, "the first the best," who themselves have had neither time nor occasion to to

> reflect on the truth and who consequently crave superficiality and half-truths if they are to bestow the reward of their approval: this is the aspiration. That is, in order to make aspiration worth anything at all, one helps along with a little untruth, men flatter each other that those assembled are very wise, that every gathering consists of the very wise ... From *Works of Love*.

Kierkegaard, like Chesterton, Pascal, Burke and *Proverbs*, held that the fall was the presupposition that provides the context for any meditation on humanity. Man is not as intended, as if what we are now is what we should be; rather we are altered – we have broken with our original state, and with everything else. The fall is like the initial bracket – we are living in the parenthesis – and God's restoration of creation forms the closing bracket. The parenthesis is so immense that we have accepted it as permanent and normal. Kierkegaard wrote of this odd, parenthetical normality that makes it harder for humanity to comprehend himself or God.

> But men (in contrast to God's memory) have long ago entirely forgotten that it is a parenthesis we have entered into, and that Christianity was introduced as the divine closure. No, we merrily live within the parenthesis, we propagate the race and arrange world history – and the whole thing is a parenthesis. From *The Last Years, Journals, 1853-55*.

Man is a puzzle and God is puzzling; to begin to understand a little of either requires humble reverence, and for many people this will mean a radically re-oriented life, although this re-orientation will probably be a quiet and gradual process; we learn slowly, "little by little". Kierkegaard wrote often about those who chatter about spirituality but haven't consciously reset their life. He said spiritual chatter is self-evading if it doesn't move beyond talk into decision, commitment and sanctity. And this self-evasion has serious consequences: it is robbing one's own spirit of its legitimate dues.

If a person ignores their own spirit, then the spirit exacts its due negatively in the form of anxiety, remorse, depression and despair. These afflictions are a vital gift to the discerning person, warning them that a crucial aspect of their self is derelict. Most people go on neglecting their own spiritual needs, stifling the symptoms with medicine, pleasure, drugs, possessions and power. This, it seems, is the condition of many individuals. Kierkegaard likened it to inheriting a mansion yet insisting on living in the mansion's cold, cramped basement.

> In case one were to think of a house, consisting of cellar, ground floor and *premier étage*, or rather so arranged that it was planned for a distinction of rank between the dwellers on the several floors; and in case one were to make a comparison between such a house and what is to be the soul of man – then unfortunately this is the sorry and ludicrous position of the majority of men, that in their own house they prefer to live in the cellar. The soulish-bodily synthesis in every man is planned with a view to being spirit, such as the building; but the man prefers to dwell in the cellar, that is, in the determinants of sensuousness. And not only does he prefer to dwell in the cellar; no, he loves that to such a degree that he becomes furious if anyone would propose to him to occupy the *bel étage* which stands empty at his disposition – for in fact he is dwelling in his own house! From *The Sickness unto Death*.

Pascal, using a similar analogy, likewise encouraged the cramped and the hesitant to investigate the extravagant promises of Christianity.

> An heir finds the title-deeds of his house. Will he say, "Perhaps they are forged?" and neglect to examine them? 217.

Chesterton admitted that many people refused Christianity not because it was too hard to believe, but because it was too good to believe. When the infinite enters the finite there's the possibility of offense because it is strange; there's also the possibility that it will reveal things so gracious, wonderful and dazzling that they seem too merciful, too satisfying, too joyful. Fine reasons to refuse a gift! God is puzzling, for man, because He is both fiercely unsentimental and so unexpectedly generous.

> What the denouncer of dogma really means is not that dogma is bad; but rather that dogma is too good to be true. From *The Everlasting Man*.

Impiety announces that if the Eternal wants our acknowledgment then certain external manifestations, of our specification, must be provided – "this evil generation demands a sign", said Jesus. When we look for evidence of the Eternal Spirit in our finite lives, we often look in the wrong places; we expect immediate supernatural action, miracles, signs, unmistakable blessings, profound intuitions and ecstatic feelings. But in the wisdom literature, the Eternal primarily interacts with us in our choices. Our everyday choices to help or hinder, to love or hate, to speak truth or slander, are opportunities to express our wills and create our lives – and interact with other lives, including the Eternal. These choices are divine tests of character, revealing what we value. We should not be surprised if we fail tests we have not anticipated, tests which have this sifting effect; they will come often in our lives, so we should expect them and be prepared. The wisdom literature is consistent with the rest of the Judeo-Christian scriptures which provide many instances of the Divine testing people to ascertain quality of character.

> The crucible is for silver, and the furnace is for gold, and the LORD tries hearts. 17:3.

> Even a child makes himself known by his acts, whether what he does is pure and right. The hearing ear and the seeing eye, the LORD has made them both. 20:11, 12.

There's magnanimous democracy in this testing because it's based on ethical behavior rather than intelligence, strength, beauty, talent, skill or age. People of any ability or disability, of any educational level, including young children, can all succeed in living well. Anybody can pass the tests of character and find favour with God. Just as we can have the good opinion of men, so we can have the good opinion of God.

> Let not loyalty and faithfulness forsake you; bind them about your neck, write them on the tablet of your heart. So you will find favor and good repute in the sight of God and man. 3:3, 4.

But man is so contrary that a person can make their own life a misery through stubborn choices, yet still blame divinity. When we refuse to take responsibility for our actions, it becomes easier to imagine that anything and everything is against us, and God becomes a repellent puzzle.

> When a man's folly brings his way to ruin, his heart rages against the LORD. 19:3.

Personal Wisdom warns the persistently stubborn. At some point, there is an end to divine constraint and the obstinate will experience the full consequences of their own actions; in the end, they punish themselves. There is irony here; and no place at all for sentimentality.

> "Because I have called and you refused to listen, have stretched out my hand and no one has heeded, and you have ignored all my counsel and would have none of my reproof, I also will laugh at your calamity; I will mock when panic strikes you, when panic strikes you like a storm, and your calamity comes like a whirlwind, when distress and anguish come upon you. Then they will call upon me, but I will not answer; they will seek me diligently but will not find me. Because they hated knowledge and did not choose the fear of the LORD, would have none of my counsel, and despised all my reproof, therefore they shall eat the fruit of their way and be sated with their own devices. For the simple are killed by their turning away, and the complacence of fools destroys them; but he who listens to me will dwell secure and will be at ease, without dread of evil." 1:24-33.

Our choices end only with death, and they determine our nearness or distance from our creator. The decision is ours.

> Besides being wise, the Preacher also taught the people knowledge,

weighing and studying and arranging proverbs with great care. The Preacher sought to find pleasing words, and uprightly he wrote words of truth. The sayings of the wise are like goads, and like nails firmly fixed are the collected sayings which are given by one Shepherd. My son, beware of anything beyond these. Of making many books there is no end, and much study is a weariness of the flesh. The end of the matter; all has been heard. Fear God, and keep his commandments; for this is the whole duty of man. For God will bring every deed into judgment, with every secret thing, whether good or evil. *Ecclesiastes* 12:9-12.

iii. REVERENCE AND DOUBLE-MINDEDNESS.

There is the puzzle of man and the puzzle of God. If we have considered these quiddities and arrived at a place of reverence, there is still the puzzle of our own dis-united heart. Reverence doesn't solve every problem; in some senses, it confronts us with more problems. Piety seeks depth and integrity, but we're prone to self-excuse, to airy justification of our behaviour. We're tempted to assume that our Creator will be satisfied with religious baubles in place of real reverence and real reform. Prayers are a Divine delight, for instance, but offering our prayers while we scorn the principles of the Decalogue is fruitless.

> The Lord is far from the wicked, but He hears the prayer of the righteous. 15:29.
>
> If one turns away his ear from hearing the law, even his prayer is an abomination. 28:9.

Where there's the presumption of religion without sanctity, then the person dabbles with the divine in a careless way: a fraught exercise. On the other hand, fulfilling the revealed laws of love and justice deepens the relationship with our creator, with temporal and celestial joy.

> Men of perverse mind are an abomination to the LORD, but those of blameless ways are his delight. 11:20.

> The sacrifice of the wicked is an abomination to the LORD, but the prayer of the upright is his delight. The way of the wicked is an abomination to the LORD, but he loves him who pursues righteousness. 15:8, 9.

God takes notice of our words, especially if we address them to him. We may utter them lightly but he considers them carefully. This encourages prayer; but it also warns us that rash promises to God are a trap we construct for ourselves.

> Guard your steps when you go to the house of God; to draw near to listen is better than to offer the sacrifice of fools; for they do not know that they are doing evil. Be not rash with your mouth, nor let your heart be hasty to utter a word before God, for God is in heaven, and you upon earth; therefore let your words be few. For a dream comes with much business, and a fool's voice with many words. *Ecclesiastes* 5:1-3.

If we have decided – and in prayer said as much – to make an offering or a gift of some kind; for example, as an act of worship after some joyful event, then we should do exactly as we said we would, without undue delay. To renege on our promise is much worse than to have said nothing; at least by saying nothing we aren't breaking any promises. It's bad enough to break promises made to another human being; to break promises made to the Eternal invites correction so true piety is learned.

> It is a snare for a man to say rashly, "It is holy," and to reflect only after making his vows. 20:25.

> When you vow a vow to God, do not delay paying it; for he has no pleasure in fools. Pay what you vow. It is better that you should not vow than that you should vow and not pay. Let not your mouth lead you into sin, and do not say before the messenger that it was

> a mistake; why should God be angry at your voice, and destroy the work of your hands? *Ecclesiastes* 5:4-6.

Piety also includes submission to the disproportionate dispensations of God. Some people have more of everything, while other people have less. Accepting differences is easy if we're among those with more; harder if we're among those with less. But a reverent person sees this disproportion and accepts it as divinely-appointed, at least for oneself. Addressing the disproportion may be warranted at times, but outright contempt for one's circumstances is rejection of God's governance. It's haughty to assume we're wiser than God, or deserve more than God has ordained. Reverence will bring a humble patience amid puzzling provision; it accepts there's more joy and peace in making the most of our circumstances rather than always wrestling bitterly with them; it delights in what it has already. Faith in divine goodness allows the fullest vision of immanent goodness.

> Better is a little with the fear of the LORD than great treasure and trouble with it. 15:16.
>
> He who gives heed to the word will prosper, and happy is he who trusts in the LORD. 16:20.
>
> Blessed is the man who fears the LORD always; but he who hardens his heart will fall into calamity. 28:14.
>
> Say not, "Why were the former days better than these?" For it is not from wisdom that you ask this. *Ecclesiastes* 7:10.

Moreover, a devout person knows that physical things, although delightful, are less satisfying than divine graces. This is the basis for monasticism, which does not neglect physical goods – historically, the monasteries were renowned for the quality of their produce and arts – but commits time and attention primarily to the sacraments and virtues. The impulse is to have less of the less satisfying (but still good) aspects of life in order to pursue the most satisfying aspects: the eternal values articulated and demonstrated by Christ. This is a rare commitment today, but it has great value for society.

Reverence acknowledges that the physical, psychical and spiritual structures of reality have an integrity and resilience that is guaranteed by their Creator, but it isn't an instantaneous guarantee. There's a delay in implementation that lulls the irreverent and tests the reverent. For example, if reality rose up the moment after some injustice or deliberate falsehood to punish the perpetrator then humanity would pursue reverence and sanctity for purely pragmatic and self-interested motives. Likewise, if reality immediately rose to reward some kind act there would be the same result: reverence for self-seeking reasons. Man's worse trait – selfishness – would be reinforced rather than corrected.

The essentially personal basis of reality precludes such legalism; love rather than law-keeping alone is desired, so human acts don't immediately garner divine response. Often, nothing obvious happens straightaway or even long after. The selfish person thinks he can get away with selfishness, but the devout person takes the delay into account, seeing divine patience operating and extra opportunities for human choice. He doesn't ascribe the delay to any divine indifference or, worse, divine non-existence. He trusts there will be a ratification of ethical reality however delayed it is and whatever the current ambiguities.

Kierkegaard likened the close link between misdemeanor and punishment as characteristic of children's schooling. In contrast, the delay between misdemeanor and correction or punishment is characteristic of adult life.

> We all go to school, only life's school is for adults. For this reason the punishment is of a more serious kind than in a children's school. It is less obvious, and therefore all the more serious; less immediate, and therefore all the more serious; less external, and therefore all the more serious. It does not follow blow for blow upon the mistake, and therefore all the more serious; one has not been spared because

it may seem as if the punishment had been forgotten, hence it is all the more serious. Yet by this seriousness punishment does in truth press one toward the Good, if one really wills it. Doubleness of mind has no desire to do that. From *Purity of Heart is to Will One Thing*.

We should not be scandalized by Goodness's seeming beggarliness when it is clothed in the slowness of time. *Proverbs* and *Ecclesiastes* acknowledge the difficulty of waiting for the ratification of the Good. There are multiple verses that encourage patience, providing assurance that the wait – the hope of firmly established justice and goodness – will not be in vain.

> What the wicked dreads will come upon him, but the desire of the righteous will be granted. When the tempest passes, the wicked is no more, but the righteous is established for ever. 10:24-25.
>
> The righteous will never be removed, but the wicked will not dwell in the land. 10:30.
>
> The desire of the righteous ends only in good; the expectation of the wicked in wrath. 11:23.
>
> If the righteous is requited on earth, how much more the wicked and the sinner! 11:31.
>
> He who walks in uprightness fears the LORD, but he who is devious in his ways despises him. 14:2.
>
> In the fear of the LORD one has strong confidence, and his children will have a refuge. The fear of the LORD is a fountain of life, that one may avoid the snares of death. 14:26, 27.
>
> The name of the Lord is a strong tower; the righteous run into it and are safe. 18:10.
>
> The fear of the LORD leads to life; and he who has it rests satisfied; he will not be visited by harm. 19:23.
>
> Moreover I saw under the sun that in the place of justice, even there

was wickedness, and in the place of righteousness, even there was wickedness. I said in my heart, God will judge the righteous and the wicked, for he has appointed a time for every matter, and for every work. *Ecclesiastes* 3:16, 17.

Kierkegaard pondered sacred providence and realised the Creator's quiet restraint allows humanity to experiment, even allowing man to enact evil and pursue self-harming futility. The absence of immediate correction allows man to explore life widely and perhaps learn from our mistakes. The expanse of freedom also permits the stubbornly erring person to pursue their ideas – they cannot say God restricted them – and engineer their own downfall. In a sense, the Divine allows man sufficient freedom and time to explore his imagination and intellect in an enigmatic universe so that, finally, weary and frustrated, man may know his limitations. If he doesn't recognise this reality and seek his true good, man cannot escape his culpability. Kierkegaard wrote about this divine constraint, which has only the *appearance* of indifference.

> For why, do you think, is He so quiet? Because He knows within himself that He is eternally unchangeable. Anyone not eternally sure of Himself could not keep so still, but would rise in His strength. Only one who is eternally immutable can be in this manner so still.
>
> He gives men time, and He can afford to give them time, since He has eternity and is eternally unchangeable. He gives time, and that with premeditation. And since there comes an accounting in eternity, where nothing is forgotten, not even a single one of the improper words that were spoken; and He is eternally unchanged. And yet, it may be also an expression for His mercy that men are afforded time; time for conversion and betterment. But how fearful if the time is not used for this purpose! For in that case the folly and frivolity in us would rather have Him straightaway ready with His punishment, instead of thus giving men time, seeming to take no cognizance of the wrong, and yet remaining eternally unchanged. From *The Unchangeableness of God*.

The ultimate ratification of the ethical and the spiritual is not human work. The humble understand this; they have no self-centred expectation that this ratification needs their help and must come in the time-frame of their life. It's rare to meet a person with this degree of consistent reverence. More common is the person with an inconsistent reverence. They've come far enough so they do not expect without fail to see in their life the reward for good choices, but their reverence is still undeveloped to the extent that they expect to be an important agent in this vindication of goodness. This is one form of double-mindedness. We fool ourselves constantly about the importance of our activities. Kierkegaard exposed the oddness of the halfway-pious person's desire.

> He wills that the good shall triumph through *him*, that he shall be the instrument, he the chosen one. He does not desire to be rewarded by the world – that he despises; nor by men – that he looks down upon. And yet he does not wish to be an unprofitable servant. The reward which he insists upon is a sense of pride and in that very demand is his violent double-mindedness. Yes, violent, for what else does he wish than to take the good by storm, and by force to press himself and his service upon the good! From *Purity of Heart is to Will One Thing*.

Kierkegaard sought to resolve this double-mindedness – this inconsistent reverence for the creator – by confessing that divine work is done in a divine way according to divine time. This often confounds human understanding, but to insist on a full, human comprehension of divine purposes is confused nonsense.

> And if he will not give up this last presumptuousness, if he, in some way, does not desire what the good wills, if he does not desire the good's victory after the fashion that the good wills it: then he is double-minded. From *Purity of Heart is to Will One Thing*.

Kierkegaard had a high view of God's majesty; his view reflects the wisdom literature which identifies God as the final arbiter of the possible: His will is never thwarted. The believer is required to live a devout life, but never as if his sacred orientation and choices constitute a "cause" that he must fight for on God's behalf, as if the majestic God is in danger of failing to achieve his goals without constant human busyness and the endless agitation of religious activism. Devout individuals can live their values and gently share their values, but without worrying about the "cause".

Proverbs reminds us that God is sovereign and powerful; he works with humanity, but he doesn't need our busy help to ensure things turn out to his credit. A flea doesn't need to jump off a lion to defend the lion against a dung-beetle.

> No wisdom, no understanding, no counsel, can avail against the LORD. 21:30.

A person must decide which will rule his understanding and will: time or eternity. If he submits to the eternal he needs to understand that his time-frames have little warrant and, further, that his capacities are not critical to the purposes of the eternal. He is finite and fallible, yet at the same time he is the apple of the Eternal's eye.

> I know that whatever God does endures for ever; nothing can be added to it, nor anything taken from it; God has made it so, in order that men should fear before him. That which is, already has been; that which is to be, already has been; and God seeks what has been driven away. *Ecclesiastes* 3:14, 15.

> Consider the work of God; who can make straight what he has made crooked? In the day of prosperity be joyful, and in the day of adversity consider; God has made the one as well as the other, so that man may not find out anything that will be after him. *Ecclesiastes* 7:13, 14.

Kierkegaard explained that a devout person accepts mystery, even accepting that silent patience through difficult trials is a special form of worship. A reverent person, humble and patient, doesn't insist on constant external demonstrations of God's power and presence. Faith is the firm hope of things not yet seen. Kierkegaard considered the neglected ramifications of the point.

> God is not a human being; it is not important to God to have visible evidences in order to know if his cause has won or not; rather it is he who should help you learn so that you become weaned from the secular life which wants visible evidences. If Christ had felt any need for visible demonstrations, he certainly would have done something about it and called the twelve legions of angels. This is precisely what he would not do; on the contrary he rebuked the apostles, who wished to see in order to believe, by saying that they did not know what spirit they were speaking, since they insisted on having a decision in terms of externalities. Decision in terms of externalities is just what Christianity does not want (except insofar as it will establish one or another mark which to the world is an offense as, for example, the sacraments); rather, by the very lack of this, it will test faith in the individual, test whether the individual will keep the secrecy of faith in the individual, test whether the individual will keep the secrecy of faith and be satisfied with it. The secular mind will always need to have the decision externalized; otherwise it mistrustfully believes that the decision actually does not exist. But this ground for mistrust is precisely the temptation in which faith shall be tested. As far as secular mentality is concerned, a far more certain way of making sure and of having positive certainty that there is a God would be to have picture of him hung up; then one could see – that God is? – or that there is an idol? – which nevertheless does not exist. As far as the secular mentality is concerned, it would have been far more certain, too, if Christ in some external manner, perhaps by a splendid pageant, had sought to prove who he was, instead of taking the shape of a poor servant without once attracting attention thereby; in this way he looked like any other man, and as far as the world is concerned, absolutely failed in his task. But this is precisely the temptation in which faith is tried. From *Works of Love*.

There is no basis for thinking or feeling that pleasing God is impossible, but he, and not humanity, sets the parameters and conditions; and because he created each person with love and to love, fulfilling his conditions is also the fulfillment of each person's life. Ignoring this love, and neglecting his parameters, is the negation that leads to the ultimate disintegration of an individual's life. Kierkegaard saw the consistency between the Eternal's love and the consequent primacy of love in the human realm.

> In the simple illustration of a house, a building, everyone knows what is meant by ground and foundation. But spiritually understood, what are the ground and foundation of the life of the spirit which are to bear the building? In very fact it is love; love is the origin of everything, and spiritually understood love is the deepest ground of the life of the spirit. Spiritually understood, the foundation is laid in every person in whom there is love. And the edifice which, spiritually understood, is to be constructed, is again love; and it is love which edifies. Love builds up and it is this which love builds up... Love is the ground; love is the building; love builds up. To build up is to build up love; and it is love which builds up. At times we talk quite appropriately about building up in a more ordinary sense. In contrast to the corruption which seeks only to tear down or in contrast to the confusion which can tear down and disintegrate, we say that a capable man is constructive, one who knows how to guide and to lead, one who knows how to instruct effectively in his field, one who is master in his art. All such persons build up in contrast to tearing down. But all such building up in knowledge, in insight, in expertness, in rectitude, etc., insofar as it does not build up love, is not in the deepest sense up-building. This is, because spiritually, love is the *ground*, and to build up means precisely to construct from the *ground* up. From *Works of Love*.

No doubt living in this sacred, sanctifying love is difficult. There's little inducement to pursue it in a materialistic society, and those who do may be misunderstood and ridiculed. No matter. A life of wisdom does not have popularity as its goal, nor does it rely on the acclaim of other people to support its search. The purpose is much greater than popularity or acclaim: the purpose is proper care for our body, soul and spirit both in the temporal and eternal realms. The difficulties that wisdom faces are immense, but it seeks an unending good. The alternatives are only relatively useful at best, and horribly wrong at worst. Personified wisdom concludes her invitation with this statement:

> "For he who finds me finds life and obtains favor from the LORD; but he who misses me injures himself; all who hate me love death." 8:35, 36.

Pascal acknowledged the difficulties of seeking wisdom and living a reverent life amid the attractions of status, comfort, power or wealth, but the difficulties are worth overcoming because the promise is a life of rich fulfillment.

> The easiest conditions to live in according to the world are the most difficult to live in according to God, and vice versa. Nothing is so hard according to the world as the religious life; nothing is easier than to live it according to God. Nothing is easier, according to the world, than to live in high office and great wealth; nothing is more difficult than to live in them according to God, and without acquiring an interest in them and a liking for them. 905.

A NOTE ON THE REFERENCES

I've used a simple form of referencing.

All quotes from *Proverbs* and *Ecclesiastes* are from the Revised Standard version, with chapter and verse given after each passage. I wanted a version that was a translation rather than a paraphrase of the original texts, and was in reasonably broad use.

All quotes from Edmund Burke are from *Reflections on the Revolution in France*. There are several editions of this work.

The essays and books for the quotes from Chesterton are given at the conclusion of each quote. Much of Chesterton's work is available online; while various publishers are re-publishing many of his non-fiction books and collections of essays. Ignatius Press is prominent among these publishers.

In the same way, the essays and books for the quotes from Kierkegaard are given at the conclusion of the quote. Like Chesterton, much of Kierkegaard's work is available online; print copies of his work are readily available through various publishers.

The quotes from Pascal are all taken from his *Pensees*. I have used the edition available on Project Gutenberg for ease of access, including the numbering system of this edition. It has an excellent introductory essay by T.S. Eliot. The edition translated by A.J. Krailsheimer in Penguin Classics is also readily available.

All italics in the excerpts are the author's own.

I first came across the story of Ignaz Semmelweis in a children's book: *Sick as: bloody moments in the history of medicine* by Gael Jennings.

SELECTED BIBLIOGRAPHY

Alden, Robert L, *Proverbs: a commentary on an ancient book of timeless advice.* Grand Rapids: Baker Book House, 1985.

Ahlquist, Dale, *Common sense 101: lessons from G.K. Chesterton.* San Francisco: Ignatius Press, 2006.

Allen, Diogenes, *Three outsiders: Kierkegaard, Pascal, Weil.* Boston: Crowley Publications, 1983.

Barclay, William, *And Jesus said: a handbook on the parables of Jesus.* Philadelphia: The Westminster Press, 1970.

Brown, Nancy Carpentier, *The Woman who was Chesterton: the life of Francis Chesterton, Wife of English author G.K. Chesterton.* Charlotte, North Carolina: The American Chesterton Society, 2015.

Brunner, Emil, *Man in revolt: a Christian anthropology.* Translated by Olive Wyon. Philadelphia: The Westminster Press, 1947.

Brunner, Emil, *The scandal of Christianity: the Robertson lectures.* London: SCM Press, 1951.

Burke, Edmund, *Reflection on the revolution in France and on the proceedings in certain societies in London relative to that event.* Edited and with an introduction and notes by Connor Cruise O'Brien. London: Penguin Books, 2004.

Camus, Albert, *The Myth of Sisyphus.* Translated from the French by Justin O'Brien. Harmondsworth: Penguin Books, 1975.

Chesterton, G.K., *A shilling for my thoughts.* London: Methuen, 1936.

Chesterton, G.K., *The common man.* New York: Sheed and Ward, 1950.

Chesterton, G.K., *The Defendant*. Reprinted Sioux Falls: NuVision Publications, 2010.

Chesterton, G.K., *The everlasting man*. Reprinted San Francisco: Ignatius Press, 1993.

Chesterton, G.K., *Heretics*. Reprinted London: The Bodley Head, 1957.

Chesterton, G.K., *Orthodoxy*. Reprinted London: The Bodley Head, 1957.

Chesterton, G.K., *Selected essays*. London: Collins, 1939.

Chesterton, G.K., *St. Francis of Assisi*. London: Hodder and Stoughton, 1960.

Chesterton, G.K., *Saint Thomas Aquinas*. New York: Doubleday, 1956.

Chesterton, G.K., *Tremendous trifles*. Reprinted Philadelphia: Dufour Editions, 1968.

Chesterton, G.K., *The well and the shallows*. Reprinted San Francisco: Ignatius Press, 2006.

Chesterton, G.K., *What's wrong with the world*. Reprinted San Francisco: Ignatius Press, 1993.

Ellul, Jacques, *Reason for being: a meditation on Ecclesiastes*. Translated by Joyce Main Hanks. Grand Rapids, Michigan: William B. Eerdmanns, 1990

Groothuis, Douglas, *On Pascal*. Melbourne: Thomson/Wadsworth Press, 2003.

Hannay, Alastair, *Kierkegaard*. London: Routledge & Kegan Paul, 1982.

Kierkegaard, Soren, *A Kierkegaard anthology*. Edited by Robert Bretall. New York: Princeton University Press, 1959.

Kierkegaard, Soren, *The Concept of Anxiety: A Simple Psychologically Oriented Deliberation in View of the Dogmatic Problem of Hereditary Sin*. Translated by Alastair Hannay. United States: Liveright Publishing Corporation, 2015.

Kierkegaard, Soren, *Fear and trembling*. Translated by Alastair Hannay. London: Penguin Books, 1985.

Kierkegaard, Soren, *Philosophical Fragments*. Translated by David Swenson. Princeton, N.J.: Princeton University Press, 1967.

Kierkegaard, Soren, *The Last Years: Journals, 1853-55*. Edited and translated by Ronald Gregor Smith. London: Collins/Fontana, 1968.

Bibliography

Kierkegaard, Soren, *The Present Age: on the death of rebellion*. Translated by Alexander Dru. New York: Harper Perennial Modern Thought, 2010.

Kierkegaard, Soren, *The Sickness unto Death*. Translated by Alastair Hannay. London: Penguin Books, 1989.

Kierkegaard, Soren, *Works of love*. Translated by Howard and Edna Hong. New York: Harper Perennial Modern Thought, 2009

Kreeft, Peter, *Christianity for modern pagans: Pascal's Pensees edited, outlined and explained*. San Francisco: Ignatius Press, 1993.

Kushner, Harold, *When all you've ever wanted isn't enough*. New York: Simon & Schuster, 2002

Lepp, Ignace, *A Christian philosophy of existence*. Dublin: Gill and Son, 1965.

Morris, Thomas, *Making sense of it all: Pascal and the meaning of life*. Grand Rapids, Michigan: William B. Eerdmans, 1992.

The Navarre Bible, Wisdom Books; The books of Job, Proverbs, Ecclesiastes (Qoheleth), the Wisdom of Solomon, and Sirach (Ecclesiastes) in the Revised Standard Version and New Vulgate with a commentary by members of the Faculty of Theology of the University of Navarre. Dublin: Four Courts Press, 2003.

O'Connell, Marvin R, *Blaise Pascal: reasons of the heart*. Grand Rapids, Michigan: William B. Eerdmans, 1997.

Pascal, Blaise. *Pensees*, Translated with an introduction by A.J. Krailsheimer, Harmondsworth: Penguin Books, 1966.

Pascal, Blaise, *The mind on fire*. Edited by James Houston. Minneapolis, MN: Bethany Press, 1992.

Peters, Thomas C., *Battling for the modern mind: a beginner's Chesterton*. Saint Louis, MO: Concordia Publishing House, 1994.

Peters, Thomas C., *The Christian imagination: G.K. Chesterton on the arts*. San Francisco: Ignatius Press, 2000.

Rogers, Ben, *Pascal: in praise of vanity*. London: Phoenix Books, 1998.

Scott, R.B.Y. *The way of wisdom in the Old Testament.* New York: The Macmillan Company, 1971.

Watkin, Julia, *Kierkegaard.* London: Continuum, 1997.

www.ingramcontent.com/pod-product-compliance
Ingram Content Group UK Ltd.
Pitfield, Milton Keynes, MK11 3LW, UK
UKHW021324180426
11947UKWH00017B/1430